D0213163

BECOMING WHO I AM

BECOMING
WHO I AM

Young Men on Being Gay

RITCH C. SAVIN-WILLIAMS

Harvard University Press

CAMBRIDGE, MASSACHUSETTS

LONDON, ENGLAND

2016

Copyright © 2016 by the President and Fellows of Harvard College
All rights reserved
Printed in the United States of America

First printing

Library of Congress Cataloging-in-Publication Data
Names: Savin-Williams, Ritch C., author.
Title: Becoming who I am : young men on being gay /
Ritch C. Savin-Williams.
Description: Cambridge, Massachusetts : Harvard University Press, 2016.
| Includes bibliographical references and index.
Identifiers: LCCN 2016015022 | ISBN 9780674971592 (alk. paper)
Subjects: LCSH: Gay teenagers. | Young gay men. |
Gay men—Identity. | Male homosexuality.
Classification: LCC HQ76.27.Y6?8 S28 2016 | DDC 306.76/60835—dc23
LC record available at https://lccn.loc.gov/2016015022

Book design by Dean Bornstein

CONTENTS

CONTENTS

Preface

Make it about our lives, our friends, our families.

(TRAVIS, AGE 15)

I've spent my career teaching courses on sexual and gender minorities, leading workshops for gay teens and their allies, testifying in court, working with political and social groups, and conducting research on sex and gender. As I look back on forty years of research, I am not altogether convinced that what we think we know always applies to today's young people. I've distributed anonymous questionnaires, organized Internet surveys, taken physiological measurements (pupil dilation, genital arousal), administered standard psychological testing, and now conducted in-depth interviews. I've observed, asked questions, and listened, often in amazement, even envy, to stories about growing up gay in today's world.

This book shares my accumulated knowledge and perspective with those of you who believe you might be gay, know you're gay, or want to find out what gay teens experience. If you care about gay youth, this book is for you. Perhaps you're a gay man who recalls his own experience as a gay youth. Maybe you're a parent, teacher, clergy member, or health-care provider. You may want to educate yourself or others about gay teens, or you may simply be curious. Unlike my last effort, *The New Gay Teenager* in 2005, which combined a limited number of life stories with scientific data, this book stays closer to the lives of gay teens as they reflect on their development: from their first inklings of a same-sex sexuality to their musings on their future as gay men. Our science about gay youth hasn't really changed much since *The New Gay Teenager*, but the lives of gay teens have dramatically changed, becoming vastly more complex and even more "normal" than was the case for their older gay brothers and sisters.

This generation, born in the 1990s, has replaced the promise of the "new gay teenager" with the promise fulfilled. The typical youth is neither better off nor worse off than his straight brother. Yes, he may have mental health problems, may be bullied, may fight with his parents, and may struggle to accept his sexuality—but how different in this regard is he from his straight friends who face life challenges such as having the "wrong" ethnicity, religion, physical size, personality, feelings, thoughts, or sexual desires? He's typical of other young people in that he has friends, loves his parents, and wants a good job, a good marriage, and good children. He's a rather ordinary teen, with a twist—a special gift that one young man referred to as "God's surprise."

As these youths were quick to tell me, today's gay teen is not particularly fond of the public image of "gay youth." That image doesn't fit him or his friends, and he wants me to correct the false information that he deems hurtful, even harmful. As 16-year-old Adrian informed me in an e-mail, he's not depressed, bullied, or suicidal, not a gay slut, nor is he unpopular. Adrian and others in this book are strong, authentic, and compassionate. Yes, too many gay teens suffer by their own hand or that of others, and this need not be the case. The "coming-out horror stories" should be told, but such negative experiences should not define what it means to be young and gay. The stories in these pages provide a glimpse into the ordinary lives of gay teens, who seek the same things straight boys do. They too desire self-fulfillment, an interesting career, and a soul mate.

The necessary corrective to our lack of knowledge is more knowledge—more understanding, more science, and better priorities, which must include listening to the actual life narratives of young people who are living their sexuality every day. Science and life stories are not always compatible. Although thousands of research studies exist, huge gaps remain in our knowledge, especially for topics that haven't been adequately covered (such as the same-sex attractions of straight boys or the adolescent romances of gay boys), and studies have yet to recruit teens who reflect the broader variety of experience, such as those who love being gay or masculine gay boys or ordinary gay boys.

1. We know little about the basic developmental needs and concerns of ordinary gay teens, especially their sexual and romantic life from first memories to young adulthood.
2. Studies have recorded far more about what goes wrong for gay teenagers than what goes right. The field is dominated by a focus on gay teens in trouble: those who struggle with finding psychological well-being, with problematic physical and social behaviors, and with stigmatization and discrimination.
3. To set things right, we need to more fully explore young lives by talking with teens about their feelings, experiences, and beliefs/attitudes—not so much through survey questions but through face-to-face encounters.

This book attempts to fill the void. What most struck me after the interviews were over was the desire of all the young men to have their real lives be the story on record—not our misperceptions. This book is their book, about their lives and their generation, rather than our stereotypes about what we think they should be. Gay teens of each generation deserve to have their story told.

To that end, I will not be altering their grammar, spelling, or style in this book so that I can preserve their experiences just as they expressed them.

Though the young men are anonymous in this book, in my life they are not. Thank you Adrian, Anthony, Asher, David, Dean, Derek, Dion, Geoff, Jake, Jared, Jeremy, Jonathan, Lenny, Liam, Nicholas, Raj, Ted, Travis, Tyler, and the other young men who opened up to me. You have taught me what it's like to grow up gay in the twenty-first century, and it is a privilege to share your stories. I hope I have been faithful in representing your life.

BECOMING WHO I AM

Anthony

My name is Anthony, I'm 15 years old, and I personally identify as gay. (ANTHONY, AGE 14)

The summer after his freshman year in high school, **Anthony** e-mailed me: "My name is Anthony." I do not routinely receive correspondence from gay teens, but when I do I always write back. Usually they share their coming-out stories or let me know how something I've written does or doesn't fit their experience. After this initial exchange, the teen usually disappears—but this was not the case with Anthony, who profusely apologized for pestering me. Although neither of us knew it at the time, this contact continues even to this day, when Anthony is a college senior.

I'll start from the beginning.

★ ★

Mr. Savin-Williams,

I hope your academic year at Cornell went well, and happy summer! My name is Anthony, I'm 15 years old, and I personally identify as gay. [Actually, he was fourteen, writing just days before his fifteenth birthday.]

I came across the New York Times article about national gay acceptance and I found it all incredibly astounding. As a gay teen at a Catholic high school, finding acceptance by others (and unfortunately, myself) is constantly a concern of mine. Through reading that article I feel an honest belief that people genuinely care, that gay acceptance will one day become the complete norm, and that I am truly proud to be gay.

Reading your biography on the Cornell website I feel what you're doing is incredible, and I want to assure you it's making a substantial difference in people's lives. Basically, I wanted to thank you for everything you do.

You are truly a role model.

—Anthony

⋆ ⋆

The next day I e-mailed back, writing in part, "Your email actually came to me on my birthday (today) and was truly a tremendous gift! Thank you so much! I wish you only the very best in your life and that you give to others the acceptance that we all want."

The irony of our birthdays was not lost on Anthony in his 304-word reply.

⋆ ⋆

Mr. Savin-Williams,

First of all, I hope you had a joyous birthday and I'm glad you appreciated the email. My birthday is actually tomorrow (one has to love the Gay Pride Month birthdays) so it was great to hear back from you.

⋆ ⋆

Though I had neglected to ask Anthony what he thought about the *Times* article, he shared his views anyway. In this second e-mail, one day short of his fifteenth birthday, Anthony reflected on the "sociological and psychological aspects of these things that can be mapped out through research," asked for an update "on any significant research you are working on," and requested information about my Sex & Gender Lab, "if you don't mind me pestering you for only awhile longer." He closed with the graciousness and courtesy I would come to associate with Anthony: "Thank you for taking the time to read this (sorry for the length!), I understand you're most likely busy with research and of course, your everyday life.—Anthony."

In follow-up e-mails, Anthony "critiqued" *The New Gay Teenager*, his millennial gay generation, and the political contributions of previous gay generations, and he celebrated the pure joy he experienced as he fell in love with Patrick, a junior at his high school. Ever the diplomatic and amiable writer, Anthony always ended his e-mails with an expression of gratitude. Over the next five years I would grow to appreciate this wonderful young man.

Meeting Anthony

I eventually met **Anthony**, age 16, at a youth conference nearly two years after his initial e-mail. He sent a cellphone picture of himself so that I would recognize him in the audience.

* *

Professor Ritch Savin-Williams,

Thank you for bringing this to my attention, and I'm planning on taking you up on the offer as it is not too far away. I probably can only stay until around twelve as well but my mom is willing to drop me off in the morning and bring me back to school after . . .

Hope to see you there. As a frame of reference I'll attach a picture of myself in case you see me in the crowd before I see you, although I understand that you may be busy at the event and I would be happy to go regardless of if I was able to see you or not—so no pressure to make time if you do not have it!

Anthony [picture]

* *

At the conference center before my talk, amid bagels, coffee, orange juice, and the colorful outfits and hair of the young people in attendance, I immediately recognized Anthony, not because of his picture but because of his non-gay-standard uniform: old Navy khakis, white shirt, tie (striped and colorful, an expression of personal identity?) pulled to the right, half socks, and brown loafers—pure Catholic school. One glance at Anthony's dark, angular looks, and you would have known he's Italian. He was "skinny" (his word) and taller than I expected, with a masculine posture. He talked softly, laughed anxiously, and earnestly intended to say what was on his mind, an intrusion for which he unconvincingly apologized.

Seeing each other for the first time, we were both a bit nervous, probably for similar reasons. After many personal e-mails, should it be a handshake or a hug? Awkwardly, it was a little of both, with small talk that felt bizarre given the intimacy of our virtual conversations. Anthony's warmth and humor were so clearly present. Then he disappeared into the huge auditorium. Despite years of experience, it's never easy for me to speak to hundreds of teenagers, gay or otherwise. Locating Anthony in the crowd eased my tension—a friendly face from cyberspace transposed into real life.

Interviewing Anthony

Six months later as a rising high school senior, **Anthony** visited my university campus, where we sat down for the interview that is dispersed throughout the book. His trip also included partying with a former high school friend and developing his suburban-restricted driving skills on the open road. The third of four children, Anthony has attended Catholic schools throughout his life. His family is economically modest and includes, in order, sister, brother, Anthony, and brother. Anthony and his three siblings are fairly close, despite their age differences. Anthony is also very attached to his mother, who had not been initially thrilled with having a gay child but has come to totally accept him. I met her when she dropped off Anthony for the interview, though it was made clear to me by Anthony that he, not his mother, had done most of the driving. She signed the consent form, we briefly chatted while Anthony fidgeted, and I hurriedly directed her to the campus bookstore. Anthony's relationship with his father is more distant, especially after his parents' divorce the previous year.

Having dropped his Catholic school uniform for the visit, Anthony was indistinguishable from the other college guys, with skinny jeans, unbuttoned long-sleeve shirt over a tee shirt, necklace, and a colorful wristband that most likely carried personal and political meaning. Vaguely anxious, with nervous laughter and an occasional slight stutter, Anthony warned me several times that I might be surprised by his answers. Turns out, unlike Andrew Tobias in his famous account of growing up Catholic and gay, Anthony hasn't lived the life of the "best little boy in the world," Catholic or otherwise.

Before the interview began, Anthony completed written exercises regarding his adolescent crushes, sexual fantasies, sexual attractions, sexual encounters, and romantic relationships, and whether they involved girls or boys. He asked tons of questions about what ought to count, and he concluded while laughing, "What a mess this is! . . . Am I cheating right now? I feel like I'm contradicting my original questions because I'm thinking about it more. Is that a problem?" Indeed, throughout the interview Anthony frequently apologized for his long answers and at times genuinely surprised himself when he revealed memories he hadn't previously shared with anyone.

Since middle school, Anthony has preferred the company of girls to guys. "I don't get along or argue with them but don't enjoy the time spent with straight guys. Don't have a lot in common." When hanging out with guys, Anthony feels insecure, so he isn't friendly with many, except for a few popular guys on the high school tennis and track teams. Earlier in his life Anthony tried sports but abandoned them, to the point that his parents charged him with being a quitter. "I was never very good so I would quit." In high school Anthony played tennis and didn't make the team, so he quit and joined the track team until junior year, when he quit that too. As he told it, "I was pretty good. Placed championship, ran and triple jump, not distance. All others got muscular and my slim physique could not keep up with that."

Anthony's description of himself was intriguing and, as I was to discover, on target. "I think I look kind of masculine and my voice isn't too high. I don't have masculine body or muscular but I don't think I come off as masculine as people think I do." At a recent high school party, Anthony was talking with a straight guy when two very feminine boys walked by. The straight guy commented, "They're so gay together." At first Anthony laughed it off, but then his friend asked, "Oh, are you straight?" Anthony disclosed, "No, I'm gay." "So he thought I was straight so anyone who is gay would know I'm gay but I can come off as a pretty normal person . . . Generally people don't automatically know." But maybe his friend suspected—after all, he did ask.

Anthony also sees himself as feminine in some respects, especially given his taste in music (Lady Gaga and Beyoncé on his iPod), his slender body ("might be an insecurity but I don't know"), and his romantic behavior ("I let Patrick take the lead, plan dates, drive"). Compared with straight guys, Anthony says he's less athletic and more romantic.

By virtue of our continued contact, I know Anthony's story better than anyone's. It is integrated into the book, usually near the beginning of each section. In the final section, "Anthony Returns," we'll get his revised take on love, gay bars, and coming out to family.

Tell Our Stories

It comes at no surprise to me that most gay teens, whether male or female, do not associate themselves with the general description of same-sex attracted teens. (ADRIAN, AGE 16)

The e-mail exchanges with **Anthony** and several other gay teens arrived as I was in the beginning phase of planning this book. I decided to ask each, "What would you like for this book to be about? What is missing?"

Travis: Make It about Us

Travis, a high school sophomore, texted me to ask whether I would mentor him on a paper he was writing on the biology of sexual orientation, and I agreed. Travis had found me by reading *The New Gay Teenager.* A few weeks later I called to ask for his advice in turn.

★ ★

R: What would you like to see as a follow-up?

Us. Make it about our lives, our friends, our families.

★ ★

I'm following his succinct advice, and that of **Anthony** and of **Adrian** and **Jared**, the two we'll be meeting next.

Adrian: Not a Gay Stereotype

I received an e-mail from **Adrian**, a 16-year-old Latino youth from Chicago. His life has been quite different from **Anthony** or **Travis** but nevertheless shared his perspective. Adrian doesn't want to be a gay stereotype, and he isn't particularly happy with the way he and his generation have been portrayed by adults.

* *

Mr. Savin-Williams,

I am a 16-year-old male. I had been questioning my sexuality since I was about 11 and since about the age of 14 have come to the conclusion that I am gay . . .

It comes at no surprise to me that most gay teens, whether male or female, do not associate themselves with the general description of same-sex attracted teens. I have always felt that we have been studied as a new species to "figure out how we work." As with any teen, and human in general, we do not all fit into stereotypes. I for one, and am sure many in my position would agree, feel that we are each unique persons, like everyone else.

* *

Adrian acknowledged that gay youths have an "added problem," in common with other teens who do not present in culturally acceptable ways, such as racial minorities. But to Adrian, it was a blessing because being gay enriched his life. Adrian is deeply religious, and he routinely thanks God for giving him this gift.

* *

The fact that we have had an added problem in our lives of discerning out sexuality to be that which is not "the norm" is simply a problem. A problem much like having divorced parents, abusive parents, or being teased about weight or height. I am not asking for sympathy for same-sex attracted teens, and adults as well for that matter, but merely for acceptance.

We didn't ask for this blessing of being attracted to the same sex (and I am going to call it a blessing because that's what it is). Like any other problem one may encounter, it is the fight through that problem from which we learn the most and for that reason,

8

we should feel blessed to have had that learning experience. But now that we have, we would simply like to live our lives as any "normal" human, although I reject the term normal because I do not believe that anything that can happen is abnormal.

I greatly respect the work you have done to further gain acceptance of the GLBT community. It is through the work of people such as yourself that we will one day be able to live in complete harmony with our fellow humans, for that is simply what we are. I thank you again, and encourage you to continue doing your work . . . I tried to speak as honestly as possible.

Respectfully,
Adrian

* *

If Adrian is reading this, I would love to hear from him again—and Jared as well.

Jared: Listen to What I Have to Say

Jared, also 16 years old but from a suburb of Nashville, Tennessee, described himself as "extremely short, blonde hair blue eyed boy who likes drama and art much more than playing football and eating chicken wings." Jared has suffered a father who tells antigay jokes and classmates who badger him with "You're a girl, shouldn't you be going to the all-girls school across the way because aren't you a girl, get ready to wear a skirt to class sissy boy." Certainly life can be challenging for those who don't conform to traditional notions of boy behavior.

Despite this abuse, inflicted more because of his gender presentation than because of his sexuality, Jared is leading a happy gay life.

* *

Dear Professor Savin-Williams,

Please excuse the spelling errors or grammatical mistakes i try to proof read as best as i could. I am a 16 male gay youth who just want to do something with his life and after i saw your lecture on itunes i realized that there are way to help and that you can be a part of something greater. If you don't have time or don't care i understand completely. But if you do just want one more in dept look at the life of one gay youth im always free to share what i have been through and feel. I do hope you read it and respond with something. I think it would be good for someone who understands or at least want to understand the life of gay youth batter would listen to what i have to say.

As I sit at my computer at 4:24 in the morning, I came across your video lecture on "The New Gay Teenager" and was completely captivated by your view of the fake perception of suicidal gay youth. As I watched the entire Q&A session my brain kept telling me to write something to this guy. I don't know why I decide to do this but I feel that if only for a brief moment someone will listen or in this case read what I have to say, and not dismiss it as trash coming from a confused and inexperienced youth who doesn't know what he wants I will calm my thirst for writing.

★ ★

Needless to say, after this introduction I was totally hooked! Without revealing details that might identify him, here's a brief overview of Jared's life.

★ ★

First I should probably tell you who I am [details deleted]. I identify as a gay youth and have been "out and proud" for about two years now. I should warn you now; I hope this to be somewhat lengthy, not a Novel but not a two page letter, I completely understand if you can't or don't have time to read and respond back. Second you're probably wondering what I am emailing you for. Well possibly many reasons but one reason I know it is not. I don't intend this to be a poor me I need help letter that is so stereo-typical of gay youth. One reason could be I just want someone to hear what I have to say and I think you'd be the guy for it or another could be because I simply want to write. Either way I'm writing [details deleted regarding his life].

If you had read this far, you professor a man I have never even met, you have done more the 99% of adults in my life and I thank you for that. For now I am going to stop writing because it is 5:21 and sleep is needed, but I would like to say this. There is so much more to my story and I could only hope you would like to hear the rest of it . . .

Yes there are happy gay teens who lead great lives but there is so much more in this area that can be done and I want to help.

Sincerely,

Jared

* *

I did e-mail back, but, unfortunately, this was the last I heard from Jared. I trust he has written his story and made a difference in his world: "I still hold hope in my heart that I can make a difference and make it now, not 20 or 30 years from now, but now when the action should be taken."

Normal, Usually Healthy

Anthony, **Travis**, **Adrian**, and **Jared** made the same point. Today's gay youths are living the life gay adults could only have dreamed about when they were young—they're proud, popular, respected, happy, and ordinary. If you are a gay teenager, we know that the number and quality of your friendships, how popular you are in school, your ability to be intimate and connect with your parents, your personality characteristics, your self-esteem, your life satisfaction, and even your life stress rarely differ on average from straight youths. The young men I interviewed confirmed this, as their stories here will attest. Ultimately, what most distinguishes you as a gay teenager is merely the gender of your sexual and romantic encounters. Yet adults, including parents, seldom celebrate your quintessential life-affirming transformation with a jamboree or carnival. Rather, it's with disbelief. Being gay is supposedly hazardous to your health.

Why aren't we affirming and acknowledging your power, strength, pride, and resilience? It's complicated. Perhaps gay adults generalize from their own hostile experiences growing up, when harassment, bullying, and family loss particularly compounded life for gay people—and your parents fear this will happen to you if you come out as gay. Because of their sexuality or gender expression, gay adults suffered, sometimes mightily, and they merely assume that your generation will as well. Or, because a caring adult works with troubled gay youths in a clinical or medical setting, his or her exposure is restricted to dreadful life stories, not those of the vast majority of gay youths who never come to the attention of social workers, public health officials, or psychiatrists.

Although it certainly isn't my intent to downplay or deny the reality of any individual or generation who wrestles with society's reactions to gayness, we must be careful not to generalize from a real or imagined yesteryear to what a gay teen experiences today. Not then nor now are you more prone than your straight boy or girl friends to suffer bouts of poor mental health. It is rare that your family rejects you, your friends forsake you, or your religious leaders lament you. Indeed, we know that on average you report equal levels of positive mental health as straight boys—and this is a good thing.

Yes, I admit that at times it's not easy being gay in all communities or in all families. It's not always a pretty scenario being young and gay, yet most of you do quite well, weathering potentially adverse conditions. Coming out and leading an authentic life can be incredibly rewarding and healthy. If you do have difficulties, please don't imitate one young man I interviewed, who is eternally thankful that he failed in the stupidest thing he's ever done.

* *

I did in ninth when I came out and at the lowest of my depression. I made a suicide attempt because I wanted to fit in and not put up with all that shit. I slit my wrists really badly, which you can still see [pulls up his sleeve to show me]. After I did it I realized I didn't want to and because I was an Eagle Scout I took care of it and wrapped it. I told people I accidentally cut myself on a pool thing. I was ashamed I did it. As soon as I did it I said this is wrong.

* *

As a whole, gay youths are certainly not in constant or universal psychological peril—yes, some are, but the vast majority are not. And be careful with gay adults who attempt to tell you what you're supposed to do or be to be a *good gay*.

Unfortunately, the reality is that we adults remain polarized about your life. Maybe the best advice I can give is to follow your own life path and that of your generation. Each of us is considerably more than our sexuality, with particular strengths and abilities that may or may not be related to sexuality. That said, you might at times need extra resources to help you cope with homophobia, but to characterize an entire generation by a few is, well, ludicrous. Many of you are simply ordinary youths coping with an adult world that doesn't always understand you. By most accounts, gay youths enjoy life and don't want to be anything but gay—as the young men I talked to corroborated.

This is true today and, despite the testimonials of adults, was true thirty years ago when I first began conducting gay research. In the mid-1980s I surveyed over 300 gay and lesbian youths between the ages of 14 and 23 from typical adolescent and young adult venues. Other than not always getting the grades, the job, the parents, or the desired romance, typical gay young adults back then weren't particularly miserable, distraught, suicidal, unlovable, or drug addicted. Most telling, their self-esteem level, which predicts success and well-being in many aspects of life, didn't differ from the national average. Though many struggled coming out to parents, only rarely were they rejected or tossed out of the home. Indeed, I was impressed with the remarkable ability of these youths to find their way through life, assisted by their creativity, interpersonal sensitivity, and self-awareness. You too will find your way and will be accepted by friends and family. Your sexuality will not be a cross to bear, but in sync with your "it's just who I am, get over it" attitude.

Undeniably, being young and gay is easier now in the Western world than it was in the mid-1980s. Whether in sports (where soccer players Anton Hysén, Robbie Rogers, and David Testo have come out), popular culture (where singing icons Adam Lambert, Sam Smith, Rufus Wainwright, and Olly Alexander are out gay men), or civil law (where marriage equality, workplace nondiscrimination, and military service opportunities have opened up), it's far gay-friendlier today than ever before.

Yet despite this new reality, when Eagle Scout and Villanova swimmer Ryan Murtha disclosed his sexuality to his swim team, it was with considerable anxiety:

* *

So this is tough for me and I apologize for taking so long to tell you guys this, but it took me forever to admit to myself and then it's been really hard to work up the courage to say it.

I'm gay. I've tried to bury this part of myself for a long time but slowly grew to accept it over the past year and a half. I want you guys to know that this isn't something that I chose. I was just born with it.

Anyway, I want you to know that I'm still the same person that I've been. I hope you guys don't see me any differently because of this. I don't think it should define me totally; it's just one of many parts that make up who I am.

But if for whatever reason you don't like me because of this, I guess I can't blame you because for a long time I hated myself for being gay, too. I made myself believe that living with this shame was worth not losing any of my friendships. But I don't want to be ashamed anymore. And I've kind of felt like I wouldn't be able to 100% accept myself and move on until I could be truthful with my friends. That's you guys. So if you're down to stick around and still be my friend, I can't even begin to say how grateful I would be.

If you have any questions or if you want to talk to me about it, feel free.

* *

After a pregnant pause from his teammates, there was applause, celebration, cheering, hugging, and they all went to eat at Chipotle. No turning their backs on a friend for such a silly reason—because he's gay.

15

Life Stories

Other than receiving unsolicited e-mails from gay teens, over the past several years I have engaged in conversations with over 200 young men, averaging 20 years of age, in face-to-face interviews. More details are provided in the Appendix, but here's a brief description of the project: young adults of various sexualities answered questions about their developmental history, from their first sexual memories to how they believe their sexuality will be ten years from now. Of these, forty identified as gay or mostly gay, and they provided the life stories for this book.

Although some had dropped out of high school or were being homeschooled, the vast majority were attending a community college, state college, or research university. Several had no career aspirations, and others hoped to be lawyers, doctors, or engineers. Some families were below the poverty line, and others were living quite comfortably. Southeast Asian, Native American, African American, Mexican American, Puerto Rican, Caucasian, Catholic, Evangelical Protestant, Jewish, Atheist, Muslim, and Spiritualist youths participated. They grew up in rural areas, small cities, suburbs, and urban centers.

But let's begin in the beginning—How did you become gay?"

Why Am I Gay?

I really don't care.   (YOUNG MAN, AGE 19)

Our sexuality is given expression by who we are attracted to, fantasize about, have sex with, and fall in love with. It affects and is affected by our personality, social relationships, and career aspirations. But how does that sexuality come about? What are its origins, and can it be changed if we don't like it? These questions likely build as your same-sex sexuality emerges during childhood then intensifies during adolescence, and you ask yourself (but not yet others), "Why am I gay?" One young man looked at his family tree, spotted many other gays, and concluded, "Genetics has something to do with it for me." Another couldn't find an answer: "It's a mystery. It's the way the universe made me."

Given his family history, including his dad's gay brother and a gay cousin, **Anthony** speculated that his genetics played a role in his sexuality, though he isn't that invested in figuring out why he's gay. He feels he just is, and he can't imagine being any other way. Anthony never chose to be gay. In fact, none of the young men I interviewed described their sexual orientation as a "lifestyle choice," although several wondered whether they are gay because they had been seduced by sexual experiences with a cousin or brother. All creditable scientists would disagree. You are not gay because of sexual seduction, sexual abuse, being called gay at school, or being overly attached to your mother or alienated from your father. Even if all were true, these experiences didn't make you gay. Sexual orientation is not a matter of choice, and neither can it be undone.

Born That Way

For decades we've explored the origin question as to why some boys are exclusively attracted to other males, and others are not. There's no definitive answer yet, but the general consensus is that it's set down at fertilization or while the fetus is still in the womb. Whatever the cause, it forever affects the neurology and endocrine functioning of the brain. It's also possible that whatever mechanisms causes one particular boy to be sexually attracted to males might not be the same for other boys.

For instance, one boy may inherit particular genes from one or both biological parents. No specific genes have been certified as causing gayness, but most scientists believe that not just one but many genes may be involved, similar to other complex human traits. Geneticist Jenny Graves called them "male-loving" and "female-loving" genes, which I like because it includes not only your sexuality but also whom you fall in love with. If, for example, your brother inherits an abundance of female-loving genes, he'll be more predisposed than you will be to mate earlier and more often, and thus to have more children. If you inherit a sufficient number of male-loving genes, you won't be predisposed to those same activities, but you might want to cheer him along (as I'll explain).

A typical argument against an evolutionary perspective is that boys with male-loving genes are a genetic dead end, the end of gayness. But that's not necessarily so. As Dr. Graves proposed there are other ways for you to pass your male-loving genes to future generations. For example, one possibility is that although you are not as likely as your girl-loving brother to mate with females and thus you'll fail to transmit your male-loving genes directly to future generations, your female relatives (sisters, aunts, cousins, nieces) who share your genetic code are more inclined to bear children because they have an extra incentive to have sex with males, courtesy of their higher dose of male-loving genes. These additional offspring compensate for the fewer children you'll have, and your genes are passed on to future generations.

A second possibility is if your female-loving brother inherits a few male-loving genes (so he's a *mostly straight* guy). The number is insufficient to make him gay but amply sufficient to increase his appeal to females. He's more sensitive, more caring, and less brutal. As a result, he increases his odds of producing a large number of offspring who are genetically related to you, his male-loving brother. In addition, this brother's chance of survival and hence having offspring is greater if his slightly elevated level of male-loving genes leads him to bond with other men for mutual protection and sharing of resources (during both the hunter/gatherer days and today). That is, having a slight bit of gayness might be advantageous—as you probably already know.

A third mechanism with evolutionary repercussions might also convey your genes to future generations. Along with inheriting male-loving genes you might receive feminine characteristics, which can help you to be more caring and protective of your genetic kin (your siblings, nephews, nieces, and cousins). By enhancing their survival you improve your chances of transmitting the genetic material you share with them to future generations.

The result is that evolution likely "wanted" a continuous distribution of individuals with male-loving and female-loving genes. At the extreme ends are your straight friends and you as a gay person, with many gradations in between. This leaves room for mostly straights, bisexuals, mostly gays, and other nonexclusive points yet to be named. You likely know many such individuals as your best and supportive friends (or perhaps you are one your-self), and they know where you're coming from.

My Gay Relatives

One clear indication that same-sex sexuality can be a matter of genetics is a family with more than the average number of gay relatives. Perhaps it's a sprinkling, but it may be a downpour. You're likely to be more sensitive to this issue and thus to locate the other gays scattered throughout your family tree. Gay youths indeed are more likely than straight youths to have gay relatives. Among the young men I interviewed, only a few could not name the fellow "gay travelers" in their families. Several suspected a first cousin, largely because they had had sex with that cousin while growing up. Later in life, the cousin might identify as straight, explaining his behavior as the hijinks of a horny adolescent or as simply experimentation, or he might even refuse to talk about it. Regardless, he apparently has some level of male-loving genes in his body.

Here is an example from one young man I interviewed. When he was an 11-year-old, he wasn't quite sure whether his cousin was gay because that cousin had been hypersexual from an early age. One night while sleeping over, his cousin made an offer he couldn't refuse.

* *

He'd say to me that he wanted to jerk me off and then he'd ask me to bend over and to see if it [the cousin's penis] fits. He tried anal on me and I said, "It hurts!" He'd jerk me off at his house but it wasn't so pleasant. He showed me what the body could do. He was always telling me that he wanted to experiment with me and this went on for several years. He said he outgrew it. It was just an experiment and he's straight.

I don't think so but that's okay. Neither of us ever said what we did is gay. My cousin was being his usual weird self. I knew it was sexual. Too bad it was with my cousin and not someone better looking.

★ ★

Several young men suspected their mothers' brothers are gay, and gay uncles frequently populated these young men's lives. In a typical case, everyone knows Uncle Fred is gay, yet everyone ignores it. He can't be gay because he's 72, has been married for fifty years, and has children. However, the giveaway is Uncle Fred's lifelong male "friend." The two spend all their time together, alone. Uncle Fred also plays piano and owns a gay bar. "My mom told me she *thinks* he's gay." Indeed, Uncle Fred belongs to a different time and generation. By contrast, another youth has two uncles who are openly gay, one of whom has been in a same-sex relationship for twenty-five years.

I will be introducing you to a number of young men who participated in my research and the one who is my best example of the family connection is **Jeremy**. He has several gay relatives in his home—his brother, sister, and perhaps even a parent.

Jeremy: The Interview

After hearing about my interviews during his engineering class, **Jeremy**, age 20, requested that I come to his college's LGBT Alliance office. Jeremy, who came from a working class, conservative town, was attending college on a scholarship. In his hometown environment, his parents stood out as not only progay and liberal, but also as practicing an organic, vegetarian diet. Jeremy was clearly nervous on meeting me, but I found him immediately engaging and thoroughly likeable. Slightly on the chunky side with dark hair and glasses, and dressed blandly in baggy jeans and sweatshirt, Jeremy fidgeted, apologized, and talked at length.

As a child, Jeremy was introverted and a loner. He played with Matchbox cars and Legos, loved science, loved being in the school band and all things musical, and was both artsy and nerdy. Never traditionally masculine, Jeremy now sees himself as being in the grey area between "gay acting and straight acting." His one athletic passion is a long-standing, intense love for skiing. If given a choice, Jeremy would prefer to be more masculine so that he "could just hang out with guys and not have to worry about boundaries because of my homosexuality. I would love to just be assimilated in with everyone else and not stand out."

Yet Jeremy does stand out in terms of his "gay family tree." According to Jeremy, he has never had a choice about whether he'd be gay because the biological evidence is so compelling. His older brother and sister are gay, though his twin sister is straight. "She's the black sheep! My father is likely gay. He is pretty, self-conscious, the gay stereotype though an engineer, reads literature, loves Cindy Lauper, sips red wine, hates sports and mechanics. My mom thinks he's gay and my older sister has tried to get him out but he says he can't be because he's married and has four kids."

Ted, who we'll meet in a later chapter, doesn't know how many gay relatives he has. Ted was conceived from sperm deposited at a sperm bank, so he doesn't know his biological father. However, from the donor's registry Ted discovered that he has, at the point I met him, seventeen half-siblings, one of whom he's met, and that half-brother is gay. "So there's got to be some gay genes on my dad's side." In addition, there is his mother. I'll let him explain:

★ ★

My mom, this is a pretty extensive family tree so I don't know if you want to follow it. My mom herself had lesbian tendencies for a while from the 70's and the early 80's. I have no first cousins because she was an only child. It's in her generation and my second cousins. It's pretty extensive and prevalent. My grandfather [mom's father] was one of eight. All of them have children and half of their children are gay or lesbian. Then my grandfather had a relationship with a man after my grandmother died when he was like in his 80s. He had a man living with him. The understanding was that they were in a relationship.

★ ★

One advantage to having gay relatives is having someone to talk to. In one case, a lesbian aunt, greatly admired by the family because "she's an artist, also a farmer, kind of does her own thing," gave her nephew the courage to come out to his parents and advice about his love life.

Bottom line: without a doubt, gayness runs in families—but it might not be genetics.

Older Brothers

Another pathway to becoming gay is through a mother's immune response to previous pregnancies, which influences the neurological development of succeeding fetuses. Researcher Ray Blanchard named this the *fraternal birth order effect*. Because some small amount of fetal cells enters the mother's circulation during childbirth or perhaps earlier during pregnancy, if the fetus is male, the mother's immune system recognizes these male-specific molecules as *foreign* (that is, not female like herself). In response she produces antimale antibodies to fight them. The probability of this occurring increases with each male fetus, such that once the mother becomes pregnant with perhaps her third or fourth male fetus, her antibodies are sufficiently plentiful to prevent the neurons in the child's brain from wiring in a male-typical pattern. So the boy becomes female-like in terms of eroticism, romantic feelings, and perhaps gender expression, though not in all respects. After all, such boys retain basic male-typical physical characteristics, such as a penis and testicles.

The theory has lots of support across generations and cultures, but it doesn't always work, for unknown reasons. That is, a boy might have many older brothers and still be straight—but not Tyler. After learning about the older brother hypothesis in class, Tyler is proud to be living proof of the theory: "I sleep with guys. I am attracted to guys. I fantasize about guys. Whereas like now that I'm gay, I don't care how I'm perceived anymore."

Unable to locate any other gays in his extended family, Tyler doubted it is genetic for him. He noted rather wide age gaps between his two older brothers and between them and him. He's at least the fourth male pregnancy for his mother.

* *

Between my two older brothers, there was a stillbirth. That explains the gap between them. The baby was male . . . I am supposed to have three older brothers. I have heard the theory and I think it makes a lot of sense, at least in my case.

I might be one of those! One of those gays that has all the older brothers and the androgens and whatnot! And feminized you as a fetus! I don't know why there is a gap between me and my next oldest brother. It might have gotten stressful having two kids that are three years apart. Maybe mom wanted to take another four-year break. I have never spoken to my parents about their sex life and I never have any desire to.

* *

Learning to Be Gay

Instead of genes or older brothers, some theories focus on the early environment. These include an overprotective mother, an emotionally absent father, an older male abuser, antigay peers yelling "fag," and gifts of girl toys. Although scientific research doesn't support any of these explanations, people believe them anyway, including Liam.

Liam: The Interview

Liam, age 25, came to the United States from the Middle East for undergraduate studies, and is now pursuing a master's degree in business administration and investment banking. Although he is now a U.S. citizen, Liam remains fiercely loyal to his home country. Liam has dark skin, dark hair, dark eyes, and is muscular and of medium height. When we met, he was dressed in casual business attire. He was reflective before answering questions, and he offered brief, compact answers. Liam's life continues to perplex him, and he is trying to figure it out. By the end of the interview, which felt like a therapy session, Liam concluded, "Guess I'm gay," though he hopes to change this "temporary status" in the future.

In Liam's religiously based private school, everyone was a friend of everybody else, and everyone knew everybody's business. He had a small group of extremely close friends, and through social media they remain in contact today. He was popular and a leader among his friends. They swam, attended birthday parties, and played (always) soccer. Whenever Liam dated a girl, either she was immediately incorporated into this small group of friends or they would break up. According to Liam, if he is a happy person today, it is because of his friends. Liam has never heard rumors about his sexuality, and he easily passes as straight. He described himself as ambitious, passionate, a Christian, a cynic, a global citizen, and a gentleman. He also loves car shows, computers, weight lifting, and dancing. Liam wants everyone to like him and to make everyone happy.

Liam fears these positives would suddenly disappear if his friends recognized his true sexuality. What puzzles Liam is that he knows his Middle Eastern friends would allow him to be gay and still accept him, so why doesn't he just tell them? Why does he have an internal drive to be straight? He can't find the answers. He traced his gay awareness to his love of dancing, which at age 17 took him to a new world in his Middle Eastern country—gay bars. After his family moved to the United States (for political reasons), Liam maintained his charade: he dated girls on Fridays, went to gay bars on Saturdays, and woke up on Sundays with the guy he'd met on Saturday. Liam juggled these two facets of his life, having both girlfriends and boyfriends and keeping the two worlds entirely separate. "The guys would text me when I was with her. When I did not come home I told my sister I had found a girl to stay with and that pleased her."

Given this history, Liam is out to few others—certainly not his immediate and extended family, who wouldn't like his sexuality but would not reject him either. However, he has a cultural obligation to marry and have children. Those who know that Liam likes boys are limited to the guys he's met for sex through Grindr, a hookup app for gay men. Our interview was Liam's first overt admission of his homosexuality.

What most distresses Liam is how he believes he "became gay"—his cousin seducing him at age 12. Throughout Liam's adolescence the two engaged in a porn-inspired routine of having sex whenever their families had outings together. According to

Liam, their sexual relationship taught him what is erotic, and it imprinted on him maleness as a source of orgasms. "I was sucked into it by him"—and he meant this literally and figuratively. In a rare moment of exasperation during the interview, Liam beseeched to no one in particular, "Why did he do this to me?" Liam is convinced that otherwise he'd not be gay today.

By way of proof, Liam argued (again, to no one in particular) that during early adolescence he was gay only in his sexual fantasies (a 50/50 ratio), but by high school he was 80/20 gay in his sexual attractions and fantasies. And, to make matters worse, Liam developed crushes and romantic feelings toward boys. The cousin was so persuasive in his seductive power that by college Liam was 100 percent gay by all sexual and romantic indicators.

★ ★

We'd sit together and it evolved where we would jack off ourselves, watching [porn] touching ourselves under clothes. Then he showed me his penis and so weird and different than mine. We then did it more openly. I could ejaculate but not at the beginning. Seeing him and interested in it and wanting to do it—within a year or two it was erotic. At one point when I was 13 we jacked off each other. Every time I see him I'd get a hard-on and we would satisfy each other. Never anal sex and never kissed but was oral sex. I reached orgasm with him and never did with a female. It was so tabooish to doing anything sexual.

What I could have experienced with a girl I reached points of pleasure with my cousin. At 13 or 14 I started an interest in looking at guys, naked pictures, gay porn and never straight porn after that. I always had a girlfriend. Through age 17 when I came to the US I felt great, but also guilty, always hesitant. Once I said I didn't want to do it anymore with him, but we continued . . . He'd put on porn and I'd get sucked into it. 15 or 16 and do it daily or every other day.

I saw him recently and didn't get a hard-on but I did in my developmental phase of sexuality. Masturbation and thinking of girls and this was all fine and then my cousin blocked my developmental system. His sexuality was complete. He says he always wants girls . . . I am jealous because he's getting married. I'm not sure I can perform with girls after him. I wanted girls and was going that way.

17 had sex with another guy . . . Haven't had girlfriends since then and not sexual with girls because I don't feel anything. No hard-on when with a girl.

I have a conservative family and it is hard to accept myself and not sure I have. Know I'm different and angry at my cousin. Why did he do this to me?

★ ★

In fact, Liam is so gay that for two years he's been dating the same guy, someone he'd propose to if he could (which was not yet an option at the time of the interview). Would he take a magical pill and turn himself straight? "I wish I could change, so, yes, to be straight. It would be easier for me to accept myself more, easier for my parents, easier for me to meet expectations of having kids, marry, and I do want kids." In his ideal future, however, Liam maintained he'd have 10 percent interest in having sex with and loving guys. He's not willing to take a magical pill to make him *totally straight*.

Liam is the one guy I interviewed who was most negative toward his gayness—not because gay sex isn't erotic or loveless but because he believes he'd been seduced against his will to be homosexual. The fact that the two cousins are genetically related, that Liam was a willing partner and enjoyed the sex, and that his

cousin might not be as straight as he claimed to be were insignificant to Liam. Why did he turn out gay and his cousin straight?
Because, Liam claimed, he had been at an earlier stage of puberty
when the seduction began, so his eroticism was mapped onto his
cousin's penis, not a vagina. As a result, when Liam had a girlfriend, he didn't want to have sex with her. Liam believes he
learned this behavior, but I have my doubts. Given Liam's cultural
heritage of mandatory marriage and children, he's in a bind, and
he knows it.

Not a Choice

Although speculations about how they became gay might be
worthy of momentary, curious reflections, more than one youth
responded, "I really don't care." One fear was that if gayness is genetic then future politicians or religious leaders will try to "correct" it to make everyone straight. Of course, reparative therapists
intent on producing *ex-gays* are themselves fervently antibiolog-
ical because they want you to believe that sexual orientation is
under voluntary control. You are to believe that if you just try hard
enough, with their help, scriptural reading, and prayer, you can
choose to be *un-gay*.

The popularity of this perspective has waned during the past
several years as evidence has mounted against the sexual orientation by choice arguments. Exodus International, the largest Christian ministry advocating sexual orientation change, closed its
doors after over three decades of diatribes against gays. The last
president of Exodus apologized for the pain, lies, guilt, and condemnation the ministry perpetuated. Having once claimed thousands of success stories, he now admits 99.9 percent of those who
attempted to free themselves of same-sex attractions failed. Simi-

larly, a former leader of the notorious ex-gay ministry Love In Action recently married his husband in Oklahoma.

The most typical response to my question—"Why do you believe you're gay?"—was simply, "I don't know. I know I didn't choose it." Ultimately, whatever causes sexual orientation doesn't much matter. It is what it is, and the real test is how you live your life with that sexuality. You didn't choose to be gay, and you can't un-choose it. How you express your sexuality is optional. You can decide not to identify as gay, not to have sex with guys, and not to date guys, but you cannot decide who you are erotically attracted to and fall in love with.

And whatever its cause, your sexuality is likely reflected in your earliest memories.

First Sexual Memory

I am uncircumcised and I think the foreskin was not entirely retracted yet, and I was just touching myself and then all of the sudden there was a lot of blood. (DEREK, AGE 7)

First memories are selective and not necessarily representative of our early life. They lack specific details, are distorted, and have unknown significance then and now. The enemy is *infantile amnesia*. We don't remember most of what happens during our early years. To have an early memory attention must first be drawn to an experience that is eventually encoded in the brain. For most of us, this includes only a few things prior to age 5. Given that a gay youth has always been gay, does he remember some aspect of this sexuality manifesting at an early age? Does he have an early *autobiographical memory* that now detects a tiny bit of gayness from before he realized during adolescence or young adulthood that he's gay?

I began every interview with the following set of questions.

* *

Please recall the very first sexual or romantic memory you have. It is not necessary that at the time you understood it as sexual or romantic in nature but now, looking back, does it have this meaning for you? Anchor your memory in a concrete event. How old are you? Is it someone in particular, a dream, an encounter, or an emotional connection? What provoked it? Did you tell anyone? Why or why not? Does this memory have significance or has it affected you?

* *

Asking for details proved particularly helpful as several young men self-corrected their first stabs at memories, almost as if a cascade had been set in motion from the one memory. I can almost see each young man relive an earlier time in his life. "Oh yes, there was the time . . ." Inevitably, a fascinating story would follow.

These questions also established the interview ambiance. The questions were unexpected, and they asked for personal information and specific details, evoked emotional involvement, and invited reflection. This turned out to be a surprising beginning: adults seldom ask a boy of any age or sexuality about his first sexual memories. Why they don't isn't obvious to me—unless adults believe a youth does not have childhood memories of a sexual nature or if he does they are inconsequential or private experiences that are inappropriate to divulge. Maybe it's simply because adults are embarrassed. The net effect is silence about the early sexual and romantic life of gay youths. This is not good.

It was not always easy to obtain answers from the young men to questions about their earliest memories, and frequently the meanings of those memories were not apparent to them or to me. Although most youths were off and running, several strained to remember anything even remotely sexual until adolescence. Also, our minds are capable of blocking from consciousness threatening or unacceptable memories, such as attraction to other boys.

The first signs of sexuality were as early as the ability to recall anything or as late as the commencement of puberty. They were sharp or fuzzy, weird happenstances without any recognizable meaning. They were mysteries or self-encounters with a profound impact on the youth's life. These memories were occasionally shared with a parent or a friend, but only rarely. Few of his elementary school teachers requested a report on this topic. Few of his religious leaders prayed for repentance or delivery from these childhood sexual memories. Later in life his feelings about these memories and what they mean might be transformed. With the new revelations that porn, masturbation fantasies, websites, and conversations can provide, the memories might acquire new significance—becoming the first indication of his sexuality. One stunned young man muttered, actually to himself, *"Obviously.* I must have been gay quite early." And he was right.

I Remember...

Among the young men I interviewed, the first sexual memory was usually about one of three things.

1. Seeing or thinking about a guy, whether real or virtual, and feeling aroused.
2. Engaging in playful sexual activities with another child, similar to what **Anthony** recalled.
3. Developing a crush or an infatuation, usually without realizing what it is.

The next three chapters explore each of these types in turn. Because the boys in each type did not differ regarding the age when it first occurred, whether they told anyone about the memories, or their reactions to the memories, I offer a summary of these memories in this chapter.

Sexual memories emerged from first recollections, during preschool, daycare, or early elementary school. The average age for a first sexual memory was 7. By age 9 over three-quarters had experienced a sexual awareness. It was a rare boy who didn't have a sexual memory until adolescence. Many now recognize these child memories as an *immature* version of what has since become far more explicit—their sexual or romantic attractions and desires.

Here is how it seems to work:

1. Your sexuality is present from birth.
2. Your awareness of that sexuality is stimulated by an early experience that creates an autobiographic memory, such as seeing a naked guy in a locker room, having sex with a cousin, or feeling infatuated with a teacher.
3. Prepubertal sex steroids enhance your awareness during middle childhood, perhaps with an accompanying increase in eroticism.
4. Puberty and its dramatic hormone escalation stamp intensity to your sexual and romantic life.

Thus, puberty doesn't create but merely strengthens what is already present. First sexual memories are laid down at any point during this process, depending on your life circumstances and developmental history. What is irrefutable is that your sexual and romantic longings and activities exist long before most parents, teachers, religious leaders, and sex education classes are willing to talk to you about them.

Disclosure and Reactions

The interview was the first time nearly every young man I spoke to had shared his first sexual memory. Although a few had told friends and a few had told parents, they were a distinct minority. Those who divulged such memories usually recalled a girl crush, a presumed universal among boys, as their first memory.

Derek, who we'll meet again in a later chapter, blended pleasure and pain in his first sexual memory.

★ ★

When I was very young, probably like 6 or 7, I think that's when I started to masturbate and the first memory I have is I am uncircumcised, and I think the foreskin was not entirely retracted yet, and I was just touching myself, and then all of the sudden there was a lot of blood, and I didn't know what to do about it.

I had no idea what it was. I mean it felt good. I really didn't know anything about sex or really I don't even think romantic attraction or anything like that. At that point, I had a very clear idea that man and woman, that's how everything went, and I would grow up, and I would have a wife or something like that.

I mean I was pretty scared. I had no idea why I was bleeding so much so I went to my mom, and I remember her asking me like, "What were you doing? Why is there blood?" And I, for some reason, I think it was in the way she asked it. I understood she kind of knew, and it was bad. So I lied, and I said, "I don't know. I just woke up like this." I think that's why it was more of a negative memory for me. Honestly, I think I forgot about it for a long time, and then I think I was actually playing truth or dare with a friend or something, and we were talking about our first sexual experiences, and that memory just popped up.

★ ★

Reactions but Few Disclosures

Derek's negative reaction was in marked contrast to what he felt—ecstasy. **Jonathan**, who we'll see more of in the next chapter, undressed and felt up a G.I. Joe doll. He knew he wasn't supposed to do it, "but there was something about it that was important to me." Others, however, were less encumbered with guilt, evaluating their first sexual memory as extremely rewarding.

Yet if the memories were positive, signaling an awareness of a same-sex sexuality, why weren't they disclosed to others? Most boys realized these memories shouldn't be shared. One confessed, "I knew this deviated from the norm, though I wasn't aware that it might label me as gay." Apparently by middle childhood most boys absorb the cultural message about appropriate and inappropriate feelings and experiences. Crushes on girls are okay. Crushes on boys are not. Sex with girls should wait, but sex with boys is intolerable. To be aroused by girls is expected. To be aroused by boys is a mistake, merely part of a phase, or impossible.

Eleven-year-old **Jeremy** didn't want to share his first sexual memory because it was embarrassing. His memory was about Sting, the musician. He elaborated, "I know, really weird. I bought *Brand New Day* and the front cover! A longing to be with him but not understand as sexual." He didn't tell anyone "because it was so absurd and like so geeky, so stupid." He attributed his early Sting obsession to his desire to become a musician.

A common theme cutting across nearly every story is the sense that from an early age each of the boys thought, *I am different from other boys.*

First Arousal

Can I look at your penis?   (BOY, AGE 8)

Sometimes we can immediately sense when a particular person is present—an energy, a mystery, a force that's tricky to describe. Perhaps our face flushes, our heart rushes, we become extra attentive and alert, and perhaps there's extra blood flow to the genitals. What is it that awakens these responses? For the straight guy, it's a girl. For the gay guy, it's something about a boy. It's a blip in an otherwise normal day, or a profound excitement that feels urgent and even life altering. Weeks, months, or years later he realizes what it was all about—and he still feels the energy.

In the everyday world of gay boys, these situations arise and are particularly important when the provocateur is another guy. For the young men I've spoken with, the experience was magical. They named a hot young schoolteacher, a winking motorcyclist in black leather, Olympic swimmer Michael Phelps wearing very little, a naked G.I. Joe, the mysterious Aladdin, an action hero in tights, an Internet model in see-through mesh underwear, a school janitor with a great smile, a varsity soccer player with amazing legs, a lingering boy changing at the swimming pool ("I wanted to peek"), and daytime soap opera stars swaggering with bare chests and ready-to-be-removed jeans.

In Dreams

One of the safest places to be aroused is during sleep. You can always claim, "Hey, I have no control over what I dream about."

Besides, you don't have to tell anyone because no one really wants to hear about your dreams, and you can easily dismiss any possibility that dream images mean anything. You might wonder about these dreams, but you'll receive no help from child and adolescent development books—you'll often find nothing but silence about the significance of sex images in dreams.

For several young men, however, dream images were a critical factor in conveying their sexual future. For example, while watching the Olympics, one boy became enamored of swimming and those who swim, especially Michael Phelps ("only because he's so good"). Mr. Phelps turned into a rich source of nighttime dreams, before shame kicked in.

★ ★

When other guys liked girls I like boys, especially Michael Phelps. Age 10, I had a dream about Michael Phelps and how hot he is and an amazing body, though he has a strange face and what's with those pancake ears? He has a body I'd die for! I liked the dream, . . . excited, and then the more I thought, the more ashamed I was for having the dream. It was wrong, and though my parents weren't religious and were never negative about gays. . . . Main thing I came to grasp with being gay, it happens at subconscious so the way it is. I dream of guys and my friends of girls.

★ ★

Lenny: The Interview

After graduating from performing arts school, **Lenny** took a semester off before beginning an internship he hopes will lead to a career in film. He had been looking forward to our interview all week—"After all, I don't have that much going on." Lenny was lean, sported an artificial tan, wore the latest style in Bermuda shorts and pricey sneakers, and had lots of thick, blond curls falling near his eyes. He arrived early, ready to talk as soon as he entered the interview room.

Lenny described himself as more masculine than your typical gay guy. According to him, he doesn't give off "gay signs" or have "a very effeminate voice. When I get drunk, it does get more effeminate which is interesting. I feel like when I get drunk I exude more 'Hey, I'm gay!' and I can't say just my voice." He's feminine in the sense of being emotional, loving to talk, and being into fashion. He named several manly (*Game of Thrones*) and girly (*Gilmore Girls*, *The OC*) television shows he's into.

Lenny vividly recalled a seventh-grade dream with the actor Leonardo DiCaprio in a starring role. What did Lenny make of it? He still isn't fully sure, but at the time it felt sexual, especially to a seventh-grader who knew just enough not to share his DiCaprio fantasies.

* *

I was way too scared. Once I had started thinking about it, I was scared because I didn't know anyone that was gay. No one else had ever talked about having those kinds of thoughts. And it was just general discourse then for people to make fun of gay people. And it was very derogatory. So it was just something I didn't talk about. I think it was a minor revelation I think because I had it in my head that I was straight before then, but I could never actually remember having any sorts of fantasies or thoughts before then.

* *

Sometimes dreams are difficult to interpret, but other times they're easy. A 6-year-old created a nighttime sci-fi world he longed to enter, but to do so he had to dive deep into the open jeans of a huge "vivid visual" guy. It was a repetitive dream, confusing yet comforting. Although he was young, he sensed that the "into his pants" dreams were best kept secret. Now he interprets these dreams as having pro-penis sentiments, and it's a reasonable reading.

In Visuals

Another context for first arousal is visuals such as television shows or movies. Before the Internet, these were primary sources of eroticism, and they still have a place in young lives. It's not so much intentionally pornographic depictions as it is common visuals that appeal to a gay boy in a way a straight boy might not understand.

Dion, who we'll meet later, found that the mundane world of daytime soap operas amped his desire. He was 10 years old when an ordinary scripted scene piqued his interest.

★ ★

First would probably have to be, it's embarrassing. So, during the summers I used to stay home, and we didn't have cable so daytime soap operas, and I remember this soap opera and I think it was like *All My Children* or something like that, and they had a sex scene and of course it wasn't like that erotic, I mean in hindsight. But there was this guy that was probably in his mid to late 30s and he was like stripping down from his suit and was like shirtless with his socks on and, yeah, that was good . . .

I felt like it was dirty and it was something I shouldn't be watching, which was probably true. It probably wasn't age appropriate. It didn't scare me you know, I felt excited and felt something that I usually didn't.

★ ★

The magazines that stirred previous generations of boys can still work their charm as well. For one 12-year-old it was the underwear ads in *Men's Health:* "I recall one of a fireman with jockey shorts. I developed a mass collection of these. I was truly obsessed with the males in the underwear ads. I was so obsessed that entirely naked males freaked me out until college. I didn't want to see men naked but in their underwear!" The effects of first arousal can be long lasting.

In the Real World

Sexually arousing situations frequently occur in the real world, with real people, often people that you know. Sleepovers with your best friends, wrestling matches, family gatherings, and rides on school buses that straight boys brush off as unmemorable can be marvels for gay boys. One notably nonathletic boy suddenly became a sports enthusiast when his best friend offered, "Let's wrestle," which was how they coded their erotic "tickle fights." These sexually charged experiences eventually became imbalanced, more desired by the gay boy than his friend.

Jonathan: The Interview

Jonathan, age 23, came to the interview slightly late, breathing heavily. His look was unique: thick, brown hair covered his forehead and ears, and he sported an unusual clothing selection of canvas shorts, button-down plaid shirt, dark socks with dark canvas shoes, and designer glasses with a hint of plaid. Jonathan was just over five feet tall, and he expressed no desire to be tall, muscular, or athletic. He immediately crossed his legs at the knees and read the consent form more meticulously than anyone else had before him, and ditto for the written exercises. Jonathan recently had graduated from a local college and now was working in student services there. He was on call, and during the interview he continually checked his smart phone. Although I never asked, Jonathan made it quite clear, several times, that he was not involved in the gay rights movement.

Throughout his life, Jonathan's friends have been girls, though now he is close to several men. He enjoys wearing dresses for fun at costume parties, and when I asked him about sports, he said, "Absolutely! Soccer, tennis, and now jogging but never team sports." Jonathan rated himself midway between masculine and feminine—his body language is feminine and his thoughts are masculine. "I feel much more comfortable moving freely, and I don't feel rigid like some other men look to me. . . . I mean not just walking down the street. In my mind, I absolutely feel like I am a man in the way I am comfortable with my biological gender, and I am comfortable with my attraction to men."

As a 9-year-old, Jonathan was on a routine visit to his grandmother's house when an unexpected box produced, oddly enough, his first sexual memory.

★ ★

We were cleaning out the house because we were moving her to a living facility, and we found all of my father's old G.I. Joe dolls. And I remember playing with them, and I was, I was in our bedroom alone, a bedroom that I was sharing with my older brother, and I remember undressing this doll and just kind of looking at it. And I spent a couple minutes feeling it, and I felt, I remember feeling, like somebody was going to catch me, that people were going to find out that I was doing this.

I felt ashamed. I mean it was part of my upbringing. I was brought up Catholic, and I didn't understand it. So I didn't feel like I had the ability to tell anybody. I didn't feel the greatest, but I felt like there was something about it that was important to me.

★ ★

Jonathan's impish delight with the naked G.I. Joe doll is a familiar one. Erotic circumstances that arouse can also confuse. They're uncertain landmarks dimly perceived as having significance at the time. A gay boy feels compelled, intrigued, but knows he can't or shouldn't share this with anyone. It's a milestone not fully understood, but one that nevertheless had been reached.

Meaningful or Not

It's not unusual to be clueless about the future meaning of erotic situations experienced as a child or an adolescent. On the bus a second-grader asked another boy, "Can I look at your penis?" A year later, he noticed another cute boy and requested, "Can I see more of you?" In fourth grade he acquired permission from another boy to "peek at his penis but I wasn't allowed to touch it." He assumed these desires were normal, that all guys must have similar feelings. Later, he lost this certainty. "I really did want to see his penis again but I didn't ask because I no longer had the confidence."

Distinctively personal circumstances can induce arousal for you but might not for another boy, gay or straight. Why a particular person, movie, or dream can have this effect and not another is unknown. We should know more about stimulating, arousing experiences for all boys, regardless of sexuality—but we don't simply because we don't ask. Yet these are part of our developmental history, surrounded with emotions, mysteries, questions, and significance.

For others, their first sexual memories were of actual sexual situations with male cousins or friends who became critical players in their lives. How nice of those other boys to cooperate!

Sex Play

I was afraid of oral sex on him, that he'd urinate in my mouth.

(JAKE, AGE 7)

Having sex with another boy can also be a source for the first sexual memory. It may not be the norm, but neither is it exceptionally rare—nor should it be shocking, given how many nongay boys are open to the possibility. Boys will be boys, and will explore pleasure with whoever or whatever is available. How do the straight boys feel about it? Are there long-term effects? Although these are important questions, we have no answers.

We practically never ask about early sexual experiences, gay or straight, except when we assume that sexual abuse has been perpetuated. Although the capacity to respond sexually is certainly present from an early age, it's rare to find research that surveys youths about their sexual activities prior to puberty. Yet some boys do engage in solitary and/or mutual sex play as an expression of their natural curiosity. Genitals, one's own and those of others, fascinate, even when you're a child.

A typical boy learns that he should be more interested in the genitals of girls than boys, but regardless is told that he shouldn't touch the genitals of anyone, of any sex. Whether long-term consequences ensue if he touches the genitals of himself or others is a source of great debate, which I won't attempt to tackle here. Suffice it to say, save perhaps for **Liam** and **Dean**, none of the young men I interviewed believed that their prepubertal sexual experiences were abusive or negative—indeed, quite the contrary.

A Swedish study of high school seniors reported that most of the boys had, between the ages of 6 to 10 years, engaged in sexually related activities with another child. The definition of these activities was rather broad, including kissing, showing or touching genitals, lifting skirts or pulling down pants, watching porn together, humping or pretending intercourse, and inserting objects into vaginas or rectums. Although putting a penis in another child's mouth (or the reverse) and vaginal/anal intercourse did occur, they were uncommon. Over half of the boys did these activities only with girls. The rest engaged in sex play with both girls and boys or only with boys. Their partners were nearly always friends and occasionally cousins, but seldom siblings. At the time the sex play felt overwhelmingly positive: exciting, silly, giggly, and pleasurable body sensations. Only rarely did the boys feel guilty, confused, scared, or angry.

Clearly, these Swedish boys were interested in and enjoyed sex. Do U.S. children experience and enjoy sex? We don't know because we haven't asked boys, although we have asked their parents (almost always their mothers) or their teachers (usually women). These adults have observed very little sex play. I'll hazard a guess here: in the United States, boys engage in sex play as frequently as Swedish boys, at the same age, doing the same things, with positive reactions, and out of the view of their mothers and teachers.

Friends, Cousins, Brothers

Among the young men I interviewed, childhood sex play was nearly always with same-age male cousins, friends, or occasionally brothers. It might be, for instance, the usual Sunday afternoon family gathering, with both boy cousins bored by adult questions ("How is school?") and conversations ("I'm on Facebook, are you?")

or they're content to be totally ignored. Both boys are curious and want something fun to do. They're left alone in a bedroom or the basement, where they're free to explore their sexuality as their parents or other adults laugh and chat upstairs, unaware that the boys are having sex. Certainly few parents would endorse prepubertal sex for their sons. If they were to discover their child so engaged, they might be mortified (perhaps blaming the other boy or his parents), hysterical ("Pull up your pants!"), or nonplussed—sighing, "Well, if he's going to do it, best to do it early then move on."

One young man recalled that as a first-grader he knew exactly what he wanted and went after it on the school bus. Without any formal invitation, a very hot boy frequently sat next to him. On one such occasion our boy suggested that the hot boy should show him his penis, and he did. Not wanting a good thing to end, for the next few weeks he convinced the hot boy "to kiss my penis. He did but I never kissed his." The first-grader, thinking his mother would be equally excited, proudly told her about it. She immediately demanded, "Stop!" Not too long afterward the hot boy didn't ride the bus any more. Our boy was sad—and maybe the hot boy was, too.

When I asked **Anthony** about his first sexual memory, he initially hesitated. He had never shared the secret he was about to tell me.

★ ★

It was actually my friend when I was 7 and he was a year older. Should I elaborate on this? He found porn on the Internet or something of that nature, and I guess he was emulating, and he got me to do it with him. Weirdly that I've never talked about this, but I'm assuming he just saw porn and didn't understand it. It wasn't like real sex or anyone getting a blowjob or anything, but I'd put, he'd just have us touch each other's genitals, put it in our mouths, but we didn't know what to do with it. I guess it was a sexual thing just from assuming things.

Didn't tell anybody because he was secretive about it and it was either in our bedroom or in the basement like you know what I mean it was never an open thing. So at the time I just assumed it was not to talk about, a secret.

I know for a fact that in middle school it haunted me. At the time I knew it was wrong, but I didn't think much about it. I remember wanting to do it, liking it. Positive.

★ ★

Liam, who blames his cousin for making him gay, at 12 years old began having sex with his cousin after he'd asked Liam whether he liked girls. Liam knew girls he liked, so he said, "Yes." Perhaps feeling a familial obligation to educate him, Liam's cousin recommended they watch porn together so that Liam would know what to do when he "likes" a girl.

★ ★

Some of my friends talked of masturbation, but before this I didn't know it existed. It was an idea in my head, and my cousin made me watch porn, and I saw how a male cums and I tried it. Very weird, so scared my hands were numb. I could not believe it! I had never seen a penis and a vagina. Not exciting but weird. I never told my cousin or anyone about how I felt. Did tell my friends that I had seen porn. I could say with confidence whatever I wanted, and so I did. I told them I had my first masturbation and how it felt.

★ ★

In Anthony and Liam's reflections on their first sexual activities, though they'd found them enjoyable, there were hints of negativity, whether from guilt or fear of doing something wrong. Dean's first time felt negative to him—not at the time, but later.

Dean: The Interview

Twenty-four years old at the time we spoke, **Dean** was working in a local café as a waiter. He was a local who'd grown up on the rural outskirts of town. While he was growing up Dean's family lived below the poverty line in a trailer park. He has a high school equivalency diploma, and he passed the licensing examinations to be a yoga and meditation instructor. Dean sported the first faux-mohawk I had seen, and he wore stylish blue jeans and several lay-ered shirts. Tattoos adorned his arms, and he carried a Starbucks cup, perhaps to prepare him for his wait shift after our interview. At times Dean grappled with remembering his past, taking his time to respond to questions that required specific memories. He was quite engaged in the process, and he hoped that the interview would help him to better understand his past, especially because as an adolescent he "didn't know how things worked. Just winged it every day and whatever happens happens."

Later I would learn from Dean's boyfriend, also a waiter, that Dean is considered the best-looking guy in the local gay commu-nity and had been voted "Best Loved Celebrity." Dean knows everyone, and everyone knows him. Dean described himself as a "crazy guy, lots of fun, in the moment, everyone has me stored in their cell phone as 'God' and they know I'll be there for my friends. So I went from unpopular to popular. I am what I make of myself and said this beginning of high school, and I can chose who I want to be with so my option is to be with everyone." To Dean, living free means going to bars at night, partying with friends until the wee hours of the morning, and socializing supersized. Being in a romantic relationship might briefly handicap him, but not for long if the relationship was to survive. Dean is seldom without a boyfriend. It embarrasses him slightly to say he is that desirable, but he has the proof.

That isn't the way it has always been. Because his family lived far from neighbors, getting out and about had been a problem for Dean. Yet he'd had a happy childhood because he hadn't known how things could be otherwise. Viewing home videos embarrasses him: "I was loud, hyperactive, annoying kid with a high squeaky voice."

His temporary childhood happiness eroded after Dean entered middle school, where he became one of those boys the other boys love to pick on. Dean was called "faggot" not because of his sexuality but because he was an easy target to bully given his small size, outsized personality, and his "badass friends." Those friends served to protect Dean, hanging out with him at lunch and recess, sitting together in class, and pairing up with him in gym. "It was all surreal." Skinny and unpopular, when Dean dated a particular girl, "one of her friends said, 'Ugh! Why you dating him?'"

Dean rated himself a seven on an imaginary ten-point masculinity scale. "I can rough it when necessary," he said, and he loves the outdoors, cars, sports, home electronics, computers, and action movies. Sometimes his friends will ask him if he's really gay—then they have sex.

Dean's best friend since fifth grade, Jan, remains a best friend today. Jan initially had struck Dean as a tomboy. "In fact, at first I thought she was a boy because she had short hair." They swam, wrote poetry, gossiped, and ran away from home together. "She was the rebellious one and she'd talk back. Helped me become stronger person. Looked up to her." Before Jan, who would later provide Dean's first straight sexual experience, pubescent Dean had his first gay sex with his teenage babysitter.

* *

He started messing around with me, and I didn't know what was going on . . . I felt neutral about it. I didn't not like it. Never penetration but touching, dry humping. It happened a lot, every chance we were alone. For a couple of years, couple times per month. Don't know why it stopped . . . At some point I got into drugs, and realized I could blackmail him, but he got into a car accident, was brain damaged, and now completely different. I feel like he got his just reward. He doesn't recognize me.

R: Did the sexual activities have an impact on you?

Sure, must have. Let me know [was] OK to be with another guy. I always looked up to him and tagged along with him and his friends. Don't know if he is gay. He's had lots of long-term girlfriends. Has this male best friend growing up, and I wondered about them. Maybe they just wanted to be together alone to smoke pot. Maybe it was sex.

* *

Nearly everyone I interviewed who'd engaged in childhood sex play had one thing in common: they liked it, though not always the other stuff that came with it, and they were disappointed when it stopped. The circumstances when the sex occurred, however, were frequently unpredictable.

Sex Happens Where It Happens

Where sex happens is necessarily limited for the very young. For one boy, it was preschool naptime: "Under the covers I kissed a couple of boys because girls had cooties." Two other boys followed each other to the bathroom during a break in kindergarten story time: "He told me to take down my pants and he did his and then got on top of me and stimulated sex." What puzzles him now is, "How did he know I wanted to do it?"

For first-grader **Jake**, who we'll meet again later, it was day camp with a fourth-grade boy.

★ ★

We would get passes to the bathroom at the same time, and so we were in this environment so nobody would walk in and we would play with each other. Going into the bathroom you had to have a stick with the key on it, and I did and he did as well—though I thought there was only one stick. He touched me and told me not to tell anyone. We'd touch each other's genitals. I was afraid of oral sex on him, that he'd urinate in my mouth. But he did oral to me, and I didn't urinate. He was a friend so I assumed that it was just like a thing friends did . . .

I knew that we were strategically being private. At this time, I had no idea that it was a sexual thing, but I knew it was something that I wasn't supposed to talk about because I knew I was supposed to ask for the bathroom pass and just go.

★ ★

This sense of doing something naughty, something that you weren't supposed to do, electrified **Ted**.

Ted: The Interview

Ted looked older than his age (22 years), perhaps because he's a big guy—tall, well built, a bit of a belly, almost imposing in his tight tee shirt and blue jeans that easily revealed his nurtured muscles. A bead wristband almost countered the big-guy look. Ted's quick and pervasive friendliness was readily apparent with his first step into the interview room. He was fully prepared to share his life, and he assured me that if my tape were to break, if I were to have additional questions, or if I couldn't understand him, he'd return pronto. Indeed, Ted was so eager to talk that several times I had to move him along, including those moments when I "lost" Ted as he swung around in his chair, not facing me, as he mentally returned to his childhood and adolescent years.

Throughout his life, for every male friend Ted has had two female friends. Despite his physical size, Ted never played team sports, though he claims to be athletic. He now enjoys adventure education, the high ropes, and rock climbing, When I asked him how masculine he felt he is, Ted was flummoxed—"at this particular moment it is hard for me to answer."

★ ★

I have an extreme sort of forward "progress, progress, progress" sort of like a Fountainhead situation. That sort of forward march thing for me is like I am not typically the most patient person. And I want to see a job done well, and I am upset when a job is not done well. I often think I can do a task better than somebody else . . .

On the feminine side I would say that I tend to have a lot more compassion. I listen more than other men around me. I can see both sides of the conversation and actually sort of figure out like this is not the way to talk about this situation . . .

But I think that now sexually and romantically, it's a little bit difficult for me to completely separate them. I see myself as a typically more masculine figure in a relationship. Where it's sort of like, "We are going to do this today." Or relatively in control, but there is also a lot of, particularly right now

I am in charge of, so many aspects of what I'm working on now or so many different things for my job that sexually it's very appealing to me to play a more feminine role. I don't necessarily mean being the bottom, but I do mean is that letting the other person take a little bit of control. That's helpful for me.

* *

Ted's first sexual partner was his best friend down the street. It wasn't a crush, but their relationship evolved.

* *

I remember we were in his house, and he had this stuffed animal that had a hole in it. I remember looking at it and turning to him and asking, "Have you ever like thought about sex?" And at this time, this is a big problem for me. I can't remember if we were 9 or 10 or 11. Somewhere in that realm, and he was like, "Yeah, why?" And I was like "just wondering," and it's interesting from a biblical sense . . . The particular stuffed animal that I was talking about was a snake, which can be emblematic of temptation or emblematic of a penis, or something phallic, so that is sort of interesting . . .

I had sort of been masturbating but not really, and it was the first time that we masturbated one another. It was very sexually fulfilling, but there was no kissing involved. It was sort of void of romance and emotion.

R: How would you evaluate the experience?

That's a little bit more difficult because there was a particular amount of self-fulfillment, which was maybe positive. Maybe not very positive but positive. And at the same time, there was sort of feeling of "We did something bad . . ." But at the time I think there was a lot of negative feelings towards it just because it was so illicit. It was extremely arousing and an ecstaticness. A tangible electric feeling.

★ ★

Ted didn't panic because he was quite aware of his sexual enthusiasm before the two began their long foray into further sexual encounters.

Good and Bad

Similar to **Ted**'s account, the most common reaction to the first sexual experience with another boy was to characterize it as "only having fun," or insisting that it had "no meaning" and was "not weird." Most of those I interviewed weren't always sure whether what they'd done made sense, but one young man described kissing his best friend's genitals when they were 6 years old as "healthy fun" that had enhanced a sense of intimacy between them. If it had been only his decision, he'd have kept going for as long as possible, as he considered it a dream come true.

But this positive reaction was not universal. For some, early sex was both pleasurable and problematic, and the young man now ponders whether the sex was good or bad. One young man, who at 11 years old had kissed his cousin, considered the benefits: "This means someone likes me. It felt cool. I knew it was wicked." Much as he'd loved the sensations, keeping the experience a secret bothered him.

Jake felt good but also *so wrong*. Beginning his sexual career as a 6-year-old at day camp, Jake built "a wall in me and not saying what I was feeling." This applied to all sexual situations, gay or straight.

★ ★

Primarily, not because he was a boy, but a sexual situation because I didn't even know that it was a boy's thing. It wasn't like, "OMG this is homosexual!" I was just completely

55

non-gendered . . . This is a subject that was very tightly held, and these early notions of like "Oh you don't talk about this" maybe then are reinforced by my parents early on . . . I knew that sex was not something that I was supposed to be exposed to. My parents had a policy of we could watch any movie with them but if sex started to happen, we had to turn our head or close our eyes or walk out of the room temporarily.

★ ★

The cultural rules and regulations, strictly enforced by parents, against prepubertal boys engaging in anything resembling sex were in place for the young men. Despite these prohibitions, many developed techniques to ensure repeat performances. Sex felt too good.

Boy Sex and More

I cannot answer the question, "Is early sex a good thing for gay boys?" It depends on many things, such as the particular circumstances, consent, safety, and repercussions. However, it is clear from the perspective of the young men that if it weren't for cultural teachings discouraging them from engaging in sex, nearly all negatives would have been positives.

What I can say with greater certainty is that participating in sex with a friend or cousin, but rarely a stranger or an adult, was a relatively common first sexual memory for the young men. It happened in the everyday world of boys and was seldom a one-time event, sometimes continuing for years and occasionally evolving into mature (with ejaculation) sexual encounters. Although many were tentative at best about discussing how the sex affected their later development, at least it delivered the clear message "I'm into sex with guys," which is what they really, really wanted. Deep inside, many also grew to recognize that the sexual activities meant *something* about who they were and would become.

If the first memory is not about the physical but the emotional, should that count as a sexual memory? To become infatuated with another boy is both easier and more complex than sex and, perhaps, more indicative of future sexuality. After all, straight boys may have boy sex, but do they develop boy crushes?

First Crush

I knew he was attractive and he was really cool, like as a little kid he was the ideal of cool and something I wanted to associate myself with.   (ANTHONY, AGE 7)

Passionate love, more commonly called a crush or infatuation, is, according to Elaine Hatfield, an intense longing for union with another—and not just a sexual union. Across all cultures and historical times passionate love has been recorded such that we now assume it is universal, biological, and entrenched with evolutionary significance. Without it, would we bond with our soul mate or engage in sex? We have a romantic orientation, which is strongly associated with our sexual orientation, but they're not always identical. Sometimes you fall in love with a gender you're not sexually attracted to, and vice versa.

Children as young as 3 years old have crushes, and these infatuations are characterized by:

- Constant and intrusive thinking and preoccupation with the other person.
- Desire to be of service to the other.
- Desire to know and be known by the other person.
- Attraction to the partner, especially sexual attraction and arousal.
- Desire to maintain physical closeness.
- Idealization of the other or of the relationship.
- Feeling positive when things go well in their interactions with the other person and negative when they don't.

- Longing to love and be loved in return.
- Desire for complete and permanent union.

If an adult knows you have crushes, they might assume they're brief, supposedly inconsequential infatuations. Or the adult might dismissively refer to these crushes as "puppy love," reflecting our cultural view of them as cute, silly, or trifling things, borne of immaturity during childhood or early adolescence. We believe they have little significance for your eventual sexual and romantic future. Although it is the rare crush that blossoms into a serious romantic relationship, that doesn't necessarily mean crushes have few ramifications for your future.

Traditionally, a crush is what a boy has for a girl, or vice versa—a friend, classmate, or someone spotted on the playground or the Internet. She may never know about your feelings for her, or the two of you may become the *cutest couple* in school. Or she is someone you know to be realistically unattainable or inappropriate, such as a teacher, movie star, rap artist, comic book hero, or a virtual girl you've never met.

Beyond these generalizations, we know little about situations in which the crush is for another boy. Do you have physical corollaries when you're with him—your heart pounds, your face flushes, and your penis rises? Is there a *magical age* when boy/boy crushes begin? Do they set a standard or style for the kind of boy you will be attracted to or who will be your future true love? Do they build your confidence, or do they devastate you? Are your infatuations the first sign of your sexual orientation, your romantic orientation, or both? That is, does having a boy crush mean you're gay? Given that gay boys frequently report crushes on both sexes, is this true for straight boys as well? Do straight boys have boy crushes? If you have both girl and boy crushes, does it mean you're bisexual? But do these crushes have to be equal in number, intensity, and meaning? Is the earliest crush most telling of your future, or is it the intensity of your feelings that matter most?

The dilemma you face is the invisibility of boy/boy crushes. Rarely do others believe that you, or any boy, can have a boy crush or recognize that your feelings for other boys are just as strong or valid as any straight boy has for a girl. I can't remember the last time I saw two 8-year-old boys holding hands, smooching behind the playground bushes, or throwing hearts at each other. A 16-year-old recently told me of cuddling with his boyfriend between classes, but I have never heard this from grade school boys. It's "okay" if you have strong feelings for your best friend, Justin Bieber, an Affleck, or a member of One Direction, unless, of course, you become overly fixated. Neither would you likely tell the object of your crush for fear it would ruin your relationship with him. You might not even recognize it as a crush because you don't have the appropriate language or models to understand it as such. Rather, you name it as something, anything else—best friend, soul mate, best buddy.

A Checklist

In terms of defining a crush, here's a list of telling behaviors and feelings. Fill in the blank with the person of your choice, and then rate each statement on a seven-point scale from strongly disagree (1) to strongly agree (7). High scores mean it's a crush.

- I stare into the distance, have little appetite, or have a hard time sleeping when I think of _____.
- I get shaky knees, clammy hands, or become tense when I am near _____.

- My thoughts about _____ make it difficult for me to concentrate on something else.
- I am afraid of being shy or that I will say something wrong when I talk to _____.
- I search for alternative meanings to _____'s words.

In these renderings, infatuations are both euphoric and anxiety ridden, with little assurance they'll last or lead to romance. Likely, they'll fade away but will happen again, perhaps many times. Whether they shed light on your life, we don't know.

Differences between Girl and Boy Crushes

So invisible are child and early adolescent boy/boy crushes that I can't find anything about them in books—who, what, when, how, or why. How long do they last, and how are they remembered? What happens to them over time? Are they good or bad, and do they impact anything? We'll look for some tentative answers to these questions in the lives of the young men I interviewed.

When I asked about his first crush, **Anthony** assumed I was referring to girls. For him, such crushes began early and continued throughout elementary school because that was what his classmates were doing, so he thought he should as well. One pairing with a girl lasted about a week. They sat together during lunch, traded lunch items, looked awkward without knowing what to say or what they were supposed to do, and maybe held hands. Inevitably, they returned to being friends.

★ ★

I think girls are so pretty, and I'm like I tell them, "You are so beautiful," like I think they're so pretty, whatever. Obviously I had no sexual attraction to them, but I always felt that way. At the time it was girls in my classes that I had crushes on, like first grade there was a girl I guess I had a crush and still friendly with her now. At the time I'd have this hand signal for love, and I'd put my hand under my desk and point it at her because I had a crush on her. Eventually I told her . . . I had guy friends I told because that was what they were doing.

At the time I rated it like happy, infatuated, positive. Really pretty, freckles, long brown hair. She was a friend of mine, but at that point she wasn't. So I didn't know much about her, and I didn't know much about her but she was really pretty, and that was the start of that.

* *

At nearly the same time that Anthony was having crushes on girls he became infatuated with a particular boy. With more passion and glee in his eyes, Anthony drifted.

* *

But I'm looking back now there was a time on vacation and I was infatuated with this kid I met in South Beach. I remember we just hung out for the day, and I was probably second or third grade. He was the same age. But I didn't recognize it at the time, but looking back on it now that is sort of how I feel about it.

He had blue eyes and black hair. I remember thinking that he was good looking, like I recognized that he was. I don't think I was attracted to him at the time, but I knew he was attractive and he was really cool, like as a little kid he was the ideal of cool and something I wanted to associate myself with. Really we only spent a day together on a beach and we exchanged screen names and we talked a little but quickly got out of touch. I remember I followed him around the beach and talked the whole time. He didn't know about my feelings. No contact with him today. Just a one-day thing.

★ ★

The one-day fling thing was not, however, dropped from Anthony's memory. They hardly knew each other, yet why does he now passionately remember the super cool, blue-eyed, black-haired beach bum?

A Developmental Milestone

The young men's stories contradict the traditional perspective that child crushes are superfluous or trivial. Rather, crushes can be a revealing developmental milestone in your sexual and romantic history. They can be intense, and may even last for years if you two become an item and evolve into a dating or romantic relationship. Boy/boy crushes also reveal a secret: I'm gay! First up, we'll talk about the girls: who are they?

Who's That Girl?

We had this jar full of different types of kisses, and at the end of when we were done playing with each other and the other one had to go home, we would pull another one out of the jar and have to enact whatever that one was.　(TED, AGE 9)

Someone He Knows

A boy's first crush might be with a real or virtual girl. If she's real, she's likely a girl he knows, perhaps a good friend, and at some point he redefines their relationship with or without her knowledge or permission. About half the young men I interviewed have had a girl crush. For instance, one friend-turned-crush scenario involved a 5-year-old boy who liked a "pretty girl with strawberry blonde hair who smiles a lot." She received several Valentine's Day cards from him with "suggestive" poems: "Roses are red, lips aren't scarlet." His stomach butterflies could not be squelched then or now, though now those butterflies are for the boys. The girl crush might also be someone a boy doesn't actually know but has fallen hard for, the pretty little thing in his class or neighborhood. He sees her, but she doesn't see him. If she knew, she'd likely laugh or worse.

Derek: The Interview

Despite a ninety-degree day, **Derek** wore a long-sleeved shirt over an undershirt, with baggy shorts, short socks, and old sneakers. Tall, lean, and athletic in physique, Derek was notably anxious as we began the interview. His answers were stark and matter of fact, but over time he elaborated the particulars of his life history. Derek described himself as fairly masculine because he'd been involved in martial arts, swimming, and soccer from early childhood through adolescence. As living proof, Derek slouched in his chair in the manner of a straight man. When Derek interacts with others, they always assume he's straight unless he tells them otherwise. When I asked how he sees himself as different from straight guys, Derek momentarily hesitated. "I think my more gay traits are certain mannerisms, my preference for music and art and participating in music and art over sports. I think about clothing and my appearance a lot more than a lot of my guy friends. Fairly typical things I think."

Derek's first crush came in second grade for a girl two years older, which would become his childhood pattern. He became totally infatuated with her, and she still affects his life. "She played the violin and because she played the violin, I wanted to play the violin. That actually became a fairly defining feature in my life. I still play the violin."

Ted's first crush was in fourth grade for the same girl his best friend was crushing on, even as the two boys were maintaining a sexual relationship with each other (recall the stuffed snake). At the time, Ted considered his feelings for his boy friend to be purely physical, though now he realizes it was more complicated (as we'll see later). By contrast, Ted's girl crush lacked eroticism (see his "Freudian" slip in the last paragraph).

⋆ ⋆

Right now, I am a 22-year old who identifies himself as 100 percent gay, or like maybe 99.9 percent, and this girl was sort of an enigma and she was very, very tomboyish. And yet at the same time I would have been called girly. It was good because we kind of met halfway. I totally had a crush on her, and it was weird. I had this other friend who was a guy and lived down the street [who had a stuffed snake]. We had this weird thing where on Sunday to Tuesday he would be her boyfriend and for the rest of the week I would be her boyfriend. Or something like that . . .

We had this jar full of different types of kisses, and at the end of when we were done playing with each other and the other one had to go home we would pull another one out of the jar and have to enact whatever that one was. And whether that was something like a kippa kiss which is Yiddish for a kiss on the forehead or like a French kiss. And again, we were 8 years old and we didn't really know what we were doing.

She had this knowledge. I have always been aroused by the sort of initiation sort of thing. Not necessarily initiation but like, "Oh let's go do something that neither of us have ever done before!" You know the experimentation thing. And she was always down for that. She was always very directive like, "Let's do this right now," and that was what drew me in. It was always very mutual . . . A lot of it was being like, "I want a boyfriend." I didn't just say that! That was an interesting Freudian slip. "I want to be a boyfriend." That was the feeling, and it didn't necessarily mean "I want a girlfriend."

★ ★

Tyler: The Interview

College freshman **Tyler** described himself as shy, yet he was brimming with excitement and loud enthusiasm about his favorite topic, his gayness. He proudly announced, "I'm definitely 100 percent gay!" and he rated himself on the written exercise as "totally gay" on every sexual and romantic indicator. Within minutes I learned, not in response to any particular question, that he is gay because of the older brother syndrome, that he is running a program for the Queer Center, and that he is on the Gay Student Board. Tyler presented himself as classically feminine. He crossed his legs at the knee, shook his long hair out of his eyes, and wore gender-neutral clothing. His jeans were white, shoes black, tee shirt purple, and physique lean. Yes, his backpack had a rainbow button. It was a particular look that shouted his sexuality and his sociopolitical beliefs. Tyler would definitely stand out in any fraternity or football team. His early exuberance settled once my questions began, and he provided spot-on, insightful, and quite extended stories about his developmental history.

Despite parental urging to do sports, Tyler wasn't interested. He predictably didn't like my words "masculine" and "feminine."

★ ★

To be honest, I hate the words masculine and feminine so much because to me, masculine is what society gives the word to men that they think men are acting the way they should be acting. If men aren't acting the way they should be acting or they are acting the way that women should be acting then they are feminine. I guess like I probably fall in between. If we are talking spectrum, from totally feminine, and I'm doing quote marks to the word, and to totally masculine, then I would say I probably fall towards the middle maybe leaning slightly more towards feminine.

For feminine, I hang out, I have hung out with more girls in the past. Now I hang out with more gay men. I do more theater over sports. So sports would be viewed as the more masculine hobby. I care about how I look. I put a lot of effort into matching my clothes and dressing well and taking care of myself. So I guess that's more feminine. I listen to more feminine music. I like Lady Gaga and the pop stars and whatnot.

Masculine wise, I am not afraid to get like down and dirty. I like to go out in the outdoors, I like camping, I would much rather run around and play in the dirt with my dog. I don't get really grossed out by anything . . . I feel like I fall nicely in the middle.

★ ★

Tyler had a first-grade girl crush, but "something was missing." His boy crushes waited until puberty.

★ ★

I guess it was just probably because as a little kid you get into these idealized things and see movies and there's like boys and girls and they are falling in love and crushing on each other and so it's just cute. She was nice, we talked, and she was really pretty. We weren't a couple. It was just cute because I liked her and I made it known that I liked her. I don't know if she ever really liked me. I mean like we never kissed or anything. It was just a cute little crush.

★ ★

Tyler denied having a "boy type," claiming to have had crushes on guys completely across the spectrum, from "flamingly homosexuals" to "guys who were big, buff, jock guys." On further reflection, Tyler slightly modified his preference for a guy who is in shape, though he can be chubby, but not obese: "Caucasian, just a preference. It's not usually a looks thing. I like guys that can make me smile, and can laugh and are willing to hold hands and who aren't afraid of being caught or found out. Just romantic guys. Nice guys in general."

Several weeks later I saw Tyler on campus, stylish as ever with flip-flops and the rainbow button. Against all odds, at least as he imagined himself a few years earlier when he was in angst about whether to disclose his sexuality, as we'll see later, Tyler is totally out and proud.

Something Is Missing

Nearly every young man noted *something* was missing with his girl crushes, and you might as well. The young men might achieve social acceptability with girl crushes, but they frequently had little intensity or eroticism. No young man reported having a boy crush for the sake of social acceptability—other motives held sway, and they ran emotionally deep.

Who's That Boy?

We would look at each other like it was the end of the world if we didn't talk with each other.　　　(BOY, AGE 9)

I just thought they were very cool people. I mean kind of like James Bond. I was just like very interested.　　　(DION, AGE 9)

Throughout a gay boy's developmental history and from an early age boy crushes are common, and they reign emotionally supreme as being more passionate, memorable, and erotic than girl crushes. Similar to the girl crushes, the object of infatuation is drawn from the ranks of friends, media characters, and superheroes. Most commonly it's a friend, perhaps a best friend, who is the object of romantic affection, but not always.

A second-grader who had befriended the most popular, cutest boy in class was shocked when the boy gave him a birthday hug, which bent the gay boy entirely out of shape. "No idea why he did it but I just wanted a boy to touch me, more than the reverse of me touching him." Later they developed a "weird game where we put our hands on each other's crotch. He started it. I didn't have the balls to do it first." This evolved to dry humping each other's back. Eventually, he confessed to his friend, "I'm gay." Although he did not receive a similar confession, the friend was okay with him being gay, with one proviso: "Don't make out with a boy in front of me." Why? Did such scenes gross him out or was he jealous?

Two fourth-graders were always, "perhaps obsessively," together, but for one of them it became erotic.

★ ★

I was feeling out and down and I had a diary and wrote that we weren't talking. We would look at each other like it was the end of the world if we didn't talk with each other. This wasn't sexual thoughts but a deep need for him in my day, in my life. Later on, I saw the physical attraction when he didn't wear a shirt. Didn't think anything wrong with it but I knew I was not supposed to tell anyone, that it was taboo to talk about it but nothing was wrong with it. I never told him how I felt. Over time our worlds grew apart, especially after I came out. He got married last week. We're now Facebook friends.

★ ★

When he was a 10-year-old boy, **Jonathan**'s attention was drawn to a new boy moving in next-door. A new chapter of his life was set in motion.

★ ★

We became instant friends. I remember one night we had a sleepover and that kind of did it for me. We shared a bed together, and it just felt right . . . He was adorable! It was a number of things. I found him very attractive. I remember, well, looking back at the thoughts that I had about him I can see that I was attracted to him. He also had a really nice personality. We clicked. I was a very quiet child and he kind of was as well, but we felt comfortable talking with each other and sharing with each other. It was easy to get along with him.

Once again, I didn't understand it, so I didn't feel comfortable bringing it forward to anybody.

He moved away at the end of fifth grade, and I was absolutely torn up about it. I got to visit his family where he had moved, so I saw him and after that we kept in touch by way of letters for a couple months, but then it fizzled out . . . From Facebook, it says that he's straight and he's dating a lovely girl.

★ ★

Nine-year-old **Dion** never shared his secret or his bed with the two more developed, tanned, and athletic classmates who he found "fascinating for some reason." At first he simply thought that his "intense feelings toward them" were because they were such cool guys. "I mean kind of like James Bond. I was just like very interested. A lot of people like James Bond. I mean I knew I had a crush on him, but I didn't quite know what it was."

First crushes can also be for an adult male, such as a coach, youth minister, or teacher. One fourth-grade teacher—a "cool, masculine, tough, a manly man"—didn't know when he stood just inches away from a particular boy's desk that fantasies were being created of the two of them together, intertwined.

Crush objects can also be media figures. Because of his Christian Evangelical family, **Asher** wasn't allowed to watch mainstream media. However, he was obsessed with the cartoon character Aladdin. "From the Disney movie. I didn't think of it as a crush. I just liked Aladdin. I was Aladdin for Halloween. I just told people he was my favorite movie character. Looking back, it was a crush."

Adolescent Boy Crushes

The nature of boy crushes changes rather dramatically when pubertal hormones kick in, when the quality of the infatuation can yield a mini-love-affair. With hormonal infusion, denying the *romantically erotic* becomes more challenging. Boy crushes scramble brains and create magnetism and an inarticulate yearning for something without knowing what that something is. The boy has no models, no resources, and only later will he realize it's about his *gay soul*. A sixth-grader wanted his best friend "to hold me and see me naked." Their purity became muddied by these newly energized bodily cravings.

When boy crushes inevitably end, especially if the object of affection is straight, the gay boy can be devastated. The mistake of falling for a straight guy is not an uncommon occurrence. A straight guy might love the attention, plus it can benefit him when it comes to finding out which girls like him and how he should act around girls. His gay admirer likely knows what to say and do because he has an "in" with the girls. However, if a straight guy dates the girl it can doom the relationship he has with his gay friend.

A gay youth might be oblivious to this reality as he invents secret scenarios by which the straight guy will eventually realize how good they are for each other and dump the girl. Later in life, he could tolerate his straight friend's wife and children (he'll be the "uncle") if he sees himself as the primary love object of the husband. Such crushes can last, unstated and unrequited, for years. Doesn't the straight boy notice your devotion, the desperate look in your eyes?

Occasionally the straight guy, the object of affection, will be deft and supportive of his gay admirer. A middle schooler was infatuated with a star athlete classmate from the "dregs of society." This iconic jock was in attendance at the drama club's rendition of *Rent*, featuring the acting and singing of our gay boy, and he gave our theater star a huge hug after the finale. They talked, really for the first time, and the actor owned up to his longstanding secret crush on the jock. Although the straight athlete had no idea (surprise!), he was delighted the gay boy found him attractive. Now, years later, they are still in contact.

Derek's epiphany of what his boy crushes meant occurred when he recognized the envy he felt toward girls who received so easily what he wanted so badly—the attention of boys. Why isn't he calling *me?*

⋆ ⋆

The first one I didn't even recognize it as a crush. It happened probably fifth or sixth grade. Just one of my guy friends. I actually had mostly guy friends in middle school and elementary school. I actually kind of cycled through each one of my guy friends. I had a crush on them or sometimes just a couple of weeks until I got pissed off at them for some reason. Or sometimes it would last a lot longer than that.

R: What was it about the first?

He had a crush on one of my girl friends and they started dating, and I was mildly attracted to her but more attracted to him. But I didn't really realize that at the time. I thought that I was jealous of him for dating her, and I think at the time, the reason I was definitely physically attracted to him. More physical attraction than anything else, and I justified it by saying, "Well I am really jealous that he is dating this girl who is the one I am really attracted to" when in reality it was the other way around . . . That just kind of flew out the window.

R: Did you tell anyone?

I think mostly just because I didn't even realize what it was and for the next few crushes on guys that I had, I just didn't even really put two and two together and realize that I am actually crushing on a guy instead of their girlfriend. I am not jealous of them, I actually am jealous of their girlfriend. And I think I didn't tell anybody because I just didn't really understand what was going on . . .

Looking back on that one and on successive ones, it took a couple years, but I started to think back and reflect on those and see the general pattern and realize, "Oh, maybe I am not actually normal," whatever normal is.

★ ★

Jake wasn't sure what normal was either, but certainly it wasn't falling in love or having sex with a guy.

Jake: The Interview

Jake, a graduate student in international policy studies, readily volunteered for the interview "to help out research." Jake wore khaki dress pants and a recently ironed dress shirt, not sneakers but brown dress shoes, and was neat and clean. By the end of the interview I was convinced that Jake is one of the nicest guys on the planet. He listened carefully to questions, reflected, deliberated (sometimes out loud to both of us), and responded in a quiet, serious manner. Leaving with a firm handshake, Jake asked whether he could help me out by distributing the study's ad cards around campus, and I gave him a stack.

As a child from North Carolina, Jake was shy, geeky, and, as best as he could determine, didn't have a sexuality because he had no idea what sex was. Yet he had a vague sense "there was something else to me, something I held back." When a fifth grade boy taunted him with "You're gay," Jake, who didn't know what a gay was, asked his parents. Their negative reactions clearly conveyed to Jake that he wouldn't want to be one.

In high school, Jake did his "dorky things" by being on the quiz bowl team and in the band. His clique was small, but smart. His senior classmates voted Jake "most likely to succeed." Teachers adored him because he was "the dependable one," the one they called on when the right answer was needed. Jake claimed he had "no inner hunter, strong ego, nor am I preoccupied with sex or procreation . . . I wish only to be more masculine if I could thus score a goal in most sports, though only for the reason to be seen as more acceptable to my peers. I don't gain direct utility from scoring."

Not unexpectedly, the adolescent Jake didn't understand his boy crush, except that it wasn't to be divulged to friends or parents. "God, no!"

★ ★

I had to learn how to mitigate the feelings. I couldn't go around all day just pining after Lloyd. Particularly because we would have such a long friendship in middle school and high school and Lloyd is a very sexual person. And I think that, it had an impact in that I wanted to be comfortable with sex, and it felt like I couldn't pull it off like Lloyd . . .

I thought that same sex attractions were wrong and they would get me in trouble . . . But we went on a seventh grade trip on a gifted students' trip and we watched porn together on the encoded porn channel on the hotel TV or something. So that's as close as it ever got.

★ ★

Consequences of Boy Crushes

Similar to girl/boy crushes, boy/boy crushes are infrequently reciprocated or consummated. As these stories attest, specifying the exact outcome or impact of crushes is tough. If they're intense, they can be catalysts for self-reflection, forcing you to think about your sexuality earlier than otherwise. Here is one youth working it out: "So I just really liked seeing him, being near him, and then I'd debate if I really liked him or just wanted to be like him, and so I decided it'd be better if I didn't like him because I knew it was wrong to like him the way I liked him." He came out as gay soon thereafter.

By contrast, after the innocence of boy crushes passes, the eroticism of adolescent boy crushes can delay the coming-out process. A nagging, internal debate was amplified for shy, awkward, insecure seventh-grader **Lenny** as he reached puberty when a new hormonally driven consciousness threatened his previous view of himself. Lenny now regrets not coming out earlier, but he couldn't find the perfect age to make it happen. Having a crush on Albert, a good-looking, confident, popular boy didn't do it, even if Albert did talk to introverts and didn't bully them. "It wasn't someone I was particularly close to. It was just someone I found very attractive and I was really drawn towards. I never had much interaction with him. I just remember thinking a lot about him." It helped that Albert "was fit. He played sports. I'm trying to remember, mostly that and a nice face."

Friends or Lovers?

First boy/boy crushes begin with the earliest of life memories, becoming sensually romantic around puberty, just as girl crushes likely do for straight boys. Girl crushes allow a gay boy to fit in with other guys even as his boy crushes confuse him. Perhaps, he argues with himself, the boy crushes are simply a meaningless bump on his way through childhood and adolescence and do not predict his future sexuality.

But I think they have it wrong. Girls are the bump in the trajectory. As I listened to the girl-crush accounts, many pairings read like best friendships. She is pretty and sweet with a pleasing personality, or she smells nice and can talk about everything. The description is usually brief, almost perfunctory with little emotion

and rather vague recollections of details. With boy crushes, however, there's angst, vivid depictions, and bamboozling of brains.
Boys are complicated, intricate, mysterious, appealing, and they
also smell nice—even erotic, he'll later decide. What is it that
makes boys so enticing? It's the mole on his face, or that he's blonde
and tanned. Or, it's the jumpsuit he wears or his rudeness—"a
cutie with bravado." It's his smile, and always it's the look. The
gay fan is captivated, and his "body quivers" as his emotions run
rampant. These boy crushes are an early sign of a boy's romantic
orientation and perhaps his sexual orientation. So if these crushes
are so vital, why aren't we talking about them more?

I've spoken about puberty several times, especially its influence
on arousal and romantic infatuations, and now we consider puberty more carefully, and what it means for your sexuality.

The Joy of Puberty

I was really embarrassed about my penis because I didn't like the bulge.   (RAJ, AGE 11)

Puberty signifies a critical biological process that profoundly affects the development and eroticization of your life, including your sexuality and your ideas about romance. It marks how you and your social world scrutinize you as a man in the making. Puberty can feel too quick or too slow, and it influences how others, especially parents and friends, respond to you. In turn, their reactions can alter your perception of yourself. For many boys, especially those who grow up in a scientific family, "puberty is merely natural bodily functions, a gradual change of my mind and body over a stretch of time." For others, puberty can be traumatic, especially if they are unprepared for the sexualized feelings accompanying puberty.

Male puberty begins, on average, around 11 to 13 years of age and lingers for six to eight years as the child's body is gradually transformed into that of an adult man. Bodily changes are initiated by hormonal signals from the brain that communicate with the testes to ratchet up their production of male androgens (especially testosterone). In response, nearly every aspect of your body is affected, from facial bone structure to shoe size. You gain height and weight, speak deeper, think more complexly, and grow hair everywhere (to varying degrees) from the face to the genitals to the legs. Of special importance, your testicles increase in size and functioning, your penis becomes longer and thicker, you can ejaculate (cum), and your sexual libido increases. You're likely to obsess more frequently about sex and respond more quickly and intensely to sexual situations.

How do gay boys respond to their pubertal changes? Are the changes good or bad? Is there something unique about your puberty that differs from straight puberty? How do you know what's happening, and are you prepared for it?

Gay versus Straight Puberty

In most respects, gay puberty is identical to straight puberty. Both gay and straight boys share the same biological events, begin at the same time, and have the same sequence of pubertal changes. What differs, however, are the consequences of puberty. Not only are you attracted to boys not girls, but also, on average, you prefer friendships with girls over boys, participate in more artistic pursuits than brutal sports, act with sensitivity rather than cluelessness, and are more feminine and less masculine than straight boys.

Whether you differ from straight boys in physical appearance at puberty's conclusion has been debated. Some believe that gay boys' bodies are less muscular, more diminutive (shorter and lighter) than straight boys, similar to girls. Somewhat ironically, others suggest gay boys are supermasculine in having longer, thicker penises and stronger sex drives (masturbate more) than straight boys.

There's reason to doubt these gay versus straight differences, largely because it's uncertain whether masculine gay boys volunteer for research at the same rate as feminine gay boys, who are likely out earlier due to being pushed out of the closet by their femininity. They might well sigh, "When everyone assumes you're gay, why not just come out?" Second, the supposed greater "anatomical bulge" among gay youths is questionable because it is usually based on gay youths measuring their own penis and reporting its dimensions. It would be reasonable to guess that gay boys might be more inclined than straight boys to embellish their penis size in response to their heightened sensitivity regarding genitalia size, compliments of gay culture, gay legend, gay porn, and their own gay desires.

Here's the bottom line: gay and straight puberty are similar in events, timing, sequence, and sex drive. Attraction to males is neither initiated by puberty nor changed by it. Puberty simply intensifies the pre-existing attraction and makes it more conscious. It's now more difficult to deny same-sex attractions—you have the evidence in your mind's eye and by looking down at your penis.

What might differ, however, is the attention and meaning that you as a gay youth associate with pubertal changes. The earliest event is predictable: body hair, pubic hair, "bigger dick and balls," and first ejaculation, whether from a wet dream or, more commonly, from "jerking off." Hair is in places "I didn't think should be," and there's an increase in sexual desires "which sucked because you're forced to grow up." Less frequently mentioned in puberty books, parental sex talks, and sex-education classes are telltale signs that the young men I interviewed recalled experiencing:

- "Lots of erections. It felt really weird."
- "I specifically remember being in the shower and noticed that my balls had dropped."
- "Pubic hair on my pelvis. I felt embarrassed at first when people found out by seeing it."
- "I became lot more rebellious and started questioning authorities and their worth."
- "Having conscious, deliberate thoughts about sex with whoever I found attractive."

The clarity of recall, a decade after its initiation, is rock solid for most, but fuzzy for a few who weren't "paying much attention to it." The young men with vivid memories tended to report an early onset, before their friends.

- "Around age 10 with dick hair growth."
- "I had to start wearing deodorant when I was 10 because I smelled bad after soccer."
- "I started growing a mustache in fifth grade. We're Italians, so I also had thick leg hair."
- "Around 11 I started to, like, growing insanely, and my face broke out with acne."

Whether you like what is transpiring depends on your developmental history and the reactions of your family and friends. You can be early, on time, or late in your pubertal onset without necessarily liking what's going on. The most common reaction is ambivalence. If you are someone who shuns the spotlight, maturing early might embarrass you or cause you to feel out of control. If your friends admire pubertal changes because they connote athletic achievement, leadership, and manliness, then an early puberty may increase your popularity. Being late is usually perceived negatively, primarily because it places you behind your friends.

Although these reactions likely hold across sexual identities, complications emerge for gay youth who don't always welcome puberty with open arms. Pubic, facial, and body hair and other signs of physical adulthood may be viewed as unsightly if you value femininity or eroticize youthfulness (the "twink" preference). Or you might not appreciate the "gay message" that is delivered to you by your pubertal development. However, one boy I spoke with loved the less-than-ideal outcome of his late-onset

puberty: he hoped that the prepubertal-looking, distinctly feminine body he retained after puberty would impress his intended
audience—straight guys attracted to femininity (and thus to him).

In contrast to those who view puberty with anxiety are the
youths who long to be a *real man*, who perceive it as enormously
terrific. For them, puberty elicits pride and optimism and heralds
a vibrant, masculine sexuality. A seventh-grader was ecstatic when
he discovered he could cum: "This was cool, like I'm a man!" Another adored his armpit hair and even combed it because he
thought a boy he had a crush on would be turned on.

Being a masculine guy into adventure activities, **Ted** predictably had positive reactions to puberty. For him, the physical and
sexual changes brought on were a colossal plus.

★ ★

It felt weird and it also felt like, "Whoa I'm changing!" I am
having these weird things going on. But then sexually, I
started to gain a lot of weight, which was weird. I had always
been this tiny scrawny little kid, and then all of the sudden
I gained like 30 pounds . . . I felt really good about growing
and getting older and getting physically older. I felt very positive about being able to ejaculate and having the ability to
be more sexual. And then like watching my actual genitalia
move and change I was like, "OMG this is cool."

★ ★

By contrast, **Raj**, an early bloomer, was embarrassed by being
the first in his class to have body hair and a "bulging penis"—until
he discovered that big penises are prized possessions.

★ ★

I had the mustache and the hair very early. It was around
fourth and fifth grade. So that would make me 9 or 10. I was
not happy about it. I remember because that was around the

time that I was learning swimming and I was more hairy than anyone, so I didn't like that. Plus when I was wearing swimming trunks I was really embarrassed about my penis because I didn't like the bulge. I would wear like two pairs of underwear to hide it. Because I remember I thought it was too embarrassing to have it hanging. But then it went away. So from the media I learned that it was good if you have that, it's not that big of a deal.

★ ★

Everyone Is Punting

Two questions I asked stumped nearly every young man: "How did you find out about puberty?" and "When you began puberty did you tell anyone?" The second was immediately perceived as a crazy question—why would he tell anyone? Isn't it obvious? Besides, who cares? It would be preposterous, one young man concluded, to announce to friends and family, "Hey, I can jerk off now and something comes out!" Another response was kinder: because puberty happens to everyone, "I guess I just saw no need to." The vast majority disclosed their puberty status to no one, especially pubic hair and genitalia growth.

As to the first question—whose responsibility is it to inform boys about what is about to happen, or is happening, to their body?—everyone punts.

Anthony first noticed his body changing around seventh grade with the growth of pubic hair. School and parents hadn't prepared him, which left him to figure it out for himself, though his parents had given his older brother a book.

★ ★

I went to a Catholic school, and we didn't have any kind of sex ed classes at all, so I really didn't know anything. Guess I was confused about it. I guess I knew it was expected, so I wasn't scared, but I didn't know so I guess I was just confused. Somewhat negative because I was somewhat confused about it. I remember thinking that pubic hair was unsightly . . .

I guess it sort of came out in my discussions with guys I was friends with, and we talked about it, and by the time in eighth grade one of the kids was like confused because everyone else mentioned they had pubic hair and he didn't and he hadn't hit it yet and he was confused about it. We didn't talk about it much because pretty conservative environment, but it came out occasionally. Early compared to others.

★ ★

So Anthony wasn't given a talk, but he did read his older brother's book.

★ ★

Instead of giving me the talk I was given a book by my parents, my mom gave it to me. Apparently they had talked about it and decided on giving that. Actually, it was they gave it to my brother, and I saw it and took it and read it like when I had seen it because I was curious about it, same time, seventh grade. I don't know why I didn't get the sex talk, I mean I guess it was just an awkward experience for everybody, for parents to do. It's a weird thing to do. I didn't get it at school because of the school I went to. So I guess it was just their way around it. I almost think it was positive because for myself I'd rather gotten more because otherwise it was like either stories or examples and backed by fact so at least I knew this book was correct. It was I knew that it was the truth so that whenever topics came up or little kids talked or my friends asked about direction I knew the facts, and I was comfortable saying because I knew it. So I knew more than some of them.

* *

I'll focus on parents and whether they fulfill their responsibility for the physical and sexual education of their son. Then I'll briefly review whether schools and friends help out before considering the pervasive power of porn to educate.

The Disappearing Sex Talk

A majority of Americans believe parents should teach their children about sex. Yet parents don't, and even when they try they are generally incompetent. The silence and ineptitude are magnified when it comes to issues regarding same-sex sexuality. Indeed, only one of the forty young men I spoke with had experienced what most experts believe is the ideal when it comes to sex education: an early, ongoing conversation between parents and child in age-appropriate language regarding the physical, emotional, and social aspects of physical and sexual development. Parents should be an open access source for questions, giving their children honest replies based on current contemporary knowledge. Unfortunately, you would be the rare boy, gay or straight, if you received sufficient information from your parents, in any language, at any point, in any sense. When parents spoke to their gay son, it was likely too little, too late, and too embarrassing.

Parent-son communication doesn't happen because parents usually punt when it comes to discussing puberty, leaving their gay son on his own. Here is a sampling from the young men:

- "The school had sex ed but my parents wouldn't let me take it."
- "My mom walked in on me in my bedroom one time, and afterwards the only advice I got was, 'It's done in private.' That was the extent of all my conversations with my parents."
- "I associated sex with HIV and didn't know why. My father tried one day when I was 15 that I would have sex with a girl and to use a condom and then throw it away. If I had any more questions ask Mom."
- "They're not touchy/feely parents."
- "My father is a doctor, and he just didn't realize I had already come to that age."
- "They're not direct people, really shy, you know."
- "They were fighting a lot and so preoccupied."
- "My mom is not educated. I don't know if she knows anything about sex."
- "Dad is a very hands-off parent and not close to me."
- "It came as an admonition 'not to do it' after they discovered I was 'doing it' at age 18."
- "They're conservative and religious."

Jonathan could not talk to his parents about anything sexual because they're a conservative family, especially when it comes to his sexuality: "It became a rule in my house that we don't talk about it. We don't mention it." I'm not exactly sure why being conservative means you don't talk to your son about puberty or sex. The beneficiary in Jonathan's case was his younger brother. Jonathan made sure his brother got the information "because I knew that they wouldn't."

Living in Kansas, **Dion**, who loved wrestling, needed the wisdom of his parents. Fortunately, his dilemma was more funny than hazardous to his health.

★ ★

Back then there wasn't Internet either. So I think that's what led to a lot of embarrassing behavior. I mean I would listen to the radio, and sometimes there would be like dirty jokes or something, but at the time I didn't know if they were jokes or not. Like some guy stuffing his pants with a sock or something, so I wasn't sure if that's what guys did and that's what I was supposed to do. I did that for a little bit, and it was just very weird because I was this little kid. So I didn't know if that was how people masturbated, with like socks or something, so do you like hump the sock? There was just a whole lot of chaffing and pain.

★ ★

Several parents made a good faith effort to fulfill their parental responsibilities, with repercussions both humorous and dangerous because they couldn't quite pull it off. One mother "used words like 'who-who-dilly' (penis) and a girl's 'cha-cha.' And my mother is a teacher!"

Other parents did slightly better. Their sons appreciated their efforts.

- "Father gave us the talk when I was 9. He's not much of a talker or emotional type, so awkward. I thought he said tentacles when he said testicles, so I didn't understand anything."
- "Our dog Susie wasn't spaded and had her period, and Mom explained what was going on."
- "I was a bit concerned when my balls dropped and went directly to Dad. He laughed a little and said it was completely normal. That was the sex talk."
- "My dad noticed my voice changing and bought me deodorant."

- "Awkward short talks with Dad when I got older like 'condoms are good.' I felt too old for these and didn't want to hear it from him."

The conspiracy of silence can be reciprocal and appreciated when neither parents nor sons want to talk about puberty or sexual things.

- "I grimaced when I had to tell my parents that I accidentally cut my face from shaving for the first time. I didn't want to discuss my bodily changes with them."
- "Would have been really uncomfortable, and they knew I would figure it out on my own."
- "They had an animated book to help them, and they gave it to me to read. They asked, 'Do you understand?' It was really uncomfortable for all of us, and I knew it already."

Many parents assume their gay son will or has already figured it out. Why create a "prickly situation"? They know he's a smart kid, an easy kid to raise, and doesn't get into trouble, and they live in the middle of nowhere, so it's not like he has the chance to do anything bad. One father tried by giving his son a book by Dr. Ruth Westheimer. Unfortunately, it didn't provide helpful information about what most puzzled him—his same-sex sexuality.

Derek's "wonderful parents" almost did the right thing by purchasing a set of books, *My Changing Body*. They conveniently left them on a bookshelf for their sons to find. The effort came a bit late and was incomplete, and yet Derek learned a lot about biology from them, but little about his sexuality.

★ ★

I think that was around seventh grade. My parents were pretty on the ball, and I do have an older brother. He's just a year older, so they got those, and I would thumb through them and read about stuff. Those books were kind of weird in that they took a very scientific approach to it. My parents are both biologists, so I think that's why they liked it. They were like, "This is the chemical change going on in your body, these are the hormones that are coming into play, and this is the effect that they have." So I understood it on that level, but I didn't understand the social aspect of it . . .

My parents never really sat us down until I was a junior and my brother was a freshman. And then they were like, their sit down was like, "Remember to use condoms. Be safe. Don't do anything stupid. Don't get anybody pregnant." And at that point, I was like no worries there.

★ ★

One mother should have received a gold medal for effort, though her timing could have been better.

- At 10, she gave him a sex talk, including "Masturbation is normal, okay, and just something that you do in private."
- At 12, at the grocery store, she asked him if he needed condoms ("which, of course, I didn't").
- At 14, he found a copy of the *Joy of Sex* by his bedside with a card proclaiming, "Lovers are made, not born."
- At 18, he concluded that his mother had been very candid with her discussions of sex.

Despite everything, she had gotten enough right.

Sex Education

If not parents, then who should teach adolescents about their sexuality? The vast majority of Americans say school, when children are around age 12, but there's one problem—most U.S. states do not mandate sex education in schools. Even when schools do teach it, the information is usually flawed, according to both youths and experts. Overwhelmingly, youths rate their school's sex education as fair-to-terrible and as impractical, failing to provide the advice they need when they need it. The topics most covered in class are biology (puberty), contraception (usually abstinence), and sexual health (don't do it), and they are rigidly taught according to a conservative value system. Needless to say, gay issues are seldom covered.

Most young men reported receiving a school-based sex education class, except those attending Catholic schools, such as **Anthony**, and charter schools run by Evangelical Christians, such as **Jeremy**'s rural school. Sex education was usually offered in middle school, perhaps in high school, and seldom in elementary school. But it was never taught in every grade. None of the young men knew why what was taught had been taught, or why it'd been taught when it was. One boy speculated, "When they suspected girls are starting to grow boobs and guys are getting horny and everything." All had quite divergent, seldom equivalent sex-education experiences. One school provided a half-hour video (boys and girls separated); another had a one-hour session in a semester health/science class; yet another had a lecture on basic reproductive plumbing with cartoon characters; another gave warnings about the dangerous consequences of sex (pregnancy, diseases, HIV).

- "Fifth grade had family life in school but cartoon drawings of genitalia, and it was a joke."
- "In sixth whenever penis was mentioned lots of giggles. I learned anatomy but not sex."

- "One chapter in physical science. Teacher laughed nervously and just wanted to get it done quickly. No mention of masturbation, oral sex, gay sex. Just reproduction for 11-year olds."
- "I mean it's not like they were preaching 'Have sex.' It was all abstinence, 'Don't do it.'"
- "Gave us deodorant sticks. In high school they told us issues of safety."
- "They showed us a condom. It was all very silly and lots of giggling."
- "I learned that babies didn't come from the belly button."
- "Eighth grade sex education combined with drug education. Not helpful."

Most of the youths that I talked to told me that the sex education they received was of limited help or useless. Information about gay sex, other than causing AIDS, was nonexistent, though an eighth-grade health teacher advised one boy's class, "Anal sex will kill you, ripping apart your rectum." (Yes, she had a teaching certificate.) This *sex is bad* perspective is also reflected in scientific research on adolescence, which portrays sex as risky and infectious. This research seldom presents sex as a positive in your life that can give you pleasure, happiness, growth, and interpersonal connection. The message is: wait until you're grown up and out of the house to partake of sex, or, at the very least, keep quiet about it.

Conspiracy of Silence

Before and during puberty, a gay youth frequently knows so little about what's happening to him, physically, sexually, and emotionally, that it's not surprising that every year "sex" is one of the most frequently searched Internet terms by teenagers. It's a conspiracy of silence among adults—let someone else do it! I'm not sure what parents have in mind, but are they referring to porn stars?

Many parents believe the school should and will teach sex education to take up the slack. One father said to his son, "I pay my taxes so they should be doing something!" Parents find it awkward, and what if they screw up? One mother protested when confronted by her son, "Your grandma never told me anything about it." Parents justify their silence with "He's a smart kid. He'll pick up what he needs to know." Some kids do, some don't, and all want more, if not from their parents then from reputable sources they can trust.

Information received from friends and older siblings is seldom particularly helpful. One middle school youth was told, "It was the boobs instead of the vagina where it happens." Another learned critical stuff at sleepovers. "Guys compared how much pubic hair they had and how long their dick is. I remember just thinking how stupid this is because then they would cut it off [pubic hair] and light it on fire."

Yet it still happens. In the absence of parents, schools, friends, and siblings, where do you search? Internet porn is the answer.

The Good, the Bad, the Porn

The pluses are that it really confirms my sexual attraction and it helps me find out what I like and what I didn't. The negatives, I guess it really raised my expectations of sex.

(DAVID, AGE 13)

Porn is often free, readily available, and tailored for every taste and proclivity. Yet few parents encourage their son to watch porn or help him to find the pornographic fantasy or erotic activity of his dreams. Perhaps the culprit is the warning parents receive about the dangers of porn wreaking havoc on young lives. According to the young men I spoke with, if their parents had attempted to regulate their porn watching (and few parents even knew how or had the stomach for it), they would have failed. They would simply watch porn undercover.

So much has been written about porn, especially whether it's good or bad for adolescents, you're likely perplexed. Lately, much of the information is about the effects of porn consumption, especially the negative consequences of frequent viewing. What is clear is that gay and straight youths rarely differ except in the content of what they watch. Porn intake usually begins early around puberty, increases with age, is higher for boys who are sensation seekers, and has little impact on engaging in risky sexual behavior.

Sex therapist and blogger Jason Winters noted that, despite the best efforts of parents, by grade six the majority of children have viewed porn, so our discussions should be less about whether porn is bad and more about the failure of parents and schools to discuss the content of porn. That's the basic fiasco. Although he acknowledged that the "evils" of porn are overdrawn, Winters was less explicit about the possible benefits of porn. By contrast, writer Maria Konnikova argued for porn's benefits: "In the absence of other options, pornography becomes a *de facto* way of educating yourself about sexuality." Most of the young men would agree with researcher Mark McCormack who categorized watching porn as a leisure activity for enjoyment, exploration, and education.

Because scientific and moral professionals are confused about porn's utility, I decided to ask the real experts—the young men who have grown up in an era of free and easy access to porn. When did you start watching porn and should you have started earlier or later? Did you discover porn by accident or by design? Has porn been good or bad for you? Have you watched so much porn that you fear you've become obsessed or addicted to it? Overall, the young men were pretty clear. Porn's negative effects have been relatively small and are substantially dwarfed by its positive effects, including sex knowledge, developing positive attitudes toward sex, having a better sex life, and enjoying many hours of pleasure.

Early Porn

Several of the young men had access to offline porn—the "old-fashioned" type such as Dad's *Playboy* magazines and adult cable shows. One youth has two gay uncles who are art collectors. "They just had like tons of art, and I was in their library looking through it. I was staying with them for the summer, and I saw, it was like Tom of Finland." In other words, it was pure, classic gay porn, complete with outsized packages.

More typical was **Anthony**, who discovered online porn around age 11. He watched it a few times and then only sporadically. What porn did for him was something porn rarely does for straight youths—it clarified his sexuality. "In the time between time [I] said bi and considering self gay, it was the driving force, and I realized had no sexual attraction to women." By peer standards, Anthony wasn't an avid porn watcher, perhaps because he had a boyfriend, Patrick.

Depending on the source, anywhere from 40 percent to 90 percent of young men "inadvertently" or "deliberately" consume online porn, and watch it at least once a week. Every young man I interviewed said without reluctance and with little embarrassment, "I watch online porn, and have done so for many years." The frequency varied, from occasional to many times per day, with many agreeing that they had watched on "most days since puberty."

Their first exposure to porn began as puberty kicked into full gear, ages 11 to 14, with 13 being the most common age. Perhaps not by accident, that's also the same age as masturbation typically began. The oldest boy to begin (age 18) waited solely because his home computer was located in the family's living room, in front of a giant window facing his aunt across the street. "If anything ever happened in my living room, she'd see it."

The Bad of Porn

Porn has a severe public relations problem, especially among parents, with the suspected negatives far outdistancing the positives. The negatives include presentations of unattainable ideal standards regarding body types (big penises, buff bodies), distorted images of normal sexual gratification (gymnastic sex, nonstop erections), and deviant behavior (sex crimes). One young man accused porn of "totally screwing me up about expectations for my body, which I'll never get over." These misrepresentations might well constitute the most negative aspect of porn.

If parents discover their son at the computer watching porn, regardless of whether the son or the porn is straight or gay, the result is usually not good. It disrupts family life and causes parent-child confrontations. If parents impose "no viewing rules," the son will likely develop more secretive techniques. Being caught watching gay porn is a boy's rudest nightmare, especially if he hasn't disclosed his sexuality yet—or has a father who promptly prints the pictures and posts them on the family refrigerator. This particular technique failed to convert one boy to heterosexuality, but it did succeed in shaming him and further eroding their father-son relationship.

Addicted to Porn?

Does porn cause mental health problems, especially addiction? Addiction is an inability or extreme difficulty abstaining from the substance (here, porn), resulting in a craving that impairs one's ability to control consumption, diminishes one's recognition of increasing problems in his life and relationships, and causes extreme emotional responses to everyday events.

Three young men confessed they might have been addicted to porn but had now recovered. However, they were using more of a colloquial than a scientific definition of addiction. There is, in fact, little if any scientific evidence that a youth can become addicted to porn.

Dion: The Interview

Dion called me to say he'd be an hour late for his interview. After his arrival he was apologetic and clearly happy to be there—so happy that his interview became my longest. At times I reluctantly had to redirect Dion to answer specific questions because he loved to talk far beyond his personal story, to relate his thoughts and experiences to African American communities, the larger world, and the universe. One of my oldest interviewees, Dion, was likely in his mid-20s (he admitted to giving different ages depending on his mood). He came from a politically conservative state and was returning to college after taking six years off to work. Dion wore shorts and a tight-fitting, long-sleeved sweater, and he obviously worked out a lot. Indeed, Dion had wrestled in high school. His parents had divorced early (though each had remarried). When Dion's mother died from cancer while he was in high school, Dion and his younger brother moved to live with their father, stepmother, and two stepsisters.

Dion was popular throughout school, though he had a problem with sports.

★ ★

I think I'm too analytical. Instead of just doing it I would be like, "This is kind of ridiculous. What's the point of this?" I did track, tennis, wrestling. These are all in high school. In wrestling, there was this guy Lewis, and him and I would usually be sparring partners and we would just end up laughing a whole lot. And they would make us do laps. I would just find it really funny that you have these guys that are calling people "faggots" but then they're like mounting each other and thrusting. I just found it funny and started laughing.

★ ★

While in middle school Dion routinely watched porn after school because no one else was around. "I mean I spend so much time watching porn." Was it an obsession or entertainment?

★ ★

I would also watch straight porn, but I always liked straight porn that had multiple guys in them. And then I was like, "I'm not gay because I'm watching straight porn." I didn't like the porn that didn't show penetration . . .

I mean it showed me what to do or like what people do. But it can be a bad thing because it sets unrealistic expectations. Especially with young guys, when they start having sex they try to reenact porn which isn't the same as real life.

I mean am I addicted? Maybe. It's a possibility. I mean I have porn on every electronic device that I own. On my computer, I have like tens of thousands of photos. So now I just upload it to the site and videos and stuff. A lot of it depends on whether I am on a mood stabilizer or not . . . If I'm off, it's just like this hyper-sexuality. Even if it's just by myself, I could masturbate seven or eight times a day, and it's just this nonstop kind of thing. And if it's with people it's just kind of like sex then I'm ready to go again with somebody else. And it kind of controls my life.

★ ★

Dion speculated that he has had more sex than anyone else I had interviewed, a claim I am unable to confirm or deny because I did not ask this question.

Rather than porn being an outlet for one's mental health problems, **Asher**, an enigma because of his masculinity, blamed porn for causing his psychiatric history.

★ ★

I have obsessive-compulsive disorder and an eating disorder . . . I attribute it a lot to actually gay culture. I saw these images of gay men on the computer, on the Internet, and I was like this is what I need to look like. I am not tall enough. I am not muscular enough. I am not thin enough. With the whole Internet thing, I don't think it became a compulsion . . . I just found those sites so annoying. I'll try it and then I'll go back in like a week and I'll check and see if there is anybody interesting, and then I'll delete it if there are no responses. Or like if I am depressed, I will leave it open on my computer screen, and I will see who messages me, which is a good cure for depression. It's better than eating. It makes you feel better pretty quickly.

★ ★

Raj recognized porn's benefits, yet feared becoming addicted.

★ ★

I thought I was addicted to pornography. I was probably not. But because I would watch it and I would masturbate three or four times a day, I thought that was ruining my life, and I was in some forum where people get together and help each other, and there was another homosexual man who was from San Francisco, and I would like talk to him and honestly really put my thoughts down. And then it was only around my sophomore year that I had, I realized that I was definitely gay . . . I wouldn't use the word addicted, but I was obsessed with it.

★ ★

For **Tyler**, porn addiction was not an individual thing. "I feel like maybe as a generational thing, our generation may be addicted to it. I don't think I have a problem."

103

Although these porn-as-bad views were not widespread among the young men, most agreed that porn fosters unrealistic expectations about sex acts and the size/shape/color of genitals, both of one's own and those of others. And because the usual outcome of watching porn is a reward (an orgasm), it is certainly possible to be motivated to watch more and more—leading to wasted time and obsessing about sex. That said, porn also has its benefits.

The Good of Porn

Counter to the porn-will-destroy-you perspective, many benefits of porn were proposed by the young men:

- Broadens sexual horizons and satisfies sexual curiosity.
- Adds zest and diversity to one's sex life by encouraging adventurousness.
- Provides new resources for sexual fantasies.
- Teaches self-exploration of body parts.
- Becomes a rich source to motivate and prolong arousal.
- Reduces fear and shame regarding kinky sex and unusual sexual desires.
- Promotes sex as a positive human desire.
- Reduces guilt by normalizing the sexual desires deemed by society to be deviant or unacceptable.

That's a remarkable list of affirmative contributions to life, gay or straight!

If they were to rank the most beneficial aspects of porn, most young men would place erotic pleasure at the top of the list. It is a ready, steady source of entertainment, fun, and relief from boredom. Second would be its instructional value, showing a gay teen what he can do to himself, and others to him. Third would be that their response to it helped them to confirm their sexual identities.

Growing up in the South, **Jake** had no positive gay role models. He knew the physics of sex, thanks to a sixth grade sex-education course, but he was not prepared for his same-sex attractions. Then he discovered websites with words like *jerking off* in them that broadcasted sex-positive messages and educational resources. For him, they destroyed his masturbatory myths (such as running out of semen), provided multiple masturbatory techniques, and taught him what a penis other than his own looked like and how to identify a vagina when he saw one.

For **Nicholas**, porn stimulated him. "I certainly don't need to watch it every time. It's not like I'm going to go watch some porn and get hard and masturbate. It's like, 'Okay I'm hard.' It's mostly, like, to expedite the process." Plus, once he "started doing things with guys," porn taught him about the many options for sexual expression.

Self-Discovery

Although knowing what to do with guys in a sexual situation contributes to your education, it also exposes you to a brand new world of sexual self-discovery. Even if their first porn was straight porn, few gay boys stopped there. Almost inevitably, straight porn was the gateway to gay porn, as **Tyler**'s story demonstrates. Before the end of ninth grade, he couldn't recall "anything sexual."

★ ★

I guess I mean I was turned on by it, which was good. The first porn I ever watched was heterosexual porn. I actually did it not because I was so incredibly interested but because my friends had actually talked about it, so I wanted to actually see.

So I guess what it told me about myself is I guess I didn't feel so different anymore. I thought I was late going into puberty because everybody else seemed to be developing crushes on other people or like going out with other people and I like wasn't very interested, so I guess the fact that I was getting turned on by the pornography made me feel like I was more normal or at the same pace as everyone else . . . And then tenth grade is when I, one night I was watching heterosexual pornography, and there was a link to the gay part of the website, and I don't know what made me want to do it, but I guess I just clicked the link, and I watched a video, and that's when it hit me that I definitely am attracted to guys.

★ ★

Tyler told no one about his "shameful" activities. He felt guilty for doing "something that I felt I wasn't supposed to do" and for breaking the law: "The website warns you, 'You have to be 18!' and I was like, 'Oh, I'm breaking the law!'"

When they came out to themselves, several of the young men took inventory of their porn collections. "I would have all these doubts and then I looked back at all the years I looked at gay porn and I was like, 'Dude, don't be silly!'" Another felt that as long as he downloaded lesbian porn he couldn't be gay, until everything snapped: "I saw a picture titled, 'Two Guys on a Tabletop,' and I just casually downloaded it with all the rest. I tried to force myself *not* to look at it, one day at a time *not* look at it. A real struggle! I can remember every detail of that tabletop."

Derek, an athlete, began porn consumption during his freshman year of high school with straight porn. Then he realized he was a lot more interested in the guys than the girls, and he discovered gay porn. He justified his switch by convincing himself, "Well, they all have great bodies, and I need to work out. I need to look like that blah blah blah." By the end of sophomore year he had blossomed: porn "helped me realize how I felt about other guys, and it helped me come out of my shell a little bit."

This sequence also characterized **David**'s journey of self-awareness. Just out of curiosity, 13-year-old David wandered onto a gay porn site and discovered, "Oh, I like dudes." When I spoke to him he still wasn't out to his parents—the one time his mother caught him watching porn, "luckily, that one time I was actually watching straight porn."

★ ★

I would turn it off when I know they are nearby, and I also deleted the history on my computer. They found out when my mom walked in on me once [while I was masturbating]. It was really awkward . . .

The pluses are that it really confirms my sexual attraction and it helps me find out what I like and what I didn't. The negatives, I guess it really raised my expectations of sex . . . Porn definitely made me think that it was going to be this other worldly experience, and I still felt like I was very down to earth.

★ ★

Ted began his self-discovery process a few years earlier at age 11, when he had inklings that he was turned on by the guys in porn. Now he knew what to do with his best friend.

★ ★

I wasn't like, "Wow! This is hot there's a girl who is totally getting fucked." It was more like that's really hot. I am empathetic for this girl. It's very different than seeing these guys with penises and ejaculation everywhere. I was like OMG! It was exciting and enticing. Watching the porn with him was what was exciting. And watching him get aroused and then having some type of . . . It was sort of an in-the-moment sort of thing. It was used as a vehicle to get us both to a place where we would say "I want your help now . . ."

A majority of the information came from the porn in terms of what sex was, and then a lot of information came from him. He had older cousins that he was close with. And also there were some websites too. They were specifically about helping guys learn about their body and masturbation.

★ ★

Watching and learning from porn can be critical for knowledge and self-recognition. And it's also loads of fun.

Not the Final Word

Today's youths, regardless of where they are on the sexual continuum, seldom think of magazines, television, or movies when they hear the word *porn*. Rather, it's online pictures, websites, and videos. Porn can have dramatic positive effects as an instructional tool, a means of connecting with friends, and, most dramatically, as *the confirmation* about one's own sexuality. The eyes don't lie, and they're watching the guys, not the girls.

Yet youths of many sexualities express concern with the unrealistic exaggerations of porn, especially the distorted images of what is a healthy and realistic body type, what you can expect from sex partners, and what you are supposed to do during sex. Lurking for many is the fear that porn consumption might become obsessive, though few would call it an addiction.

I'll close with **Jonathan**, who remains eternally grateful to porn for helping him define himself, establishing him within a community of similar others, and providing many hours of pleasure. Yet he worries that porn is negatively affecting his ability to develop same-sex romantic relationships. His task is to find the balance.

★ ★

I have very mixed feelings about porn. I sometimes watch it just because I'm interested, like I had a couple of my standard websites, like I know when they post their new videos so every now and then I'll go and check it out. If there's somebody that I find especially attractive to me I'll watch the video, but it's not something that I focus on since so much of the beginning of my development was so focused on porn. I spent pretty much ages, I mean 13 or 14 to 18 or 19 relying on porn as kind of my in to the gay world and for masturbation purposes. But more so to feel connected, because I didn't. My community that I grew up in was very, I don't want to say very religious, but very conservative. So not a lot of people talked about it. There were two out gay people in my high school, so I didn't really understand it, so the Internet was my big connector to the gay world . . .

I mean I think there is a negative because so much of my understanding and upbringing or introduction—I shouldn't say upbringing. Because so much of my introduction to the gay world was pornography that I feel like it has colored my own development sexually. It's negative in the way that I have trouble mixing sexual and romantic feelings for people, so I tend to have solely sexual encounters, and my romantic relationships are few and far between. And the romantic relationships that I do have don't last that long because—I don't want to say I have unrealistic expectations about sex, but since I have these expectations about sex that are, "It's only about pleasure it's not about connection." It has a lot to do with, there was a long period in which I thought the only way that two men could have sex together and find pleasure with each other was through intercourse, and so many other things have not become apparent to me that I have never thought of before. And that's been my journey for the past two years.

★ ★

To Internet porn detractors, who argue that porn distorts what sex and love are all about and that it can feed obsessive attention to sexual release, I say, "Yes, it can." But far more prevalent are its contributions to the lives of gay youths. Besides the hundreds of hours of pleasure that porn provides, porn teaches you what can be done during sex, and it can be a crucial barometer of your sexual proclivities. As such, porn may contribute more than any other factor to the self-recognition if not the self-acceptance of your gayness. If that's true, we owe a lot to porn.

After we've dispensed with the gratitude, we need to correct the distortions by openly discussing sexuality in our families, schools, and religious institutions, not as a substitute for porn but as a commentary. Why are young men relying on porn to find out what being gay means and how to do gay sex? Why should we take away something that is so exciting and pleasurable? Why not provide a diversity of gay porn, including those in which the actors demonstrate love, caring, safety, kindness, honesty, and commitment? Let's maintain a variety of porn, with real-life loving and caring adults available for discussion. That revolution is within our reach.

OMG! A Wet Dream

I didn't really feel the need to. Obviously, it's natural. You can't help it. But at the same time, it's not dinner table conversation.
(GEOFF, AGE 12)

A wet dream is a spontaneous, uncontrolled orgasm with ejaculate (semen) emitting from the penis during sleep—hence the technical term "nocturnal emission." Wet dreams are brought on by the hormonal changes of puberty, especially the large increase in testosterone and the subsequent buildup of semen that creates a pool of ejaculate (the "wet") released during sleep. What elicits a wet dream can be physical, such as rubbing or humping pillows, or mental, such as an erotic fantasy (the "dream").

Wet dreams are a one-time, occasional, or frequent feature of adolescence, especially during early adolescence, after which their frequency wanes. Not all preteen or teenage boys have nocturnal emissions or have them at the same age. You might wake up at the beginning, during, or just after a wet dream, or in the morning to a messy, gooey substance on your pajamas, underwear, or bedsheets. An erection is not necessary for a wet dream, and there's no evidence that you can will a wet dream into happening or prevent one.

When recalling the physical pleasure, you may want more, but that's tough to arrange. Engaging in other means of eliciting ejaculation, such as masturbation and partnered sex, reduces the frequency, intensity, and volume of wet dreams. Once you masturbate as a regular feature of life, wet dreams become history or so infrequent that they are a surprise when they do occur.

Neither is it likely that you can stage, choreograph, or direct the dreams, including who is in them, what takes place, or the color, sound, location, or dialogue. You might be pleased ("I'm a man!"), confused ("What's this all about?"), or disturbed ("It was a guy in my dream!") by the fantasies or wonder if they mean anything at all. If you're gay and not yet prepared to acknowledge that fact, male images might upset you and create fear about your sexuality. It's far more likely that you won't remember the images—you'll just go back to sleep or get ready for school.

Information about wet dreams is difficult to come by largely because, no surprise here, boys are seldom asked the pertinent questions. Several medical websites provide information about wet dreams and encourage questions. They're reasonably consistent in their advice.

1. Foremost, wet dreams are normal, common, and don't mean you are a sexual deviant.
2. Masturbation slows down or stops wet dreams. If you want a wet dream, stop masturbating.
3. Just because you dream about having sex with a baby cousin, sister, pet dog, male race car driver, female cheerleader, or exposing yourself on the gridiron doesn't necessarily mean you are into pedophilia, incest, bestiality, homosexuality, heterosexuality, or exhibitionism.
4. There's no need to feel guilty, embarrassed, or sinful because of a wet dream. Most boys have them.
5. Enjoy them while you can because they taper off with maturity or sexual activity.

Bewildered and Bemused

About 60 percent of the young men I interviewed recalled a wet dream, although many could not actually remember the essential details. They were not sure how old they were when they had the dreams or what the dreams were about. Of those who remembered, the first occurred between ages 10 and 22, usually before entering high school. The go-to period tended to be ages 11 to 13. Some had the wet dream of their dreams. One boy's fantasy was with a group of attractive guys with erections in a locker room shower. "But I knew I couldn't invite them up my ass." He was ecstatic until he woke up to the mess. "Then I was mad because I had to get out of bed to clean myself."

Anthony's first wet dream was in eighth grade, and "it was weird" but not unexpected. He had read a book about sex, so his reaction "wasn't oh my god!" However, he didn't tell his parents. "In my house, not a thing to talk about."

The first wet dream might occur late. When **Jonathan** was 20 or 21, he had a very specific dream about having intercourse with a woman. "I woke up and I took a shower, but the image that I remember in my mind was a woman's stomach. Like the exterior, I could see the stomach, belly button, but I didn't see anything below it. It was candle lit, so I just saw her and I saw myself entering her, and then I woke up." Yes, wet dream fantasies can be bewildering and make little sense, though it was noteworthy to him that he couldn't see anything below the woman's belly button.

More common were the young men who could only guess at their ages or their dreams' images. Their reactions to the dreams, though, were vivid—perhaps puzzlement or immediate recognition. One boy's dream wasn't "intense but thought my wetness was sweat but then lifted my boxers. Pretty cool, but damn messy."

As a 14-year-old, **Nicholas**'s experience was mildly embarrassing because he thought he had wet himself. "The first few times it was mildly embarrassing, then I realized 'Oh, this is what's happening.'" Fortunately, his mother had taught him how to do laundry.

But did Nicholas tell his mother why he was doing the laundry? No. As in **Anthony**'s family, wet dreams weren't routine topics for family discussion. **Geoff**, who had his first wet dream in sixth grade, assessed the situation and didn't feel the need to tell anyone: "Obviously, it's natural. You can't help it. But at the same time, it's not dinner table conversation."

Several young men couldn't recall ever having a wet dream but wanted one. One tried to bring one on by abstaining from masturbation for six weeks, "but it never happened. I have had strange sex dreams though." In contrast, one young man claimed he managed his wet dreams by not masturbating or having sex for prolonged periods of time and by focusing on a mixture of men he knows and hot celebrities. Another wanted more wet dreams to correct his tendency to be shy around the guys he was attracted to. By his thinking, if he couldn't do it real life, maybe he could learn how to do it in his dreams.

Another youth attempted to prolong his wet dreams because they were so thrilling he didn't want them to end. "They tend to be vivid in terms of emotions and sensations. I often feel everything you would in real life, but I also realize I'm dreaming, and so I try to push the dream to last as long as possible, but I ejaculate. The dreams themselves seem to last but five seconds, and sometimes the dreams start out with me already in the act."

Perhaps he should just masturbate—then he could better control his fantasies and how frequently he has orgasms. It's masturbation I turn to next.

Masturbation

*Just playing around and it felt good, so I kept going harder.
After a bit an explosion and I freaked. I had no idea what was
happening. I figured I'd wait to see if everything was fine.*

(BOY, AGE 12)

More frequently than wet dreams or partnered sex, masturbation elicits a boy's first emission. With the first sexual hormonal urgings, stimulating yourself becomes almost unavoidable for many boys. Nearly two-thirds of boys aged 14 to 15 have masturbated, and nearly all men have by young adulthood. Although we don't know whether there are sexual orientation differences, I doubt that there are. At the very least, we can say that nearly all boys regardless of sexuality masturbate at least once (if not multiple times) during and after adolescence, and it's the exceptions that need explanation.

Nevertheless, is a gay boy more likely than a straight boy to manipulate his penis and do so earlier and more frequently? Some say gay youths are the winners in the masturbation sweepstakes, but why? One explanation is linked with the unique status *male qualities* have for a gay youth. What he has is what he wants. That is, because what he is most attracted to (maleness) are the very features that he himself possesses, the erotic stimuli are always just a touch, sight, or smell away. As a result, he's aroused earlier and easier. It's having an erotic Shangri-La available in the simplest and quickest way possible—with himself. One telling but unknown factor would be whether he's more apt than a straight boy to jerk off in front of a mirror.

Another view is that because a gay boy is by his very existence a *sexual outlaw* in Western culture, you're more likely to develop a wary and dismissive attitude about what mainstream culture says you're supposed to do. Because you're already an outsider, traditional rules don't apply to you. You might as well exploit the rebel label and have fun doing so, breaking sexual taboos by masturbating earlier and more frequently.

Regardless, whether sexual orientation differences exist is questionable. We already know gay boys don't begin puberty earlier, have a thicker and longer penis, or have a greater hormonal motive to masturbate. Among the young men I interviewed, the frequency of masturbation proved quite variable, depending on the availability of other outlets or alone time, or on their study habits, computer availability, temperament, sex drive, and so forth.

Given these realities, my interview questions focused on other issues—when and why he began, what his masturbatory fantasies were, whether he told anyone, how he felt about it at the time, and what impact it had on him. Although it would be intriguing to know why a youth who doesn't masturbate restrains himself, I can't answer that question because none of the young men I interviewed reported that they had abstained from masturbation for long periods of time. Several did acknowledge feeling uneasy about their activities even though they continued "the habit," and their reflections offer insight into masturbation reservations—religious/moral self-discipline, obsessive fears of overdoing it, potential harm to their penises, and substitution for finding sex partners.

One other point to make here is that when talking with the young men I detected no hesitancy to disclose information about their first masturbation experience. In this, **Anthony** was more characteristic of the present than previous generations.

★ ★

I had watched a movie, and I was around seventh grade, yeah. Watched a movie and remember in the movie, I think it was some movie where a guy lost his job and lived in a house with another person and they caught him masturbating like with a sock like in their room or something, and I didn't know what it was until this point. Oh, like what is this? I was curious and quickly excused myself to go to the bathroom, went to my room and tried it. No one else was there. I was just talking to myself. Very positive. I didn't tell anybody. Anything related to the genitals at the time in seventh grade and I was in a conservative school and my family wasn't there, but the ideals were set by the middle school I was at, so I assumed it was really something not to talk about.

★ ★

I Did It

Unlike the first wet dream, nearly every young man vividly recalled the first time he masturbated, and frequently he had a comical or entertaining story. Here are three examples.

- "I was 12, the age when genitals are more stimulating and want to be touched. We had a massager for shoulders and back. I used it on my genitals, with a surprising ending."
- "One day I found it felt good when my erection was rubbed, so I rubbed it up and down with my palm. Sometimes you get the precum, and one time I was like, 'Oh, I am going to keep doing this because it feels good,' and then the next thing I know, it's everywhere."

- "Just playing around and it felt good, so I kept going harder. After a bit, an explosion and I freaked. I had no idea what was happening. I figured I'd wait to see if everything was fine."

One boy had the benefit of his family's pay-per-view porn channel and his older brother. Late one night he secretively observed his brother "do something to his dick that he really seemed to enjoy." He imitated him on nights when his brother wasn't around. Only later did he discover, from his parents' outrage, there was a charge for pay-per-view programming. He'd blown the budget.

Whereas in childhood touching the penis felt good, now with an orgasm in hand it felt fantastic. First masturbation began as early as age 5 and as late as age 14, but usually it began between 11 and 13, with 13 being the favorite age. A few could not explicitly remember how old they'd been, with one declaring, "I've done it way too many times since then to remember."

One of the youngest was **Raj**, who'd been concerned with his early puberty and its consequence of a bulging penis. From an early age, the importance of Raj's penis as his stress relief was apparent to the family. "Whenever I would get nervous I would hold my penis or pull it. That was like a joke my parents would say." His theory was different—his penis preoccupation was caused by his gayness. Maybe that was true, but many kids hold or pull their penises, and I doubt all of them are gay. Nevertheless, at first nothing came out, but it wasn't long before something did, in fifth grade. Raj then established a bedtime routine, with gusto.

★ ★

I did it all by myself. I was under the covers. I didn't have my own bedroom actually. I guess I just I started touching.

It started with me every night before I went to bed. Going to bed was an exciting thing. Because when I was in my bed for like one or two hours I would imagine all these elaborate scenarios where I am trying to save this guy from that accident, then I am helping him, and then he is my best friend. He's doing something sexual with another woman, and somehow during that I start touching myself and then I masturbated.

★ ★

At Boy Scout camp, seventh-grader **Asher** heard a new word from the guys, and being an industrious boy, he used Google to look up "masturbation." It seemed like a good idea to him, so he quickly closed the laptop and followed directions. "I don't think I had any images at that point. It was more just enjoying the feeling." For fifth-grader **Dion** the images were men from soap operas. For high school freshman **Jonathan**, "It was one of the gentlemen on the soccer team I was thinking about. He was quite developed."

Regardless of when a boy began, how he found out what to do, what the images were in his head, or what his strategy was for doing it, he had mixed reactions to the first and subsequent episodes. Masturbation not only brought great pleasure but also sometimes an undeniable message about the direction of his sexuality. Perhaps it was a first realization of a connection between his erotic interests, what he was fantasizing, and what he is—gay. For some, the revelation was not always welcome. Later, masturbation would serve other functions such as relief from boredom or tension, a sleep aid, an antianxiety medication, and, of course, always pleasure.

Joy and Shame

After the first time, you might well want to choreograph a repeat performance, unaware of the "refractory period"—the time between an ejaculation/orgasm and when the next one is physiologically possible. This is when the nerves and muscles in the penis are again capable of responding to stimulation. As a teenager, this can be a matter of five minutes, but the time increases with age. By age 30, it can take thirty minutes between orgasms.

Although some of the boys might have vowed to refrain from masturbating ever again because of orgasm guilt, none of them followed through on their pledge. **Jeremy**, an early maturing youth, first masturbated at age 10 and was traumatized by his mother walking in on him halfway through (she ran out)—and he also feared that "my semen was pus." Yet he characterized his first orgasm as "amazing," and he arranged many repeat performances. Indeed, masturbation was never a one-time event, even among the most guilt-ridden boys. Whether the masturbation was accidental or orchestrated, the description of that initial physical sensation was always glowing: "Awesome!" "I almost fainted," and "I was in awe, like, wow!"

With something this good, you'll want to share the news with your parents, right? Wrong. This almost never happens. Most youths I interviewed insisted that there was no need to tell, that it wasn't an appropriate conversation starter, that it carried a negative stigma, or "I have no scenario of telling someone and seeing them like punishing me or something." No young man had an in-depth, supportive, or honest conversation with his parents about masturbation, even when the parents were capable of having such conversations.

Tale of Two Boys

I'll close this discussion with two fairly typical young men. First is **Jake** from North Carolina, who was 12 when he began his masturbatory career.

★ ★

So I actually learned how to masturbate from Lloyd at school. My fantasy was also of Lloyd . . . It was a shock, and I was wondering like what was happening. I think my reaction was to clean it up, and it wasn't so much to get a handle on whether it was a good thing. There was no appropriate forum to talk about it. It wasn't appropriate at home or at my lunch table where my friend was teaching everybody how to do this. It wasn't like, "Everybody try it, go home, and report back," but it was more of like, "I can do it now!" If asked, if somebody was like, "Do you do this?" I was like, "Oh, I do . . ."

R: What did you like best about the first time?

That it was wholly new and that it was undiscovered and you could discover it by yourself at the shower.

R: What did you like least about it?

That I didn't know what to expect. That this glob came out. It was a weird consistency. I didn't know if I should be okay with it or not.

R: Did it have meaning for you at the time?

I knew that it was sexual. I knew that something about sticking a penis inside a vagina caused a baby, and I assumed that this was the load of transmission.

R: Do you think it had an impact on you?

Oh yeah. Partially, I still have a very vivid memory of that. When your brain goes into strange situations, it records all the possible information. It's still very easily accessible. I don't talk to

Lloyd, but he's still in the fantasy rotation. So getting back something of that surprise and newness. It was just very exciting.

★ ★

Tyler was 14 and ill-prepared. He wasn't fond of his late-arriving puberty, his masculinity, or his first orgasm.

★ ★

I was freaked out when the orgasm happened because I had no idea what it was basically about. I kind of knew because I knew the mechanics, but I didn't really get the whole sexual attraction or stuff like that.

R: *Who did you tell?*

No one. Because who wants to admit to that? It's just embarrassing! Yeah you want to take it as "Oh yeah! I'm becoming a man!" But like it's also embarrassing . . .

I didn't really know the mechanics of masturbation. I heard guys talking about it, but I didn't really understand it. I was just like, "Oh, you rub yourself and then you feel good." That doesn't really make much sense to me. I watched the porn and I did get erect, and I remember rubbing it through my shorts or whatever I was wearing, and all of the sudden orgasm, and I was like, "OMG! What's happening?"

R: *Do you recall what you were looking at?*

I assume you are not very judgmental, so I will just be completely blatantly honest. I really didn't know how to find pornography. I looked up things on Wikipedia . . . Then I think I looked up pornography, and there was actually a link on Wikipedia, and when I came I think I was cumming to a video that I found on that website. It was male and female in missionary position. It was dark and low quality . . . I think it was more the act itself. Later on I realized when I was watching straight porn, I would actually be focused on the male, but I think that first time it was more just about, "Oh my God, I better not get caught doing this!"

★ ★

What Have I Just Done?

Our culture arranges for self-stimulation to be kept private, even secretive. Supposedly, no one wants to know whether you do it, when you do it, what your best technique is, or what you're thinking about. You're to be ill prepared and ashamed by what is natural and feels so good. Masturbation is likely to be something you'll be doing for the rest of your life and will provide you with tons of pleasure, relief, and recreation. Are you equipped? Do you know the best lubricants to use? Do you know the remarkable variety of pleasurable styles and techniques? If not, you can search the scores of websites devoted to masturbation.

Does it really need to be such a big deal? No, not really. When the silence is broken, it can be a blessing—you learn that you're not alone and you're not deviant. It doesn't have to be this way, but until a cultural about-face occurs, masturbation will remain as it is, so you must tackle your questions and feelings on your own. You survived the first masturbation, for better or for worse, with little or considerable impact on your notions about your body, your emerging sexuality, and your first sexual experience with a girl, a boy, both, or neither—and that is what we'll talk about next.

First Girl Sex

It was expected that I do something. She was kind of like, "We might as well at this point." I just kind of did that to her and I was like, "I'm done!"　　　　　　　　　　(ASHER, AGE 13)

You might expect this chapter to be brief—gay boys having sex with girls. Nationally, about half of gay youths report at least one sexual experience with a girl, primarily during adolescence. First they're friends, then they're dating. Sex might feel obligatory, if not by him then by her because that's what dating teens are supposed to do. He complies, though not always with enthusiastic initiative. He experiments and has fun, or simply considers it about time. Some gay youths find straight sex satisfying both emotionally and physically. Others conclude, "I could live without it" or never take the first step.

Although they are not currently that into girl sex, one-third of the young men I interviewed had had sex with a girl/woman, but very few rave reviews followed. Of the two-thirds who had never touched a girl's vagina, the vast majority had no intent of changing that status. Some expressed disgust with vaginas, and others speculated that it might be interesting to try sometime but had no plans to do so any time soon. Maybe they'd dated girls in high school but just didn't go further.

First I'll consider the *heterosexual virgins*. Next, I'll discuss the youths who have had *minor sex* with girls or women. The young men with *oral or real sex* (vaginal intercourse) experience close the chapter.

I Never Had Sex with That Girl

A gay boy might date but never have sex with girls during adolescence. They begin as best friends, and he appreciates her personality and beauty. Because it's a boy/girl combo, others assume they must be dating. The two comply with public assumptions and call their friendship "dating." Usually after a relatively brief period of time, they return to being just friends again. Both, especially him, are okay with never progressing to sex.

What motivates you to date under such circumstances? Perhaps it's the status you attain as *normal* in the eyes of peers and, conceivably, yourself. Like most boys, you're not immune to the pressure to consider girls sexually. Or perhaps you're less than certain about your sexuality and want to give yourself a fighting chance to be straight by dating a girl.

Tyler dated his next-door neighbor and best friend. They hung out nearly every day, went to middle school dances, and agreed to be boyfriend and girlfriend. She was attractive, had a nice personality, and represented a status symbol. In school they were an item, though Tyler soon realized that, despite the social benefits, dating his best friend was costly and was putting their friendship at risk. After several weeks they "floated back" to being just friends, without ever having had sexual contact. They never formally broke up, just tapered off. They were much better suited as friends.

Tyler and his friend were lucky. Others found that their friendships did not survive dating because she recognized their relationship for what it really was—he was using her for his own personal or social gain. High school wrestler **Dion** considered dating his beautiful friend to be a dilemma. Although he understood it might ruin their friendship, he also thought that if he didn't date her, then he might lose his one slim chance to be with a girl. To try to convince her, Dion would wear her jersey while she played volleyball. Although others thought they were dating, she didn't. Over the school break she went out with another guy, and Dion "just got really nasty. I think I was bitter, and we stopped being friends until senior year, and it was kind of sad. I still sleep with the stuffed animal she gave me when I was 17." Did Dion blow his one chance to be straight? No, not really.

Nicholas had long considered himself straight, despite his same-sex attractions. One of his girl friends was a desirable catch, so why not date her and see where it led? It would give him an answer to his vexing sexual orientation question.

★ ★

I do remember back in high school there were some like, "okay she's good looking" while I was still confused and trying to figure it out. I did have two girlfriends, quote-unquote girlfriends, who were more like best friends who happened to be female.

R: Did it become physical?

It's just not the sort of thing either of us would have done, especially her. She was more of a conservative. I don't want to say Catholic because I am pretty sure she wasn't religious, but sort of in that way how they are supposed to wait and all. Maybe perhaps old-fashioned might be the right choice.

R: Who broke it off?

It was kind of mutual. We just saw each other less and less, and that was kind of right around the time I eventually came to the, finally accepted that I was gay and all.

★ ★

Even if they dated girls, most of the young men had zero sexual desire for them. At the extreme end of this continuum were those who were disgusted with the entire notion of female anatomy.

- "Just don't find vaginas appealing. They gross me out."
- "I'm one of those repulsed by female genitalia, and I don't care what they do with it and I have no intention of finding out."
- "Because a vagina is really repulsive, I'm not sexually attracted to any girl, unlike other gay guys. Rather Brad than Angelina."

Tyler was in this camp. "No desire. I have never even seen a vagina in real life, but I saw a picture on the Internet, and I was like 'I don't want to go near that!' Once that I accepted that I was gay, the thought never crossed my mind."

That's not to say that all boys resisted genital contact while sorting things out. Some enjoyed these excursions while others were highly disappointed. It wasn't "great sex," especially when compared to guy sex.

We Touched, We Explored

Those who engaged in genital contact with a girl prior to puberty seldom defined it as sex then or now. It was almost a random event or a curiosity, an opportunity that had presented itself so they went for it.

For example, the first-grade boy who'd had another boy kiss his penis on the school bus also made out with a girl when he was 5. They kissed on the couch and played doctor—"I'll show you mine if you show me yours." When I asked about the significance of his experience with the girl, he said the thrill of maybe getting caught trumped any sexual excitement, a different answer from the one he gave when his object of desire was the boy on the school bus.

Closer to puberty, several boys touched girls in order to answer the age-old question, "What do girls have?" **Anthony** was one of these, going about the average distance (fingering) for those who had adolescent sexual interactions with girls. Why did he do it? He said it was primarily because he wanted answers to his curiosity—was he missing out on something important?

* *

Happened twice with two different girls, both friends of mine. First one, we were good friends. Freshman year I fingered her, and we were both drunk, and that goes with that. [It was] before first time with the boy. She was the whore of our class and a good friend of mine, and I said I was missing out on something, so it was really nothing . . . Did not impair the relationship. It should have, but it didn't. Very close friends and had worked together over summer, and so sleeping in same bed several times per week. Other girl was same thing, and not actual sex . . .

Just because of our friendship that should have not happened. These mistakes are psychological for me because I feel guilty. So maybe not worth it, okay. Weird position to put her in because people knew what was going on, so like they looked at her that she had done something with a gay guy.

* *

For sports-oriented eighth-grader **Asher**, it was just "one of those things where you slip it under a skirt." He fondled a girl, didn't enjoy it one bit, and that was his first and last genital contact with a girl. Asher developed a strategy to protect himself.

* *

It was expected. I went to an urban middle school, and most the kids by that time had had some form of sexual contact. It was expected that I do something.

R: Did she ask you to have sex?

Yeah. She was kind of like, we might as well at this point.

R: Did she touch you?

No, because I just kind of did that to her, and I was like I'm done! So that became my M.O. I would date a girl until the point where it got to we should have sexual relations, and then I would break up with her, and then I would date another girl. And then eventually in high school, I dated another girl who never requested sex, which was great because I found out that she was a lesbian later on, so it worked beautifully.

★ ★

Maybe that's the answer! If you must date a girl (for whatever reason), date a lesbian who doesn't want sex with you. Or date a religiously conservative girl committed to abstinence. Several boys found a third alternative: first get drunk or high before sex. However, that turned out not to be a wise choice. One teen, drunk at his senior prom, wondered whether having sex with his best friend and prom date would "mess up our friendship." His second thought? "It grosses me out." Both happened: while dancing and making out, she grabbed his hand and inserted it down her pants for ten seconds. It didn't lead to further genital or, unfortunately, continued friendly contact.

Middle schooler **Derek**'s "girlfriend, quote unquote" was dating a boy named Dom, and it was Dom who was the real object of Derek's romantic and sexual desires. "I kind of stole her away, which created a lot of drama." Without the girlfriend, Dom would turn to him, right? But it didn't work out that way. Derek never even kissed his girlfriend—or Dom, for that matter.

Derek tried again his sophomore year of high school. By that time his motives were not wanting to be left behind as well as assuaging his sexual curiosity.

★ ★

At least in my group of friends, having a girlfriend was a status thing. There were the couples, and those were kind of the center of the group, and then there were the single outliers, and for me, I was at this point starting to get confused about who I was attracted to and what was really going on there. Is everybody like this or is it just me? I still didn't know very much. The status thing was important for me. I was nervous, I didn't really know what was going on, and it was a traumatic time in most kids' minds anyway . . .

Throughout most of that year, the only thing we really did was made out a lot. We would hold hands. We would cuddle. We would watch movies and things, but there wasn't any sort of genital contact. My friends were starting to have encounters with girls, my guy friends. So I started to feel like I was kind of behind the ball in that aspect. Part of it was just the mystery of it. I don't have a sister, so I didn't know anything really aside from pictures in a book. So I just kind of went for it. She actually was kind of uncomfortable about it because it went from making out to me sticking my hand down her pants. I had no interest at all in it. And she was pretty taken aback by it . . . [Later they tried dry humping, and he achieved an erection.]

Actually I think my underwear might have still been on. No, maybe hers was. I can't really remember. I would consider it genital contact, but it wasn't anything that exciting . . .

R: *Was she encouraging you to do more or less?*

After that, I tried to re-initiate it on subsequent occasions, and she probably, two or three other times I tried to get something like that going again, and she would just kind of gently shut it down.

★ ★

The prospects of having sex with a girl can terrify any boy, gay or straight. One 13-year-old shook uncontrollably as he rubbed against his date. "She played with my genitals. I wouldn't have known what to do with hers." During high school he dated a girl he loved. "It would have been very appropriate. I did nothing, and she was upset." His heart belonged to a boy, even as he faked the straight relationship to feel and appear normal. Disgusted with himself, he came out to her, and she, of course, understood. He vowed, "Never again!"

Gay youths confront the dilemma of dating girls who want sex far more than they do. Some comply because they feel they owe it to the girl to have sex with her after they've been dating for so long. But if he fails in the act, will she guess why? Will she tell others? Will this be his last chance to prove he's not gay? An eighth-grader saved himself by creating an erection just in time. Seeing the obvious, she inserted her hand down his pants and caressed his penis. However, erection or not, the entire experience disappointed him. Even though he was in great demand, the "girls usually broke it off because I wasn't into them. They would say, 'It's just not working.'" To the persistent girls, he would excuse himself with, "It takes a really long time for me to become aroused." Eventually, he attempted another line, "I'm bisexual." This didn't work either because the girls laughed it off: "Me, too."

I Had Sex with That Girl

In contrast to those who escaped with only minor scrapes were the youths who engaged in oral and vaginal sex. Although sex with girls is likely becoming less common among today's gay youths because a greater percentage of them recognize their same-sex sexuality at earlier ages, it's not totally absent. The motives are complex, and so are the circumstances and assessments. We know that the girl is usually a friend or dating partner as opposed to a random hookup or someone found online or at a brothel. Sex is a one-time event and only rarely does it continue for years. In all cases, girl sex doesn't begin to compare with the excitement and eroticism of boy sex. But then, that's what we might expect.

Dean experimented with a play date in the woods when he was 8 years old, again to answer the ancient question of what a naked girl looks like. (He found out.) Throughout middle school he was popular with girls because he was masculine but not macho-masculine, athletic but not a jock, and knock-dead gorgeous but sweet. Dean had a series of clingy girlfriends but no strong sexual desires for them. Jan confessed to the 14-year-old Dean that another guy wanted to have sex with her but she'd rather lose her virginity to someone she cared about—like Dean. Being an accommodating kind of guy, he viewed it as a reasonable request from a friend, but it didn't turn out so great. "I came over, and we did it. Neither of us had an orgasm. I had a condom on so did not feel much. It was all right. Both of us were nervous. Nothing heavy or lots of physical motion. Just okay. Neither of us were having a good time, so we stopped. We remained best friends. Only time [we did it]. Just a weirdness between us." The experience didn't pull him any which way, because Dean was already on his gay path.

One boy continued his charade of dating girls during his teen years because it was absolutely essential to him to appear straight. "It was my beard, my cover, at least to myself." Then for his sixteenth birthday his girlfriend offered him a blowjob. How could he refuse? She delivered the gift, which proved pleasant but rather boring—a chore. He ran the test the opposite direction a month later by returning the favor and going down on her (granted, under the influence of alcohol). His reaction was again blasé: "This is it? I thought it was foul." Later, for bragging rights to friends, the pair engaged in intercourse. Over time, however, "screwing deteriorated, and I could no longer deny my low sexual desire for her. I'm never becoming straight, and nothing I can do about it."

Not all was lost, as this realization paved the way for his eventual gay self-acceptance.

Similar to his friends in the Middle East, **Liam** dated girls and proclaimed himself good at kissing, though he somehow missed the point that he was supposed to go farther. While he was dating the most beautiful girl in school, Liam repeatedly told her that despite his strong feelings for her, he was not in love and thus wouldn't have sex with her. After five months, while fondling her breasts, something at last moved for him. "I was very hard. [I] felt good and proud of it." He fingered her, and she became very wet. The next time proved to be the charm, and they had vaginal intercourse. Though he found it sexually satisfying, it didn't compare with the sex he had been having since age 12 with his male cousin and other boys. Sex with guys was explosive for him, but sex with his girlfriend was routine. The situation was resolved when his family moved and he cautioned his girlfriend "not to wait for me, and she has since married. She could never burn me or hurt me like my current boyfriend can. I would get jealous if she was with another guy but indifferent if we were not together."

Raj's pattern was similar, except he waited until college to have his first sex with a woman. Although he had been having sex with guys since early adolescence at his private school, he decided to try it with a woman. He was living in a sexually progressive residence hall, and at a naked party an opportunity presented itself.

* *

She initiated, and I was happy in the sense that she was the cool girl of my social group. I was just happy that an American white girl wants to do me . . . I would actually perform oral sex on her. She would do it, I thought sort of reluctantly, on me too. One time she wanted to have anal sex, and we tried to do it. We did try because it didn't work. I guess because we were drunk and it was just painful, and after a while it didn't happen. The sexual part of our friendship lasted three months. We were not dating but hooking up apparently.

* *

Jake's lengthy tale exemplifies several complexities with having sex with young women. Growing up in a rural Southern community where premarital sex was scandalous, Jake copped a breast feel at age 14, but didn't have his first straight sex until college, with a woman he knew from high school who was one of his best friends.

* *

We lived in the same building and hung out. She gave me a backrub, and this is where it transitioned. I got "excited" and she noticed. She initiated it by asking me to roll over. I did, and she said she shouldn't, but she had the evidence. She undressed and that continued from a backrub to a hand job to sex. I orgasmed, and I think she did. Actually, I have no idea. I was flustered, felt very unsure and wary of where it'd go. There were no romantic or physical attractions to her. I was happy to have my virginity gone. I thought I should have sex with a girl. It may have been coinciding with, maybe I'll like having sex with girls and this will make me not have attractions to guys. At that time, I still wouldn't have applied the "I'm gay" label to myself.

I didn't tell anyone for at least a year, and it continued mostly under a "we're not dating but when we hang out if it goes like that we'll have sex." It has played on ever since, peaking for three years as friends with benefits . . . I tried to break off the sex, but then my fear was that it would dissolve the friendship. Neither of us wanted sex, but it just happened, even several times after we broke up. At a certain point she had become emotionally invested with it, and I never did.

I miss not talking to her now because we were such good friends. Now no sexual tension, and we make jokes about it occasionally. I would say I was sexually attracted to her but not physically. I could have an erection, and it would work fine, but I wasn't particularly interested in doing it that often . . . If I didn't move away, there would be a not insignificant probability that we would be married now.

★ ★

These interactions illustrate the dilemma young men face among friendships, emotional connections, romances, and the role of sex in each. If Jake had married his friend, would he be less gay? No, but he might have been considerably less happy than he is now.

Reconsidering Girl Sex

These stories are not strong endorsements for gay boys or young men to engage in genital touching, oral sex, or vaginal intercourse with a girl or woman. Several had "real sex," and several expressed disgust with the entire concept of female genital anatomy. Between them were the boys who tolerated having a hand on his or her genitals and those who were content to do without. Regardless, they seldom considered it worthy of a repeat performance.

The youths with heterosexual experience had understandable motivations—peer popularity, curiosity, relief from boredom, obligatory bragging rights, and the proof they desired that they weren't gay. For the latter, if they enjoyed the sex, as some did, perhaps their biggest fear couldn't be true.

Less toxic were the benign reasons for having sex with girls. Several young men simply confessed, "It's something I wanted to do before I died." Others felt they had been somewhat manipulated by the girls. For instance, maybe she was everything he wanted in a lover—kind, attractive, available, great personality—but he had limited desire for sex. So when the two had it, she had to initiate it, and it wasn't an everyday (or monthly) event. From one young man's perspective, girl sex wasn't his main thing because something huge was missing: "Girls just didn't do it for me. I like girls in a gay way, idealizing them." For him, boy time was so much more erotic and pulsating.

Blurring the lines between friendship and romance is risky. If her feelings haven't been too hurt, maybe the two can remain friends, but not always. Why put her through his personal conflicts or indecisions? She can legitimately accuse her young gay lover of being insensitive to her needs because she isn't his priority. She may wonder, is she so unattractive or undesirable? And even though the two of them have such an emotional connection, he still doesn't want her? In the best-case scenario, after his explanation, she becomes his best friend and strongest ally.

Although it's not surprising that gay youths usually refrain from girl sex, the usual percentage who try it is likely plummeting as boys become aware of their gayness during middle school and high school, and apply a name, an identity, to it. There is less need these days to drag a girl through his angst, to experiment with the nonpreferred sex, or to contemplate "maybe I should have sex with a girl to tell me whether I'm really gay." Before the issues of coming out to self and others take center stage, let's make the comparison with boy sex.

First Boy Sex

First time I said something sarcastic, and he said, "Suck my dick," and I said, "Whip it out," and he did and I did. I didn't have an orgasm. He didn't do anything to me, so it was his orgasm.
(DEAN, AGE 13)

The parallel to first girl sex for straight guys is first boy sex for gay guys. The stereotypes are out there for first boy sex—it is abusive, happens with an older feckless partner, and the sex turns him gay. To counter these foolish, homophobic misperceptions, we need to know more about why a gay youth has his first sexual experience, when he has first sex, who he has it with, and how he feels about it.

The "why" question was addressed by focus groups with 14- to 18-year-old gay teens. He might have *personal reasons* such as horniness, physical pleasure, curiosity, experience, or love. Also at work are *social pressures*—everyone else is doing it, to keep a boyfriend, partner insistence, and media/cultural focus on sex. On the negative side, the reasons not to have sex include fear of disease, traditional morals, not being ready for sex, and waiting for a connection, the right guy, a special occasion, or love.

As to the "when," "who," and "how do you feel" questions, among the young men I interviewed first gay sex for the majority occurred between the ages of 13 and 16, and it was usually a positive, at times playful, experience with a same-age peer, often someone he knew such as a best friend or cousin. If he waited until college, the partner was more likely to be older than him, a stranger from online, and the entire sexual encounter was less enjoyable. The one answer that was consistent in a survey of gay youths I did thirty years ago was that having first sex at an age-appropriate time was a far more positive experience than having it later, in, say, college.

This chapter will be organized around age of first sex with another male, from the earliest to those who haven't had any (that is, gay virgins). Because earlier I covered prepubescent sexual experiences, only first-time sex after pubertal onset is included here.

Early Adolescence

The timing of first sex depends on circumstances, such as can't-miss opportunities, attractive male cousins, willing best friends, working parents (being home alone), a particular personality style ("let's try anything" versus "too scared"), and sexual desire.

Given the scarcity of neighbors, 13-year-old **Dean** frequently hung out with his male cousin.

★ ★

First time I said something sarcastic, and he said, "Suck my dick," and I said, "Whip it out," and he did and I did. I didn't have an orgasm. He didn't do anything to me, so it was his orgasm. Felt a little giddy, amped, weird a little because I had known him a long time. We were both for it. It was the first time I saw someone else have an orgasm. I had already had one, so knew what it was.

From then on for a couple of years, two to three years, not often, like once a month. Saw him five years ago at work, and we talked. He said he "goes that way" but has a girlfriend. Seemed like an invitation.

★ ★

More common sex partners during early adolescence were the best buddy, the guy across the street, or the friend of a friend. A 12-year-old wanted his friend to be more than a friend, so inside the fort they'd built they kissed, removed their clothes, touched each other, took a shot at oral sex but didn't know how it worked, and attempted *actual* sex—which they thought meant rubbing up against each other. Their sexual relationship lasted a year. Our gay boy was "giggly thrilled," but the other boy was less so, "probably he wasn't gay."

Other pairs of 12-year-old boys had similar experiences. Typically they had known each other for years, and with the onset of puberty new physical things began to happen during sleepovers or in hot tubs. It would start as play and then evolve. One youth felt no shame or guilt but knew it wasn't okay to tell. Then the day came when "he was uncomfortable and so it ended. It was the physical sensation I wanted."

For the hot tub pair, the ending came much too early for our gay boy.

* *

We were in the hot tub and he said, "I have a boner" and he put my hand on his dick. Both of us ejaculated. No regrets, satisfying. He felt the same but didn't want to put a label to it. To him it was not gay behavior. I gave him a blowjob, and we mutually masturbated each other three times total. Then seventh grade began, and it was awkward. He denied anything happened. He admitted to one of my friends that he's bisexual, but he retracted that and says he's heterosexual. He definitely is not.

* *

Although physical pleasure and curiosity were the usual motives, the initial drive could become complicated over time. For instance, two boys engaged in sex-for-pleasure as merely *filler* until girls made themselves available, then the boy/boy sex had to end so that each could head down the heterosexual highway. This sounds good for the straight partner, but what about the boy who unexpectedly became romantically attached?

★ ★

He initiated the first time. Me and him would vacation together every summer, and one time he put my hand down his pants and asked, "What's this?" We had been rafting together and were getting ready to shower together, and there was touching, testing, whatever. I supposed we were both figuring things out, and I would only talk to him about things like sex, dicks, hair.

Initially I felt awkward. Why am I doing this? But I did like it, so not a negative. This continued off and on through eighth grade. We would masturbate each other but no oral or beyond. He became less interested as he got more into girls. I just became the filler for him . . .

He's straight. I was just convenient for him and available, and we were exploring sexuality. Once a week at the max. He was my super best friend so always sleeping at each other's house. Not something I had to do. Things fundamentally changed the summer after eighth as we grew apart and didn't see the same people. As I thought of it as I got older, I recognized it as abnormal in that others weren't doing it and that it might mean I might be gay. But I had no comparison with girls either. I had an emotional attachment to him at the end, and so he wasn't just a friend with sex. He did not reciprocate the emotional attachment.

★ ★

Neither **Raj** nor his *special* next-door friend intended for their sexual relationship to last beyond initial exploration in sixth grade.

* *

We would play around and fight, and after a while we developed a game where it was like Tom and Jerry, and it was like fake kissing and making a really funny sound, and we started doing that, and that ultimately turned into doing something sexual. We would just meet up and just make out and kiss each other on the necks and stuff. Now I find it really bizarre that we don't talk about it as being, we would never talk about it, but we would do it regularly. Then we, there was this big time when we first showed each other our penises, and I think we got naked and rubbed each other. I also remember it lasting for like two or three months . . .

R: How did you feel about that?

After the first excitement went, I was not really that into him, and then he would try to do it. There was a significant period of time when we would always get together, and I would constantly avoid having that happen, but he would push it and it would happen.

R: Did you ever have an orgasm?

No, we actually did not have an orgasm. And we only had like oral sex. We never even had full oral sex. One time, I tried to put my penis in his mouth. It was mostly just cuddling and kissing. I don't think he liked it that much, and I didn't really think about taking his or performing oral sex on him.

R: Do you know what his sexual orientation is today?

I'm actually confused. He is straight. He has girlfriends, and he is back in India. He is very masculine, and I think he's one of the bad kids, but he's trying to become a cop, but he's very different. Sort of like I know him on Facebook.

* *

In the stories thus far, there was no long-term future to these sexual relations. Even if the sex continued for years, the two rarely developed a lasting relationship. **Ted** was a slight exception.

Ted's first partner was his best friend (the boy with the stuffed snake), and sex between them began with puberty and persisted until age 15. They shared many things, though never an official romantic relationship. Today, they remain "really good friends."

★ ★

It was planned that we would have a sleepover every Friday or Saturday night. And on Fridays we would sleep over his house, and Saturdays we would sleep over my house. Because my parents would make us breakfast on Sundays, and I had a bigger TV so we could watch cartoons on Sunday mornings. But his house was close to middle school, so we would go there on Fridays. It was strategic . . .

We would do something like we were playing a video game that had a particularly sexually arousing scene and then we both got really turned on, and then we would go watch porn or something, straight porn.

R: *The genital contact you were having with him continued?*

I wouldn't call it gentle!

R: *I meant genital.*

Oh yeah, genital . . .

R: *Did it evolve into more than rubbing?*

Starting from when we were 11 we went very quickly from mutual masturbation to oral to full on penetrating sex, in both directions.

R: *Why did it stop at 15?*

He was growing more wary of having sexual relations with a guy. He's black. His parents were going through a divorce. He put a stop to it. I had some health issues when I was 16 that I needed

144

to sort of take care of, monitor. But he is now identified as gay. He has had a long-term boyfriend for two years who is white.

★ ★

Boys who first had sex with other boys around pubertal onset usually did so with cousins or friends. Sex was seldom a one-time thing but continued for years and involved rubbing, mutual masturbation, oral sex, and occasionally anal intercourse. Kissing and cuddling were possible. Universally, neither boy told anyone about their secret. If the partner now identifies as straight, why did he engage in gay sex? Perhaps it was experimental or pleasurable, or something he knew he'd outgrow. The gay partners now express doubts about whether these sex partners are totally straight.

Middle Adolescence

For **Anthony**, his first gay sex was during his freshman year of high school, via a new smart phone with a gay hookup app, a spring day, a deserted beach, and not much else going on. Anthony idly pulled up the app on his phone, "Just wanted to see who was in the area." It wasn't that he *intended* to do anything with anyone, of course, but the rest, well, was his maiden voyage.

★ ★

I've since deleted [Grindr], obviously, first day had it found [a] 17-year-old in my area. Of course we were both skeptical at first, but we had a mutual friend . . . I blew him on the beach. He had orgasm, I didn't . . . It was enjoyable experience, and I enjoyed it. I wanted the sexual experience, I guess. It was cold. It was like very long. That is why a somewhat uncomfortable situation, but I wanted the experience, so was positive. I told my friends.

★ ★

145

Later, I asked Anthony for his single most significant sexual or romantic experience. He named two (of course). "The lesser of the two would be with the first guy I had sex with, just because it was the first time and I needed a first experience and it fulfilled that need. Second was the first time I bottomed for Patrick because such an emotional experience and it led to what I want romantically. I wanted more of an emotional thing."

Anthony's timing of having first gay sex during high school was common. His strategy of going online has become a familiar one, even customary, among millennial youths. The location might be a car, library, park, home, or wherever is convenient. Feelings about the sex ranged from disappointingly awkward to "rocked my world." If the first sex was with a first love, whether before or after it became romantic, it was judged to be "totally awesome." Sex with emotional closeness often reigned supreme for young lovers.

A 15-year-old boy was assigned at summer camp to the same tent as a drop-dead heartthrob, an out 17-year-old who initiated sex with him the first night. The younger didn't exactly know what he was supposed to do, but he learned quickly. Soon they were enmeshed in a flurry of kisses, hands, and orgasms, and his life took on new meaning. No one had ever been that attracted to him! His fear? "Mom will kill me!" But until then, he'd live it up. For two weeks they were passionate, with secret hookups multiple times per day throughout the campsite. Although ultimately they went their separate ways, the youth's life had been transformed. "So happy to have years of pent-up feelings released."

By contrast, another 15-year-old decided it was "way past time to do something with a guy," and he went online to find a partner. He later wished he had saved himself for someone he at least liked.

★ ★

I went to a chat room and found a guy my age. I could tell by his online name. We IM'ed and talked for a few days, then exchanged phone numbers. It happened the first time we met. His parents weren't home. We made out and did some oral stuff. No big deal. We dated for a few weeks, hanging out at the mall. He was a strange one, and I wasn't that attracted to him or his personality. I was not out to anyone at this time.

Felt happy because made out with a guy, but I didn't feel anything for him. It was exciting because was with a guy, better than with a girl. But no further sex after that. I saw what a typical gay was like, and it was everything I didn't want to be. Definitely not me. He was very negative, rebellious, didn't care about school, did bad things to his parents, very out and proud of it, no ambition, into rap music, smoked pot.

* *

This was not an uncommon theme among those who met guys online: the sex was not that great, and he missed liking the guy. Jonathan, age 17, took this one step farther by falling in love with his first sexual partner, but it was not to last.

* *

We had been talking for a while, and he invited me over so we could have sex, and it was my first time. So I went over to his place, and I remember it being kind of odd. Just the first time I saw another man's penis was kind of thrilling, and I remember hesitating, but then it just felt natural. Since I had been masturbating myself for a number of years, I felt like I knew what to do.

Mutual masturbation, blowjobs, he eventually penetrated me. I don't remember it too vividly because I realize now that I was infatuated with him. Just very strong desire for him because he was my first, but literally the day after we had sex he told me that he can't see me again so that kind of ruined it. He sent me an email saying his therapist said that he shouldn't be hooking up with people. So I just kind of took it as it was. I got very upset, I shut down, and that had a major impact on me since at the time I thought that I loved him.

* *

Most gay high schoolers, however, knew their partners either because they were friends or because they had been dating for weeks or months before sexually engaging. The long-term prospects for romance were meager.

One young man and a best friend attended the senior prom together—each with a date in tow.

* *

After the prom we took the girls home. I spent the night and slept next to him, wanting him to do "something" to me, but nothing happened. Next day we got Chinese, and he said he liked me more than as a friend. I agreed. His uncle had a nearby house, and so we went there to eat and put our sleeping bags in the loft. He made the first move as I felt scared shitless because it was something that had opened something up and I knew I couldn't go back. Not that attracted to him, but he was a guy and this really fucked with my head. Maybe not attracted to all guys but just to each other, which confused me. I couldn't be gay because just sex with him.

We dated for three months and had sex once a week. Did not go further than oral. All of our friends knew we were having sex. Then I decided to cut it off, and it was a mess. He was upset, angry, emotional, a horrible thing. I still have all the letters. Sex made me more comfortable with my sexuality, what I wanted from a person and a relationship, and it wasn't him.

★ ★

Here's a better outcome. A newly out high school sophomore couldn't take his eyes off a fellow swim team member. They were first friends, then sex partners, then temporary lovers, and now best friends with benefits.

★ ★

We didn't know how to show that we cared about each other, but after a swim meet he hugged me and we knew. A week later we had sex. First time was oral sex, both ways, and it felt good and I wanted to do more. For a few months, about every day we'd go back to his room once his roommate was gone. It was a boarding school. Penetration first time at 16. At first I did it to favor him. You do it for the other person. Now I'm accustomed to it, but it wasn't easy. After a while it got more enjoyable.

I depended on him and told him all of my problems, and this got to be tedious. He ended it because it was tedious. I had feelings for him at one point. He's one of my best friends today. I'm visiting him with my boyfriend next weekend. We continued to have sex several times after we broke up. I needed it to feel better about myself. Last time was a month ago. Actually, it's happened a lot. He used to regret it afterward but not now. My boyfriend knows he's my ex.

★ ★

Many of the young men didn't count sex as sex until it was *real sex*—which meant anal penetration, "the big nasty." A 14-year-old decided once he and his boyfriend were "officially dating" that it was time for "a butt check, which seemed gross to me, but I wanted to try it to see if I'm really gay." He passed the *gay test*. Wondering if he was too young for this, he asked his girl friends, who were supportive because they, too, had recently lost their virginity. The two 15-year-olds had been in a three-month relationship and decided it was time. "He was on top of me, but the first time it didn't work out. We didn't know what we were doing or how to do it. Felt horrible! It hurt! 'Get that thing out of me right now!'" They were in love, so they could laugh about it. Two weeks later, success!

Asher, who had the crush on Aladdin, found it difficult to arrange his first sexual experience. He didn't blame the usual suspects (conservative religion or parents) but the "worst gaydar known to man" and an inability to flirt—"I am very bad at it." To Asher, everybody looks preppy, like your "stereotypical homosexual." At his school being gay was "fine as long as you didn't hit on the straight guys. So I worry about hitting on straight guys." As we'll see later, his junior year he discovered Danny, a senior.

Although Asher asserted he has no gaydar, he's the exception. Although mistakes are made when gay youths hit on straight guys or miss sexual overtures by other gay youths, most have a sixth sense about who is gay or not. Research has shown that sex-atypical features, such as feminine body movements, voice, and facial features (particularly the eyes and mouth) are the giveaways. Youths who prefer the receptive role in sexual encounters tend to be more accurate than those who are tops—perhaps because they have more to lose if they're wrong, or they're simply more sensitive to subtle cues.

After experiencing his first adolescent gay sex, a boy might determine that it wasn't great sex but it was good enough to satisfy erotic pleasure, end his virginity, promote a romance, or learn what to do (as a supplement to porn watching). The partner might not have been the love of his life, yet it felt right at the time. Although these initial flings had an expiration date, they were appreciated for what they confirmed: "Yep. I'm gay."

Late Adolescence

A youth might defer first gay sex beyond his high school years. But if first sex has such significance, why did they wait? The young men suggested a number of possibilities.

- Circumstances at home not being conducive to having sex.
- Avoidance of perceived peer or family condemnation.
- Uncertainty about whether he's really gay.
- Not being ready for sex.
- Personal moral or ethical standards.
- Struggles with his sexuality because of religious or cultural issues.
- Absence of out gay youths in his high school and not wanting an anonymous hookup.
- Not having yet met the right guy.

Once he graduates, however, having gay sex might rise to the top of a young gay man's agenda, with motivations such as pleasure, curiosity, hormones, ego boosting, or getting it over with. Perhaps he decides what he needs are explicit *tryouts* to test his gayness. Even if he passes his own test, by delaying sex has he unduly hampered his erotic development?

Jake, at 19 years old, contemplated sex with girls versus sex with boys. Was it to satisfy eroticism or who he *should* be having sex with? He received the answer that he'd expected but didn't really want. Similar to his first girl sex, he chose one of his high school friends, now his roommate.

★ ★

It was just a talk about sex late in the evening led to masturbation just in front of each other, and then it kind of developed into a masturbating each other over a month or two. Then over an-other month or two, it was oral sex.

The mindset through all of this is, "I'm not gay!" I have attrac-tions to men but I don't necessarily want them or in fact I actively don't want them. It would be easier if I didn't. It altered our friendship because he wasn't comfortable being intimate with a friend . . . It felt good to be sexual with a person that I was actu-ally sexually attracted to. But it was tainted with the fact that I thought that I shouldn't.

R: Of the two, how would you contrast these two?

So with the girl, it was much less heavy because I thought I should be having sex with a girl. With the guy, I couldn't have a conversation even with him really, outside of sex, about having sex. And so again, it was just stifling the atmosphere around the event. It was much more erotic with him.

R: And frequency?

I had sex with both of them an equal number of times. Once to maybe twice a week, and it was easier because he and I shared a dorm room . . . He was very conflicted about it, and I was some-what conflicted. I knew that I was attracted to him, and I think he really didn't want to be attracted to me . . . I was always disap-pointed in the guy because I wanted more emotionally anything. Even more friendship would have felt better. But it never even got close to romantic.

★ ★

A 21-year-old decided he'd go to a gay bar to settle his gay truth. Though the partner he picked wasn't especially cute, they went home together, had anal sex that "felt right, more right than sex with girls," and he had his answer. "Huge impact. Realized that what I was wondering was true, and so it changed my life." His friends "had already known I was gay. I had felt insecure since late high school because always called gay when I was little, and now I was nervous about being gay."

Another young man, just two weeks into his college freshman year, couldn't believe his luck in math class where he met his first sex partner. He found the same answer, though he told no one.

★ ★

He tells me he's having trouble with his girlfriend. I wondered about him, so I told him I might be bisexual, and I asked him if he had experiences with males. I was closeted at the time, so I told him in a whispering way, "We can experiment." I was shaking internally, but he said, "Sure." That night, it was oral sex. I had an orgasm, and I assume that he did. It was our only time because he transferred colleges. That night I said, "Oh my god that oral sex is good!" Plus, I had finally done something and explored a new facet of who I am. I did feel dirty because I let my hormones take over my rational self. I was almost out as gay to myself and this was one leg over the fence.

★ ★

Others were half a step beyond these young men, knowing they are gay but without the opportunity to have sex. Its absence felt like an albatross around their necks. This was **Derek**'s situation during the summer after high school graduation. He felt he had to be "experienced" before college, so he chose the most flamboyant guy in high school.

★ ★

He was very attracted to me, and he kind of figured out that I was gay by that point. And kept like trying to be my friend and talking to me and stuff . . . He and I messed around on two different occasions. All that really happened with him was just like we masturbated together and I think we had oral sex . . . He was fairly notorious for having flings with

153

different guys around the area. I was kind of ashamed of it because I didn't find him that attractive. I felt like it was just like a dirty thing to do. I was pretty convinced at that point that I was gay. For me it was more just an experience. After it happened, I could say I am not inexperienced.

* *

However, waiting late need not be a negative experience as **Lenny** and **Nicolas** demonstrated. Lenny, a filmmaker with an identical twin, prizes his first time at age 21 with a sexually experienced college student. This friend of a friend took the lead with a hand job.

* *

I had an orgasm but he didn't because the tide came in. We were on a beach and the tide came in. Just to bring some context.

R: *What was the impact for you?*

It's funny because it's something that I always thought about for so long. When is this finally going to happen? While it was happening it was great, but it wasn't this huge, it was very in the moment. We were both pretty drunk. I think afterwards, I thought, "Wow. It actually happened. I've done that."

R: *Were there future interactions between the two of you?*

That was the last time. We're not in contact . . . I really really, by my current definition, fell in love with him. I knew it was silly to think that way because I haven't spent that much time with him. I had never really been that infatuated with a person before . . . I guess he just kind of lost interest and continued on. And then after that I sent a few messages to him saying, "This is how I feel." It was a nice ending.

* *

Nicholas, from a conservative, rural town, didn't know any gay people in high school, though he'd wondered about a few boys. As a result, few opportunities presented themselves to help him

figure himself out. The annual collegewide "Homocoming" celebration did the trick.

* *

I met a guy. Like I knew him kind of from Outreach. I talked with
him and going back to his place and hanging out, and then one
thing led to another. When I went with him did I think it was going
to happen? No, but I definitely knew it was a possibility at that
point. But I wasn't like, "We are definitely going to do something."

It was my first time, and he said he had only done anything like
once or twice before. I mean it wasn't that awkward, but it wasn't
like completely smooth like you would see in porn or something.
It was nice to know he found me attractive, and I was like he's
cute, and neither of us really knew what we were doing, so.
R: How far did it go?

There was making out, oral, and then mostly mutual jerking
off . . . I remembering being at the time being like, "Oh this is interesting. I've never done this before." And I really didn't have any
idea what I was doing, but it was kind of learning how to fly basically . . . We ended up dating for about a month. Roughly.

* *

Also from a conservative community, **Geoff** told no one in
middle school about his boy crushes, and in high school he avoided
all things gay. In his college freshman year he met *the* guy in his
dorm. From the beginning they had their suspicions about each
other.

* *

We knew we liked each other, but we weren't sure if we wanted
to date each other . . . He moved my hand down there. Not that I
was opposed or anything. I didn't jerk away or anything. But I
didn't want to come across as being too dominant or aggressive
about it, so he kind of made the first move.

R: How far did you guys go the first time?

Nothing beyond touching. It started out above [the belt] then below. No orgasms . . . At the time I didn't really know what we were or if this was just a one time thing or if it would evolve into something more. I was kind of uncertain about it in that regard. But I enjoyed it.

★ ★

The physical became more regular and one step led to another, culminating in oral and anal sex. "We didn't really negotiate anything. We could just talk about whatever. We were very comfortable with each other, but at the time it was just whatever happened happened." The two progressed from acquaintances to friends to first sex partners to romantic partners to life partners. We'll return to this rarity and to Geoff's unique transitions.

Gay Virgins

Of the forty young men I interviewed, two had not had genital contact with another guy. For both of them, romance trumped sex. One was totally out on Facebook and attended Gay Straight Alliance meetings, and everyone he knew was aware that he is gay. He wasn't opposed to gay sex, but he wanted his first sex to be with the love of his life. In this, he believed he stood alone among his generation. "If I really like a guy I will fantasize being romantically with him, but sex is the least part of the fantasy."

The other gay virgin, who was sensitive to his Puerto Rican roots, didn't want to get stuck in one position. It was an emotional not sexual or romantic connection he desired.

★ ★

I have homosexual attractions to other boys, but I also realize it might appear to be sexual, but really it's an emotional

need for same-sex friendships rather than a romantic relationship. A few people know my struggles. Ideally, I don't
get sexual attractions to either sex. I like healthy friendships
with both sexes. I don't want to be turned on by either sex,
no crushes, no fantasies. I get sexually attracted to other boys
and not girls. I wish there was a boy I could get emotional
and rely on and be around all the time. I've had no sex with
boys or girls. It is a priority, but I won't do it. If my desire
changes from homosexual to heterosexual, then after we
marry I'd like to be changed, but I'm okay if not get changed.

★ ★

You have to hope he'll find the emotional connection he's searching
for.

Simply a Hookup?

Your options for first sex include having it at the onset of puberty,
years later, or never, or soliciting it from an online app or one's
best friend, teammate, or cousin. It can be pleasurable or not,
meaningful or meaningless. Sex is a one-time event or something
that has no end. It is a hookup that means little except pleasure and
a way to wile away the time. Sex can be with a date, a romantic
partner, or a soul mate. Perhaps it's a statement about yourself, or a
means to establish what you have long suspected—the defining
event that proves forever your gayness. Or it's something to get
under your belt, or an opportunity to connect with the love of
your life.

Some gay boys are virgins after high school graduation, perhaps as a matter of personal choice or as an unwanted condition.
Maybe a young man is intent on losing his virginity but is flustered because he's highly selective and the gays he knows have

undesirable physical or personality characteristics. Perhaps he is having difficulty setting aside religious or cultural objections because he's not going to do it with just anyone or he fears catching a disease. He may be unsure about how to take the first step. Perhaps he'll terminate his virginity once the love of his life appears or perhaps he'll miss him.

The critical issue is remaining true to yourself because otherwise regret rules. One valuable lesson is that first sex is better if you're attracted to the guy physically *and* as a person. First sex can't be undone, and honestly, for the rest of your life you'll remember the first time. In earlier generations having first sex usually preceded a gay identification by two years, but today sexual awareness and gay identification nearly always come first, before the sex. Why the generational reversal from the sex-then-identification sequence? Guys in your generation know they are gay at increasingly earlier ages. You don't have to have sex as a prerequisite for self-knowledge. You know from your fantasies, the porn you watch, the people you're attracted to, and within your heart of hearts. Let's now turn to that awareness.

I'm Gay—Probably, Certainly

I was like, "Okay, that guy is kind of cute." Am I appreciating the fact that he's good looking? (NICHOLAS, AGE 12)

As I listened to each of the forty young men talk about his *gay journey* from first awareness of same-sex desires to where he is now, I was struck by the near absence of anything resembling an inevitable trajectory of how a gay boy becomes a gay man. No one followed a series of universal stages from cluelessness to out-and-proud as traditionally envisioned in the coming-out models proposed over thirty years ago. The prototypes fail to capture or make sense of what you likely experience when moving from *thinking* gay, to *doing* gay, to *being* gay. They don't map onto real lives—that is, few youths, including the young men in this book, stick to them in the predicted sequence and with the same consequences. For example, some *do* gay before *thinking* gay, and others *think* gay before *doing* gay.

If these models are discarded, as they should be, what else is there? One alternative is to view your life as processing various gay developmental milestones, especially coming-out-to-self, at various ages with skips, slips, and stalls.

It's Not All the Same

Recognizing yourself as gay might well be the most memorable developmental event of your young life, a culmination of all that has come before as well as a marker of your future, from which you cannot readily, without great cost, retreat. Emotionally, it may feel like schlepping through a quagmire of uncharted, extremely dangerous territory with potential repercussions to face from family and friends. Will it be denial, rejection, acceptance, or celebration? Or will it be a breeze, seamless in its continuity with all that has occurred previously? Yes, there are websites, YouTube channels, and television shows and films that normalize or even glamorize the process and offer support from famous people, anonymous others, and agencies.

You might also feel as though your situation is totally unique. You have no story, no angst, and no dramatics because you've always known about your gayness, as apparently everybody else did while you were growing up. Your transition has been an ongoing inch-by-inch, cascading process over the course of months or years. Are you dejected because you have no coming-out story, though you've read and heard about such exciting stories? But it doesn't happen to you. You've negotiated your gayness in a straightforward manner and have had the needed resources with gay-friendly friends and family. You calmly accepted your predestined pathway with barely a blip in your lifestyle.

Or perhaps you have a dramatic coming-out story because at a particular and sudden point in time everything came together. You remember the exact moment and even today celebrate the anniversary to mark the spark when your life suddenly made sense and was set on its inevitable course.

Under such varied conditions it's difficult to suggest the best trajectory for you to take toward your goals of recognition and acceptance. This is the intent of this chapter—to provide you with examples of personal, internal journeys from first suspicions to the moment when you accept your sexual and romantic reality. A bisexual phase might not be unusual, if even for a day or a year. When and how you disclose this new reality about yourself to others are addressed in subsequent chapters. Be prepared for many variations on an uncommon process.

Early Going

Attractions to other boys through emotional crushes, erotic arousals, or sexual activities typically begin many years before puberty, perhaps forming some of your first childhood memories. Perhaps you immediately understood *I'm gay* after a night's sleep, or perhaps it took you a decade until the eroticism of puberty again delivered the gay message. The key element might have been feeling vaguely different from other boys throughout your childhood and adolescence. You didn't fit the masculinity prescribed for boys, or you were more enamored than other boys with boys.

What instigates the process of gay awareness? When and why this happens we don't know, but it's quite early for most youths, although it is without clear signposts along the way. Inklings of gayness exist, yet you might wonder why you would ever want to spend the rest of your life with a boy. Boys can be, as **Jeremy** told me, all about "beer, getting chicks, World Wrestling Federation, drinking, and hunting." However, similar to girls, boys also have an inner world, like to listen, and can provide what you want.

These prepubertal and early adolescent feelings, with or without clear sexual and romantic components, are critical for many boys to activate the self-awareness process. To varying degrees, things are clarified rather dramatically with the increased level of pubertal hormones and subsequent erotic feelings. By pubertal onset, you might be willing to forgive boys for their rude and crude ways as you realize you *really like* guys and want to be around them, which can be scary. What's that all about? Could it mean *I'm gay?*

Maybe Bi?

Among the young men, freshman year of high school was the average time for first becoming aware that the romantic and erotic inclinations have a name. This revelation could come as early as age 8 or as late as 19—the latter was a young man who said he was "still working on it." Before they acknowledged that they're gay, about half filtered through a *bisexual phase*, similar to **Anthony**.

Anthony couldn't tell me the exact moment when he first realized he was sexually attracted to guys because it had been such a gradual process. By the end of seventh grade he recognized a basic fact—his attraction to girls was primarily emotional, but his attraction to guys was both emotional and erotic. First, however, he passed through a bisexual phase "to hold onto" being at least a little bit straight. Unfortunately, his model for bisexuality was a middle school kid who was unworthy of emulation.

★ ★

We were never close. He was very different from me. Even now I was with a popular crowd and he had anger issues, so he wasn't a person people go to for things. We talked a little about it. He told people he liked kissing guys but not anything else, so in my head he wasn't actually gay. Wasn't harassed. At the time each of our respective friends knew. He was out to a good amount of people, but anyone who might have cared didn't know.

★ ★

Transient bisexuality, as opposed to true bisexuality, is a false start toward gayness. It might last only a brief time, but serves an important purpose for some boys—providing cover with a more socially acceptable, less ostracized alternative to being totally gay. "Bisexual" is easier and safer to say to friends, including girlfriends, who might also claim to be bi. Bisexuality in some circles is more edgy, a mysterious status symbol, at least for girls.

Appealing to bisexuality seldom works for long. Although a gay boy might dupe his friends, he'll be less successful with himself. Deep inside, one young man admitted, "I knew I just liked men. I was trying to force myself to like women and fantasize about them sexually but it just never worked. It seemed less bad than being gay." He thought he was a little bit abnormal as opposed to being totally abnormal.

If he's not bi, how does he make sense of a limited but genuine emotional and physical attraction to girls? It's likely to be less than the overwhelming, erotic, lusty, infatuations he has with boys, so he essentially splits the difference and says he must be bisexual. One 12-year-old noticed the duality between his erotic and emotional attractions. "At different points I was bi, straight, and gay and then I said I'll just wait to see what happens. I knew my sexual interests were with boys and my emotional ones with girls and if a guy ever did the emotional one then I'd know." The truth arrived for him in ninth grade when *the boy* appeared and the anticipated gay repercussions were confirmed. The two were voted "cutest couple" at their high school. Other youths maintain a level of romantic and erotic interest in women that is sufficient to identify as *mostly gay*. I'll elaborate their lives in a separate chapter.

Aha, I'm Gay

Whether initial same-sex awareness creeps into consciousness to confirm a gay identity or passes through a bisexual phase is difficult to predict. The time frame from *maybe gay* to *absolutely gay* can be instantaneous or it can take a lifetime. It's exhilarating or depressing, a moment of joy or panic when a long-fought battle is finally lost or won, depending on your perspective. Although at the time of my interviews, most of the young men had progressed quite far, their evolution to self-acceptance was still a work in progress for several. I'm puzzled (as they were) about how they will get there.

At first **Jonathan** interpreted his early erotic fascinations and multiple boy crushes as normal boy stuff. Suddenly everything changed in ninth grade when he heard the word *gay* out loud, as if for the very first time. Immediately he sensed its enormous significance and rushed to a private computer room in the library, tucked away in the back so nobody would see him searching the Internet for "gay." He found a young lesbian online, and through instant messenger they talked late into the evening. This eventually led Jonathan to finally realize he has gayness. Jonathan's gay life started late, proceeded at lightning speed, and then cruised until his mother intruded on his therapy sessions (more on this later).

By contrast, **Anthony** transitioned from "not gay" to "yes gay" shortly after the onset of puberty. By eighth grade he knew his gay reality, and at the halfway point of high school he was out to his best friends and parents, accepted himself as gay, had sex with other boys, and began a committed romantic relationship—and eventually e-mailed me.

But we're getting ahead of ourselves—the important point is that, while their personal journeys made sense for **Jonathan** and **Anthony**, no other youth followed either of these exact treks. Neither pathway was typical or customary except for one feature: puberty, at which time sexual desire threatens to acquire meaning. Although this wasn't universal, it was nearly so as over three-quarters of the youths *knew* shortly after the flood of sex hormones. This didn't necessarily mean, however, that they *accepted* their gayness.

I'm not sure what to call this milestone when lifelong sexual and romantic feelings and arousal are given their initial meaning—perhaps we can call it the *aha moment*. Sometimes there's no resistance, and the ripple effect is instantaneous. Or it is quickly dismissed (call it suppressed, if you like), and the eventual, predictable recognition must wait until young adulthood—as it did for several of the young men I spoke with. I have divided the young men into two groups: those recalling *erotic* aspects as critical and those persuaded by *romantic* aspects.

Erotic Focus on Guys

Whether during fantasy head-trips, porn, or sex, a youth eventually realizes boys not girls erotically turn him on. This recognition seldom leads to an immediate gay affirmation, but it does enhance the process. On the cusp of puberty, one boy eyed "super developed, naked, nice looking guys," but he wasn't ready to say he was sexually attracted to them—that would have been too abrupt and gone too far. "I just knew I liked looking at them." He remembered a fifth-grade sleepover as the time when the most developed boy pulled down his pants and danced naked. Anxiety about whether the other boys might notice his sexual excitement meant our boy was unable to fully enjoy the moment.

Although porn is a common slayer of assumed heterosexuality, additional conditions also play a role. For example, because of his gay uncle, **Dion** knew what it meant to be gay and suspected that he might be, too. At age 14, he observed his preference for straight porn featuring multiple guys. That was strike one, but he needed further confirmation. Late one evening he snuck downstairs to watch *Queer as Folk*. Strike two! At age 16, he experimented with two guys he'd met online. The sex wasn't great sex, but it was sufficiently telling. Strike three! Several of his friends suspected. "It was kind of like an Anderson Cooper, you know, he may be, but he has a crush on this girl."

Erotic kissing was sufficient for **Asher**. He had no suspicion about his sexuality until he was 12 or 13 when on a church youth group trip he got wasted with several guys because "you know, that's what you do on church trips." After making out with a 14-year-old ("We sat and kissed for like five minutes"), the next morning Asher woke up to his new reality. "I was like, 'Fuck! This is probably [it],'" but he ignored it and dated girls until he was a junior in high school. That's when he ditched his charade. The instigator was again erotic making out: a session with the co-captain of the track team sealed the deal.

Nicholas exemplifies how long the process can take. At age 12 he questioned himself: "I was like, 'Okay, that guy is kind of cute.' Am I appreciating the fact that he's good looking?" At 14 while masturbating he realized, "Okay this is happening easier when I am thinking about guys or looking at guys as opposed to girls." At 17 he acceded to the meaning of everything, and accepted it.

I Want to Be a Boyfriend

A potent and telling sign of gayness is the persistence of boy crushes, moving beyond mere infatuation to a desire to be in a relationship with a guy. Girls don't do it for a gay boy. He needs more passion, which boys, usually one in particular, can offer.

Similar to **Nicholas**, **Tyler** bridged the erotic/crush divide. There is no universal sequence of events, but Tyler did the usual progression in reverse—first the crush, then the erotic, with an assist from an ex-dating partner. Tyler's earliest sex memory was rather late, a ninth-grade crush on a really good-looking theater kid who was so comfortable with himself, so irresistible, so cute, that he pulled the girls and Tyler into his orbit. Tyler speculated, "Maybe I wouldn't mind kissing a guy." Confirmation came in his junior year *by accident:* "I don't know what made me want to do it but I guess I just clicked the link and I watched a video, and that's when it hit me that I definitely am attracted to guys." Tyler entered "what I like to call my bisexual stage." The process shifted into high gear with the help of the girl he was dating when she posed *the question:*

★ ★

"Are you sure you're not gay? You haven't really ever talked about girls?" Then I had to think, "Am I sure I'm not gay?" And so that set me into just really thinking about it and really trying to figure it out and I guess over a span of time, maybe like a few weeks or whatever, I just started to really question hard whether, "Am I actually bi? I don't really think about girls that often?" I am really not sure the moment I officially said to myself or knew to myself, "I am definitely 100 percent gay . . ."

Maybe the right girl would come along. I didn't want to rule that possibility out. Maybe the first time I knew I was gay was the first time I kissed a boy. Up to that point, I had kissed girls. That was a boy named Joseph, and that was the very beginningish of my junior year. When I kissed him, I felt like this means a lot more to me than any time I ever kissed a girl.

* *

For **Derek**, his junior year provided his Big Epiphany: the absence of romantic feelings toward girls. His best girl friends observed, "You're not exactly the same as all of our other guy friends. You haven't tried to date us yet."

Geoff: The Interview

College sophomore **Geoff** immediately struck me with his intense eye contact and traditional masculinity. He looked and acted straight. Initially, I wondered if he had come to the wrong interview room. Throughout the hour-long interview Geoff had difficulty expressing himself, yet he was fully engaged in the process. Green shorts with a blue Hollister shirt, flip-flops, a buzzed haircut on the left with curly, thick strands on the right falling over his ear, Geoff looked to me like an All-American athlete in some alternative sport. He chewed gum throughout the interview. Geoff grew up in a small Western town, and he'd had an uncertain career path although he now knows that he wants to combine science with business. His first smile waited until I asked if I could tape the interview. "Of course!" he said.

Geoff has never had a large group of friends, just a handful of really close ones. Because his father was the baseball coach, Geoff played school sports. "I was forced to. I mean not under whip and chain . . . The whole parental Little League kind of thing, so I was made to play basketball for three years. And I just hated it." He eventually replaced the competitive and distasteful nature of team sports with sports for fun, such as biking and running.

* *

I don't know if I differ too much [from straight guys] in terms
of interest or just the way I act or the way I talk or whatever.

People mistake me for straight often, not too often. I don't think there's a huge distinction between my personality and that of a straight person's . . . Well, I've never really been into guy things, so to speak. Not that there is a right and wrong, but I'm from Montana and a lot of people are into like hunting and all those outdoor things. That's never been my thing at all. I've never been athletic at all. I was more into music and stuff. And art.

Kind of looking back on it now, it seems like you're going through this period of time where you are expected to become a man, but in my area, the people around me, their definition of a man was not what I was at the time. They wanted men who dressed in camouflage on weekends and who played basketball and video games. And that just wasn't me . . .

The guys from where I am from are kind of sloppy, not to make sweeping generalizations. But I always did my hair and didn't wear sweatpants and a tee shirt every day. So in those ways, I think I am more feminine. Then I think I am more masculine emotionally. That's all I can really think of at the moment.

I am not stoic and emotion-less. But I don't know, the way I'm thinking is that there are like jokes about women being emotional but I don't have a lot of mood swings and I am just pretty chill, go with the flow.

★ ★

Geoff traced his gay feelings to boy crushes, although initially he attributed them to a male buddy phase he heard all boys go through during puberty. Not to worry, Geoff thought, because he appreciated boys in a mental not a sexual way. He couldn't initially say *gay*, but he identified as bisexual until the end of high school.

169

But his boy crushes were not fading. Although eventually Geoff was able to say, "This is just who I am and was more open and comfortable to it," two years later he was still not totally comfortable with his sexuality. "Not that I hate myself or anything. Just because society is not comfortable with it."

Similar to Geoff's considerable child and adolescent boy crushes, Ted was also not prepared to say, "I'm gay." Classmates thought otherwise and teased him with "You're so gay!" Ted believed it was because he was weird and belonged to the theater group, a mini-college within his high school for the visual and performing arts. The theater geeks protected him when the gangsters and jocks called him "fag." Despite their support, it remained difficult for Ted to accept his sexuality.

★ ★

The time that I really recognized that I was gay was with that guy with the heart, and he was very close with a friend of mine that I had been best friends with when we were in school together before middle school and we hadn't seen each other for four years and then all of the sudden in high school again. And at the same time, the black friend of mine who I had been friends with since I was 2 and involved with since I was 11 . . . He and I sort of stopped having sex at around age 15 . . . I was really getting used to the fact that I was no longer interested in women . . .

After middle school I realized, "I am interested in men." And it was internal, and I remember being very sort of disconnected from that feeling when I was in public. But when I was in private, it owned a lot of me. I started only watching gay porn, no more women in porn. There was a level of disgust for female genitalia and figure. And then my relationship with him and the other jocks in school. It was sort of a floodgate where there was this sort of specimen of men was very attractive to me. He was very confident, very sure of himself and not necessarily aggressive but contrarian in a way that I found attractive. But in that contrarianitivity I saw that as aggression and sort of masculine strength, which to me was attractive. He listened to a completely different kind of music. A little bit rebellious. And all of those things led me to realize that and to me it wasn't necessarily about sexuality. It was like I want to be a boyfriend for that person.

★ ★

To Have Sex, to Love

Although a variety of factors instigate the name-my-sexuality sweepstakes, it's usually coming to terms with the motion of your penis, your heart, or the two conjoined. Either can be first, though ultimately the clincher is the synchrony of the two. This realization may be a revelation, though cultural issues such as small town America, conservative values, and religion frequently handicap it, as happened with **Raj**. The dilemma between sex and love continue to weigh heavily on **Raj**.

Raj: The Interview

Believing himself to be several minutes late, Raj apologized, "I lost track of time." A computer science junior, Raj was from what he called a warrior caste family who lived in a small town in India. Raj gave me a brief history of the various Indian castes, quickly segued into how people didn't realize he was Indian because of his light skin, and then highlighted his other Indian characteristics (dark hair, short stature). Raj wore a white tee shirt, plaid shorts, and short hair. He was slightly stocky and, to use his words, "a bit nerdy looking because I'm often too much into my head." Though he is clearly quite intelligent, at times I was uncertain which question Raj was answering or if he was unaware of what he had just said or where he was going. He'd pause and apologize: "Sorry, it's my issue."

Educationally, Raj attended an all-boy's school in India and thus had few interactions with girls. In his neighborhood Raj played street soccer, where the children kicked a stone as if it were a soccer ball. Their play was pretty intense, and Raj proudly confessed he was actually quite good at it. But cricket is the sport of India, and Raj admitted that he was bad at it, so he didn't rate himself as being athletic.

Culturally, being gay was a big problem for Raj. "Ideally, I would like to be heterosexual, absolutely because I think it would make things a lot easier. So that's how I feel. I wish I was white, Caucasian, straight male, born in Switzerland with rich parents."

Raj first became aware of his same-sex romantic feelings in late childhood when he began developing crushes on other boys, especially a rather outstanding Bollywood dancer. Raj struggled mightily with his Bollywood crush.

★ ★

I had had certain fantasies about certain men. My sister is six years older than me and she had some friends, so about them, in terms of I didn't know about sex but I did know about this Wedding Night. So in Indian customs is a big night for doing romantic things, and they kiss leading up to something. So I would imagine doing all of those things leading up to that something with that guy . . . He used to dance in our school. Bollywood dancing was a big deal. I remember I really really liked him. I think I was in fourth or fifth grade and he was in ninth or tenth grade. I didn't tell him I had a crush on him. I couldn't even think about it. It was not a possibility. I didn't tell anyone. I really wished I could be like his good friend . . . I would think about him, and I think it was hard because I was starting to realize that I should not be attracted to him but I was attracted to him. I knew that it could never happen. I could never have a romantic connection with him or sexual connection with him, which was very very disappointing. I grew up watching Bollywood, and I had this really romantic idea for my lover. I really wanted to dance in front of the Pyramids, and the first ambition I guess that I formed was that I would have the greatest of love stories that I would see in the movies . . .

R: *What was it about him?*

He had a very good way of speaking. He was very good looking, that's one thing. And he was composed in a way, even until now, I like people like that in the same way. People who are not too, he was very confident and he really didn't have to try hard and he seemed very comfortable in his skin and I was really attracted to his body and his physique was also attractive.

★ ★

Acting on his crush, however, wasn't an option for Raj, and a lustful passion for girls never materialized—much to his chagrin even today. "I would feel like my love [for girls] would be a lot more pure because it's not sexual. I would explain it to myself that way, and it was going to be all good." Raj was optimistic he could do this until he visited a cyber café and went online to porn sites. He would like to blame porn for his gayness, yet he chose to watch porn guys, not porn women. By college, he was ready to say, "I accept myself as gay."

It's a Process

Whether the time lapse between the *aha* moment and *I'm gay* acceptance will be speedy (**Anthony**) or delayed (**Raj, Geoff**) can't be predicted. What happens during the gap? Is it simply *time passing*? It's as if something inside you has to do its thing. Now that the construct (being gay) has been set in motion, you have within yourself a place to interpret your viewing patterns at the beach or the locker-room and your porn selections.

Many *maybes* make this process easier for you. If no one really cares whether you're gay or not, if you live in an environment with supportive friends and/or family, if you fall head over heels for your dreamy boy, if curiosity with boy sex propels you toward multiple access opportunities, if you're living with so much stress that you have to do something quickly or you'll explode, or if you're dating a girl who says, "You're gay, aren't you?" then it's time to accept your basic sexuality.

Nothing is programmed about these developmental milestones. There is nothing to indicate that they should proceed in a certain sequence. There is no one correct or healthiest coming-out-to-self process. There are no rules, no universals, and no predictability about when you accept these insights or when you disclose them to friends and family. Coming out to others, however, requires another process, and it is this to which we now turn.

Something to Tell You

My friendships have gotten stronger because of my self-acceptance. My smile is a lot more genuine and surfaces much more frequently.

(NATIONAL SWIM CHAMPION TOM LUCHSINGER)

Many youths, but not all, have a coming-out story about the first time they disclosed their sexuality. Some stories are quite memorably scary, but others are merely a pro forma event—"Oh yeah, I probably should have told you." Taking place anywhere from early adolescence to adulthood, they range from accidental to planned, a necessity to a luxury, and monumental to "I've suspected." Specifically, this is where we'll be in this chapter: coming out to someone.

Various coming-out-to-others tales have been chronicled in coming-out books and on social media, websites, and videos. Unfortunately, many are wrought with rejection, verbal abuse, and physical attacks. It can be a horrible chapter in one's life. But if these narratives don't feel familiar or are difficult to relate to, it's because they are not the norm, not now and not ever. That isn't to say that coming out to others is always easy or without negative consequences. It can be difficult or even dangerous, but that isn't typical. It's a huge blunder on our part if that's the only depiction you have seen of what it's like to come out to another person.

What we know is that most of you are pretty savvy. First you disclose to a safe person, a best friend, or someone you're confident will be supportive. It may become the quintessential developmental marker of your life, forever registered in your memory, not only because of the initial uncertainty about how the other person will react but also because of what it says about your personal journey. This moment is tentative or dramatic, a private affair with whispered pleas not to tell anyone or shouted to everyone on Facebook.

Coming out is nearly always a relief. It can immediately follow your first awareness that you're gay, or it can wait years longer until you are utterly, positively convinced you're not even a little bit straight. Perhaps it helps you to accept the inevitable with trepidation, resignation, relief, or joy. However it goes, you won't likely forget it. If you're ever stuck in an awkward situation with a gay person and you don't know what to talk about, just ask him for his coming-out story and the evening will be consumed.

The benefits of coming out are massive—better friends, happier days, authenticity, and boyfriends. Free at last! It's not about saying the words out loud but about you accepting your sexuality. National swim champion Tom Luchsinger is our witness. After a torturous adolescence and young adulthood, he concluded,

> My friendships have gotten stronger because of my self acceptance. My smile is a lot more genuine and surfaces much more frequently. I laugh a lot more. My body has time to recover from a workout because I'm actually an easy-going person. I have found qualities—both physical and emotional— that I like about myself—though that's still a work in progress. My number of good days far outnumber my bad days. I'm still the same person I have always been, just a hell of a lot better at it.

It is noteworthy that when he disclosed to a fellow gay swimmer, an older brother, and his best friend Kate, all accepted and supported him. As for how Tom's parents reacted, see the next chapter.

Other coming-out narratives pose critical questions and provide sage advice on what to consider before publicly coming out. Why are you sharing this information, at this particular time, to this particular person? What do you hope to gain? Is it to increase self-acceptance and self-respect or to garner sympathy and support? Or is it simply about time to do it?

Before coming out, please consider five points:

- Make sure you have a sufficient level of self-acceptance, especially about your sexuality.
- Rehearse what you're going to say.
- Tell someone safe, someone who respects and likes you and has been supportive in the past.
- Don't take a negative response personally. Those are about the other person, not you.
- Have an escape route in case things don't go well.

Coming out frequently leads to a positive transition in your life and those you disclose to.

Anthony first disclosed to a safe female friend who was also his primary source of information about sex. By eighth grade Anthony was ready to tell her he is gay. "[I was] shaking and being so nervous and never did it in person, not face-to-face, but by text. I never got a bad response." If it wasn't progay, Anthony's high school was at least gay benign.

The Basics

The average age of first disclosure among the young men was 16, with the earliest at 11 and the oldest a decade later. Two first publicly came out during their interviews with me. For **Liam**, it was his first opportunity to *publicly* say the words out loud, albeit somewhat tentatively. Prior to my interview, he had implicitly disclosed to his sex partners. The second youth had also grown up in a sexually conservative community with family obligations to marry. Rumors abounded among his friends about his sexuality though they would never have rejected him for it. Even so, it remained too scary for both youths to come out.

The words "I'm gay" seldom were a surprise for the other person, and the disclosure nearly always elicited supportive assurances. A friend told one youth, anticipating his disclosure, "If you're gay I'll still love you." Another youth, with heart pounding, hands shaking, voice quivering, and with courage he didn't know he had, received from his best friend, "Duh!" In one situation, the two first came out to each other and began dating as 16-year-olds. Needless to say, their first disclosure went quite well. Only occasionally was the first outing to a family member, as we'll discuss in the next chapter.

Within this range of *big event* to barely registering was a mix of reactions, disclosure ages, and questions, the most perplexing of which was, "Why did I wait so long?"

Wasn't That Bad

Counter to websites, most of the young men I spoke with reported that their first disclosure wasn't "that bad." Many experienced a rather smooth process without any trauma. Helpful to many, to varying degrees, were having an internal sense of well-being, comfort with, and certainty about their same-sex sexuality, having supportive friends, having a crush on another boy, and attending a school with a positive climate. These conditions weren't rare, so why did some wait so long after the *aha moment* to tell someone? It's complicated.

David: The Interview

For twenty dollars **David** was willing to give me a few minutes of his time, but if the interview took too long, he told me, he'd be gone. At first David couldn't find the interview room though when he called me for directions, he was just outside the door. So I heard him in a duet: on the phone and on the other side of the door. When I invited him in, he was busy reading his smart phone. He glanced up, faked a smile, and spoke quickly, asking, "Whasup?" and "How long will this take?" He then texted someone about something. David, age 19, wore the college fare of flip-flops, white tee shirt, black shorts, long sideburns, and a large silver necklace. Despite our rough start, he put everything aside, became quite engaged, and answered questions in detail and depth. When he was leaving, David accepted the cash, paused, flashed a huge smile, and said in an authentic tone, "I really enjoyed it."

David, who grew up as an only child in San Francisco, had only recently begun to readily identify as gay. He claimed to have been a "really normal kid," with the same interests as his friends, especially volleyball and swimming. He ran track in high school because track required the least amount of coordination and effort. "I really was just too lazy to go through practices and compete. I took short cuts all the time." At his private school David was an extremely popular, funny guy. "I think I was friends with everyone in school." David began eighth grade as straight, and he exited as (closeted) gay. His same-sex feelings "suddenly blossomed. One day I didn't realize I liked men, and the next day I did." The assist came from a gay porn site.

David had difficult moments beginning in eighth grade after he *accidentally* hit a gay website and became forever gay. He concealed this fact for several years. Though out gay youths were in abundance at his San Francisco high school, David wasn't one of them. "I kind of was in denial a little bit hoping that it would change. Thinking like why did this happen to me? All my friends are growing up the same. I felt like I was going to be ostracized right from the get-go." Yet the other gay youths at his school weren't being shunned or shamed because it was a safe place to be gay. Still, David didn't come out despite several "very obnoxious gossipy girls that would be like, 'Are you gay?' and I would be like, 'That's an uncomfortable question.'" Over time, after he had several sexual experiences under his belt, David was ready to come out his senior year. How did his friends react? With complete indifference: "'Oh,' as if they knew, which they probably did."

Despite differences in where David and **Dean** grew up—one in San Francisco and the other in Appalachia—their experiences with coming out were both positive. As a child Dean was bullied for being skinny, living in a trailer park, and possessing a know-no-boundaries personality. Then, in a ninth-grade New Year's resolution, Dean decided to stop pretending. "I was going to be more popular and say what was on my mind and that I could be an asshole." Though he was one of the "badass" guys, Dean became quite popular.

* *

The guys were tough and didn't take shit from anyone. The girls dated but they would not hold back, smoked, mouthed off. Having a constant boldness who went where I couldn't because I was taught how to behave. I enjoyed watching the dramatic . . . Started figuring who I was and experimenting and getting to know the ritual. Some guys called me a "faggot" but just in a derogatory way. In eighth and ninth I was coming out and wasn't shy about it, so everyone knew.

★ ★

It was not having sex with guys, which Dean discretely had in abundance, that convinced him to come out in his freshman year, but rather his infatuation with a particular cute guy. First he disclosed to his bisexual best friend: "Awesome!" The cute boy was less enthusiastic, yet also positive. "He was cool with it, and he said he wasn't gay but he let me hold his coat while he played sports." Likewise, **Geoff**'s crush on a straight boy wasn't a disaster, but it was met with *indifference:* "It didn't change anything between us."

Even though **Derek**'s masculinity sheltered him from coming to terms with his sexuality, he came out to two best girl friends ("You haven't tried to date us yet"), and then he went silent for over a year before telling anyone else. Why did he wait? It wasn't fear, because even the flamboyant boy he fooled around with hadn't been ostracized. It was because of the adults around him, including a teacher who, the day marriage equality passed, became "so pissed off that he cancelled class and refused to teach the rest of the week." Although school climate in general receives a bad PR rap, nationally the vast majority of gay youths have reported feeling safe in school, at least among their classmates.

So, too, **Tyler** wasn't the only gay teen in his high school of 1,500 students, and the others were completely accepted. In four years Tyler had been called "faggot" twice in a whisper. Both times he had to persuade his friends not to take revenge and beat the guy up. He was never physically bullied, despite his expressed feminine behavior and fashionable appearance. He first told his two best girl friends, "You know if I have a crush on a guy some day or something or fall for a guy it wouldn't be the worst thing ever."

By junior year he had "told everyone that I was gay and then it felt really good because I felt more okay with myself and being able to talk about it." Tyler's biggest regret was not coming out earlier, and what held him back was sex. "Even when I knew I was gay there was always the question of 'How will I feel after I sleep with a guy?' And it was the best feeling. I was thrilled and it felt right."

Asher: The Interview

Different in appearance and temperament than many of the young men, 22-year-old Asher almost didn't make the interview because he misjudged the time and location. He smiled and apologized for being "a bit manic" and "a bit outgoing." Asher had a modified faux-mohawk haircut, skinny jeans, a black tee shirt, and a thin yet muscular body and unshaven facial hair. His creative writing teacher once told Asher that he was "a lesbian trapped in a man's body, and she said I was very very confused." One of his parents was Jewish and the other Catholic, so the family became Unitarian (a religious joke). Asher was working a part-time retail job until a better opportunity came along.

Throughout his childhood and adolescence, Asher's best friends were his fellow athletes. His sports were soccer, gymnastics, martial arts, pole vaulting, hurdles, sprinting, cross-country, rugby, crew, and wrestling. Given his athletic abilities, Asher was fast-tracked through high school, and he competed internationally in gymnastics and martial arts. He eventually accepted an athletic scholarship at a sports-oriented college, which he graduated from the previous year.

Asher's internal battle with coming to terms with his same-sex sexuality was handicapped by his masculinity. According to his ex-boyfriend, "I am extremely masculine for a gay man. I am outdoorsy. I hang out outside. I can't pick out clothes to save my life. I like ecology. I do ecology. I am scientific. I am unemotional, whatever he wants to call it. I like sports. I like watching sports and doing sports." In high school he was a guy's guy, and guys like that didn't have crushes on other guys. To protect himself he interpreted his crushes on his soccer teammates as "bromances," without romantic or sexual intent. He later changed his analysis.

Because Asher didn't come off as gay, other gays didn't believe he was gay. To find gay guys, he had to rely on "stupid dating web-sites which are totally ineffective for dating." What was he looking for? After first denying that he had a preferred type, Asher described several:

★ ★

I like it if you are either lean and well muscled or if you [are] one of those frat boy types. But then I usually don't like frat guy personality. Usually for Asians, I like leaner but again toned. But then I generally love any type of Middle Eastern man who is mostly fit. More importantly, I like guys who are outdoorsy. This is to date. If I am going to date you, you need to be outdoorsy. If you are athletic, you need to be intelligent. You need to be able to hold a political, intellectual, or artistic conversation. Something. You need to show some kind of interests.

★ ★

That was Asher's formula. However, he couldn't find those guys in high school.

In terms of his coming-out process, Asher did not initially come out in high school, even though bullying gays was rare at his school. Asher heard his teammates use the words "fag" or "gay" in a joking manner on the playing field and thus he harbored lingering fears those taunts would be directed at him if he came out. No one even suspected Asher might be gay until alcohol, "a really great facilitator for many things," did him in at a junior class party.

* *

One of my friends is a twin, and his sister, the female twin, we just got elected co-captains of the track team for the next year. We were leading warm ups for the last like two or three weeks of practice. The party was at their house. She comes down and confronts me at track practice. It just traveled, and I was like "fuck." She caught me making out with her brother! Sorry I left that part out! And so after that, it kind of spread throughout the school, and I might as well just accept it at this point. It was this slow pace of acceptance for me. But it was good because my friends were really supportive. Nobody cared. My teachers agreed to keep it from my parents.

* *

Asher was the first athlete to "get out," and two others would follow him a year later. In his school, pretty much everyone hung out or wanted to hang out with Asher's clique. If anyone dared harass him, Asher knew his friends would "take care" of it. Given this level of support, why did it take him so long?

* *

I had this view that everybody else was against it . . . It's a Republican area. There are a lot of churches that say that it's wrong. But I didn't give my peers as much credit about how progressive they were. I went to a high school that was 25 percent African American, 25 percent Asian, 25 percent Latino, and 25 percent white. It was a forced integration school. We were bussed in from the rural part of the county. These are groups that you don't think should be accepting, but everybody was like, "We really don't care who or what you do at this point. There are bigger issues." There was maybe one girl who cared. She was a Baptist and tried to convert me for a long time. I am Jewish. That's my religion. And she was insisting I could be saved. And then she got terrified of me when I came out.

R: *Do you have a positive gay identity?*

Yes . . . I think my life would be much easier, especially in this country, in parts of this country I mean if I was straight or if I could pretend to be straight.

* *

Positive peers, crushes, being tired of living a lie, and time also motivated **Nicholas**. Although no one in his rural school was out, he suspected several of being gay. "I am pretty sure they were gay but they certainly didn't, I don't want to say it was obvious because they weren't flamboyant really but if you had to guess you could probably guess one or the other."

Nicholas didn't come out until his senior year. "But it definitely had been lurking subconsciously, and I finally accepted that." Unfortunately, the motive was a crush on a straight guy. "I don't remember exactly what I said to him, but it was definitely along the lines of 'I think I'm gay and I think I like you. Not as much think but more pretty sure.' Probably looking back, not the best way to do it. This was probably early senior year. It turned out that he did not like that at all." Nicholas took it back and returned to the closet, having learned his lesson. "So I was definitely much more careful about who I told. I kind of like vetted them before so I knew it was going to be mostly positive responses, and that's what it was." Smart guy.

Though the youths usually reported a positive climate among their peers, several waited until after high school to reach public openness.

Escaping High School

Dion did not come out in high school, and neither did anyone else in his school. Yet once he was out, the road cleared for Dion to fully embrace a gay life.

★ ★

I feel like in the six years so much has happened. It's so much different how people view gay people in general. And in high school people didn't take their boyfriends to prom. It was possibly unsafe . . . I mean there were several guys that I had a feeling were gay or had same-sex attraction. No, nobody was out in my high school. Even the really really flamboyant guy that everyone knew. Everyone knew! They would point fun at him because everyone knew that . . .

There was this guy, we were all out and we were waiting in the car, and he was known for being kind of an ass, says inappropriate things and always wants to talk back, and he really liked to make people feel uncomfortable. I was like wearing shorts, and he put his hands up my leg, like straight guys do that like a game of chicken. And I let him go all the way up, and then he was just kind of looking at me. I guess he was interested. Then he kind of whipped it out . . . and I went down on him.

R: *Who was the first person you told?*

I met this guy, and I first thought that I was attracted to him, and then I thought we would just be friends and I really wasn't attracted to him. And I told him that, and he asked if I was gay and said that "maybe" and "I didn't know." Then he outed me at work and told everyone that I was . . . and I went from not having told anybody, not even my closest friends in high school, I didn't tell anyone, to being completely out and living like a life.

★ ★

186

Lenny accepted his same-sex attractions in middle school but didn't come out then or in high school, despite one friend who kept asking, "Are you gay? Are you gay yet?" At first, Lenny attributed his resistance to the fact that, as an athlete, "I knew they wouldn't exile me or anything, but I knew it would just be weird being on the team and letting them know I was gay." It wasn't the school climate that closeted him but his personal issues.

* *

I thought that I would maybe change or just be able to go on without being sexual at all. Since people actually thought I was asexual. Like in high school I refused to get involved with girls in any manner. That was mainly because I did not have any feelings for them. But also not wanted to. It's kind of like I set the path for myself to come out, but I wasn't comfortable with idea of being the gay kid. Especially in high school I didn't want to be the gay kid. There was one gay kid that I knew. He definitely set a positive example. But I just wasn't a fan of him as a person. Not a terrible person. He wasn't quite flaunting it. The story that went around school was that he had this big fight with his parents and they were really angry about it, and he was very like, "Oh well I don't care." He came off kind of arrogant. Just not quite the role model for me.

* *

Instead, Lenny postponed coming out until his senior year of college when he Skyped his best friend who was, as expected, "super positive so I needed that. But it was a heart beating for the first hour before the conversation. I was extremely nervous. I took my laptop off into a dark corner and had headphones in and was like whispering to her. But it was amazing. It felt great."

Lenny was aware of his sexuality at an early age, but why did he delay so long? Perhaps it is related to his identical twin brother, as we'll see in the next chapter.

Benefits of Being Out

Given the angst and possible repercussions of coming out, what are the benefits of being out? One is realizing that you can be both gay and popular, perhaps not in middle school but in high school. After disclosing his sexuality to three friends—who shyly confessed, "We know"—one youth's coming-out experiences were relatively smooth. Then a guy named Fodder, who was not a popular guy, made sure the entire school knew. But it backfired on the bully: the victimized youth soon discovered that his avenue to high status was his sexuality. "Even the good-looking guys hugged me and were supportive. One whispered 'fuck Fodder.'" Thus protected, he started a Gay Straight Alliance club at his high school and attended a gay pride march with his parents. He only regretted not being out of the closest earlier and "being a better human being."

Another benefit is that it helps in developing honest relationships with others. This weighed heavily on one young man who bemoaned not being truthful with his best friends and especially forsaking intimate, fun friendships with other guys. As a college freshman he assumed that being gay would eliminate him from having a straight male friend ever again, which caused him inordinate anguish. Then at a frat party he met a "typical frat guy, very good looking, very comfortable, talk about anything, first person I told. I was very closeted but decided to experiment and act on my impulses." It worked, and now he and his straight male friend "go to dinner, study breaks, parties, gay bars, weekend New York

City trips, late night gossip, and cuddling." With this friendship and coming out en masse, "I feel self-fulfilled, like Maslow's final stage of psychological well-being."

A straight-acting, closeted athlete decided he had to come out to his best guy friend, who was initially aghast, "You've seen me naked! Are you attracted to me?" The young man assured him that gays aren't attracted to every male. With much relief the two enjoyed an improved relationship with fewer boundaries, even hugging and spooning—"Well, if we've been drinking."

Being out enhances self-development by increasing a sense of authenticity, self-knowledge, and sexual acceptance. It relieves you of your greatest fears, unburdens the stresses of always being careful about what you say and do, and brackets the shame plaguing you for years. When your fears are no longer toxic, you can emotionally blossom, as indicated by several of the young men.

- "Deeply rooted in my sexuality is my relationship with myself. Now I'm out to everyone."
- "I'm developing more deeply and examining my own life. I can appreciate my values and those of my friends. My struggle taught me so much."
- "I could feel the weight lift on me. Now everyone I know knows. I'm out on Facebook."
- "Solidified my commitment to myself and helped me stay away from drama and conflict."

It's a Journey

In his coming-out story, which is both entertaining and heart-wrenching, one young man was aware of his sexual attractions at 13, and two years later fell madly in love with cool, talented, straight Eric in his school's theater group. He feared telling him because he didn't want him to think he was hitting on him. "I couldn't pee next to guys because guys would think I was looking at them." With Eric he tentatively confessed to having a crush on a cast member. Excited, Eric listed all the girls, and each was denied in turn, until the youth confessed, "It's you, Eric." His straight friend didn't run away, and neither did anyone else, including his parents and anyone who mattered. Yet despite being out early and fully, in the intervening five years things were even better. "Now straight guys are more open and accepting, and this is refreshing. I'm not worried about offending them or touching too much." At a theater party a group of fraternity guys staggered in. "This one came up to me and asked who was the best looking guy there, and I said he was! He loved it that a gay guy found him hot." This young man was "enormously happy being gay, beautiful same-sex relationships and friendships, with shared experiences. My sexuality makes me unique and I'm proud of it." It frees him, allows him to be himself, and lightens his life.

If coming out is nearly always positive, why not do it earlier? Must you first fall in love before you recognize how central your same-sex sexuality is to you? Why internalize negative cultural notions of what is "normal" when being gay isn't commonly viewed as negative among your generation? You can maintain or even increase your status. Schools are essentially safe, and friends are hugely supportive, but what about those parents? Why is coming out to parents frequently fraught with so much angst?

Hey Mom, Dad, Bro, Sis

Guys, I'm gay. I'm gay as fuck. (TYLER, AGE 16)

Swimmer Tom Luchsinger originally wanted to tell his parents face to face, but instead he called them on the phone. "I'm gay. And I'm scared." Their response was incredible. "Are you the same man we raised for the past 23 years?" "Yes." "Then, who cares?" Tom believes he "lucked out to get them as my parents." Yes, him and many others.

Coming out to parents is usually forever etched in your memory, the final chapter in your developmental progression from early sexual memories and feeling different to accepting and integrating your sexuality into your life. Among the young men I interviewed, the average age of disclosing to a parent was 17, typically three years after knowing he is gay, over one year after accepting this fact, one year after coming out to a friend, and six months after feeling positive about his sexuality. Eleven of the young men hadn't disclosed to either parent, and two are out to only one parent. Of note, because of its rarity, one first disclosed to his parents before his friends, sex partners, or siblings.

Why is coming out to parents one of the last developmental milestones? Is it fear that parents will kick you out of the house or refuse to pay for college? Is it because you simply forgot to tell them, but you're promising yourself that you'll get around to it? Is it because of their enormous significance in your life? Is it because you want to be absolutely certain that you're inevitably and totally okay before sharing? It's all of the above, though as always, it's complicated. Perhaps most telling, the young men's coming out to parent stories are among the longest and most emotional accounts I heard from the young men.

One obstacle among some families is they keep secrets, one of which is that not everyone is the presumed heterosexual. The lesson you are supposed to learn from this? Keep quiet. For example, **Anthony**'s paternal uncle was "probably gay," but his family doesn't talk about it. Coming out to his family was not particularly horrendous though it didn't go according to plan (actually, there was no plan).

★ ★

He [brother] found out because of conversations on Facebook that I was bi with conversations from middle school. He thought I was lying about it, just trying to be different, and we talked about it several times, but I was angry at him obviously because he accused me of it and obviously now never true but that he said I was making it up . . .

Sophomore year told mom . . . She'd say if, you'll never get a wife if you don't learn how to cook and things like that. She was joking around like a mother, and I remember at the time talking to my friends about how I wanted to tell her. Like, "Well I won't have a wife so it won't matter." But I think something came up about kids and me saying that I probably didn't want them, and I was at least, I might not be able to have kids and I didn't want to tell her, but eventually she asked what I meant and I told her and I told her not to tell my dad. Apparently she told my dad the next day. She thought I was being self-righteous kind of and she didn't want to hear it, but I had already known [I am] attracted to guys for a year so I was pretty confident. She like probably wanted me to doubt it but I was, didn't let her talk me out of it . . .

She asked before that point. She was like, "You were acting weird . . . If you are gay let me know." She did say that. But interesting how her reaction was different when she said that in seventh grade than sophomore year of high school. Apparently from what she told me, her and my dad, late at night, cried together not because didn't want me to be gay but my life would be harder.

They both know about Patrick. I would talk to my dad about Patrick if something happens or going somewhere, and I'll tell him I'm hanging out with Patrick for whatever reason. Don't talk about the relationship itself. My mother asks if I'm a virgin, and I never answer her. I don't care. I can be more open with her and talk about my relationship but don't go to her for advice . . .

Have little brother and older sister. He doesn't know, and my older sister I just told my mom to tell her after I told my mom. I just assumed she wouldn't care. When same-sex marriage [became legal] my mom texted me and said, "Great news."

* *

They were so not bothered by Anthony's gayness that they would definitely come to his wedding.

Haven't Yet

One quarter of the young men I spoke with hadn't disclosed to their parents, not because they anticipated rejection but because they predicted it would make life more difficult. Perhaps a young man likes keeping his own special secret from his parents, or "I'm unwilling to take the risk and open up a can of worms." It's more complicated if the family is religiously, politically, or culturally conservative. He may want to protect the family from embarrassment, or he doubts they'll understand. When his parents visit, one young man "tells my friends to butch it up."

David was the one young man who most feared rejection because he is the "sacred child in an extremely traditional Chinese family. My dad is condescending, and my mom is outrageously homophobic." Eventually, he'll tell them, but only when he is in a long-term, committed relationship. Then, he will have someone else in his life. "Like I won't be left alone."

Also for cultural reasons, **Raj** is publicly out to friends in the United States but not in India where his extended family live. The ultimate family coming-out process will never occur for him because his father died before Raj could tell him. The two had debated Indian legislation legalizing homosexuality, and although his father agreed that homosexuality shouldn't be illegal, "he would argue that we [his lineage] are genetically superior because we have never interbred." Raj delayed coming out to him until he could win their argument by becoming "super successful," but his father's premature death denied Raj his victory.

Nicholas: The Interview

Coming a few minutes late and somewhat hurried, **Nicholas** wore the summer fashion of the day—cargo shorts, tight-fitting tee shirt, and red Nikes. Nicholas immediately told me he was not tall. In appearance he seemed a solidly Midwestern blend of English, Scottish, and Irish, with blond hair, blue eyes, and a two-day stubble. He was committed to remembering the particular details of his life, and after many questions Nicholas looked at the ceiling, slammed his eyes shut, and in halting speech conveyed a memory. His life was a blur to him because no one had ever asked him about it. At the end of the interview I feared that it had been too much effort for him, but Nicholas surprised me by saying he liked talking about his life because he doesn't really understand it. I found him a totally likeable, explicitly charming guy, but the prolonged silences made for an uneasy interview.

His mother remarried when Nicholas was in fourth grade, and the new family moved to a conservative rural town. Nicholas played sports, participated in quiz bowl, and developed friendships with boys, though he reminded me that he was using a rather liberal interpretation of friend as "in someone who I get along with and I see on a semi regular basis at school." In college, he had "lectures bigger than my entire high school. There are some classes here that are bigger than my entire school district and my freshman class was bigger than my entire hometown." In terms of sports, Nicholas "sucked at it. But it was a good learning experience even though I am not sure what I learned."

Nicholas said he is not much different from a straight guy—"I play sports. I watch sports, that sort of thing"—and he bridges masculinity and femininity.

★ ★

On the whole, most people see me and are like, "He looks straight." I do have my feminine moments but not so much that most people are like, "Oh, I never would have guessed you were gay!" But not like super masculine . . . I do have my moments. We have karaoke every week in the dorm, and I will never pass up the opportunity to sing badly in falsetto. Just stuff like that . . . I definitely express more emotions sometimes. Stuff you would normally say, "Okay females do this," I will do that . . . Watch those chick flicky movies. Not all the time but only if they're good.

★ ★

He is different from straight guys, however, in trying "to figure out sexual identity and stuff . . . who I am attracted so and who I have sex with. Other than that, not that different."

Both flamboyant and supermasculine guys turn Nicholas off. He is attracted to guys "kind of like me"—masculine or feminine or somewhere in the middle. Body hair is "a complete turn off, which is really weird considering I have a fair amount. I am attracted to smooth skin and stuff like that." The body hair thing makes Asian men particularly attractive to him. "Putting those aside, I have no real preference."

Nicholas named losing his virginity as one of the most significant events in his life. "I am inclined to say the first time because it's given me something to say like, 'Okay, I've experienced it,' and now I can start to understand everything else." Now, he feels he has some idea of how sex "should be done."

Nicholas is out in college, but he hasn't "gotten around" to it at home, though he knows they'd be fine with it. He told me he has loving parents.

★ ★

I am pretty much out. If anyone asks me, I will be open about it. It's not like I'm going to go flamboyantly running down the street like, "I'm gay! I'm gay!" But if anyone asked, I am not going to skirt around the details of that.

Back home . . . I am still very much in the closet . . . I have been meaning to for the longest time, and I feel like it's the sort of thing I ought to tell them in person, but I don't want to be like, "I'm gay!" I want there to be a good reason behind it. I have been meaning to, and I haven't gotten around to it.

I'm sure my mom would be fine with it, and I'm going off the fact that we've had our share of disagreements, but what parent and child doesn't? She will be like, "However you piss me off you are still my son and I will still be there for you."

* *

Nicholas is less certain about his stepfather, who is more "old fashioned, conservative-ish."

Went a Bit Rocky

Among the young men who had disclosed to their parents or were outed to them, a mixed response was common. Later, we'll visit the families in which reactions were positive, even celebratory.

I'll start with an unusual set-up. **Geoff** is out to his conservative father but not to his mother, and how his father found out is also exceptional. Everything went fine, perhaps because his father's sister is lesbian.

* *

The guy I'm dating . . . we met up a few times this summer for a couple days, and I accidentally left a hotel receipt in my room and my dad found it. Stupidity on my part. He didn't care. He wasn't like, "Yeah! Good for you!" but he wasn't like mad or anything. But he's like, "It's fine. It doesn't change the way I feel about you." He used to work at a hospital, and he said there were a lot of people who would come into that hospital and it really ate away at them because they were unsure of who they were sexually. That it's good that I know this now rather than letting it bother me and then eventually hating myself for it.

I should have known something weird was coming because he was at work. It was just this last summer, and he texted me, "I'm going to the supermarket to get a steak for myself, how about I get some scallops for you?" Not that he is mean or anything, but he certainly hasn't went out and bought me expensive seafood before. So we were together in the kitchen, I was cooking the scallops . . . He was just like, "This was found [the receipt]" and then he said, "You're 18. You're an adult. You get to make your own decisions. I hope you're safe."

He asked if I was gay. Sorry, I should have said that initially. Yeah, but it wasn't, it was kind of just conversation for us. It wasn't this dramatic thing, and it quickly passed. We went back to cooking and talking like we had before. It was maybe a two-minute interruption.

R: *Have you guys talked about it since?*

Not much. He asked me, well I asked him, now that he knew I didn't feel like I had to sneak around and drive for hours. I could just say, "Hey I'm going there . . ." When I got back he asked me about it. Once again, it wasn't this long, drawn-out conversation just, "How was it? What did you do?"

R: *And your mom?*

He said he wasn't going to tell her [mom] until I was ready . . . I suppose I have to tell her sooner rather than later. But I don't have a scenario set out in my head for how I'm going to do it.

★ ★

Parents react in divergent ways, sometimes unexpectedly, which can be sufficient reason to tell one and not the other. One youth came out to his parents in his senior year of high school, and surprisingly his mother was less positive than his father. "Mom asked, 'Why do you want to be that way?' She thinks it's a choice, and she doesn't want to talk about it." His father was stunned because "he can't fathom turning away from all the great looking college women."

Jonathan's father also reacted more positively than his mother. In the face of a family crisis, a compromise was enacted between Jonathan and his parents—silence from his mother and an offer to talk from his father. I've had to reduce the following account from its original due to the level of detail Jonathan related.

* *

I told my parents when I was 17 . . . I was insanely stressed in high school. I was dealing with understanding my body as well as trying to understand my sexuality as well as dealing with homework and teachers. So I was a little bit of a mess . . . I kind of hit a breaking point. I got really, really stressed out, and my parents sent me to my doctor to just kind of have a chat. Nothing about my actual condition but just as a way to let off some steam and get some more insight into the world . . .

[We talked] and the first question that my mother asked me as I walked in the door is, "What did you talk about?" And I told her we talked about school, homework, and stress. And she was like, "What else?" and I said that I don't want to talk about it. And she said, "Well why?" and I said, "Because I don't have to." And she started getting very defensive, and when my mother gets defensive she starts yelling. So I started yelling back, and it eventually got to the point where I screamed, "I can't tell you because if I tell you you'll throw me out of the house" and I stormed off to my room and didn't come out for hours . . .

[The next day] my mother is sitting on the porch in negative ten-degree weather in her winter jacket and earmuffs and reading a magazine, and she point-blank asks me if I am gay. And I said, "Yes," and she asked me how long I had known, and I said, "I don't know" and we leave it at that, and I walk inside and she doesn't really talk to me for the next two weeks . . .

Based off of the screaming match that my mother and I had, my father guessed that that was probably what was going on. So he knew, but once again, I asked my mom to be the one who told him and I did. He told me everything that they had talked about the night before, and they kind of figured that this was what was going on and he offered to talk to me about it, but I was not at a point where I could comfortably talk to my father about it. He was a lot more accepting. And I don't know what to accredit that to . . . It might have been a religious difference. It might have just been a parental difference. I honestly have no idea.

★ ★

This state of affairs persisted until Jonathan invited his boyfriend home for dinner. "They ended up liking him a lot, so it was a lot easier once they saw that it was a good thing for me and that he was a good influence on me."

Critical for some youths was not whether to tell parents but when and how. What is the perfect time, the perfect strategy? What if they ask how he knows—do they really want to know about his masturbatory fantasies or sexual encounters? What if afterward they say absolutely nothing?

Lenny intended to tell his parents in person, which was difficult to arrange (and again I have shortened his extended account).

★ ★

It was pretty tricky because, at the time, I was planning on telling them as soon as I got back . . . They were kind of just sitting downstairs and watching TV and I am pacing upstairs just thinking how do I initiate this? Just extremely nervous about it . . . As soon as I just started telling them, I just started bawling. And my dad is half asleep but I'm just like looking at the floor. And when I finally got it out, my mom comes over, she is crying and she hugs me.

It's hard to describe. It was more negative than positive. But there were definitely positive aspects. Like, oh, I finally told them but well for one, my dad didn't say anything. And he is not one to communicate well to begin with, but he didn't say anything. Not a word. And my mom was saying a lot of things that made me upset. She was being supportive but at the same time, I guess being kind of discriminatory. It was hard because she was saying things that I was preparing myself for like things that someone might say without really meaning it. The very first thing she said was, "Are you sure?" not "Oh, I love you" or anything like that. As if I hadn't thought about it before I told them! "Yes!" Mom, "How do you know?" At the time I said, "Well, I masturbate to guys." She was saying things like, "I hope this didn't have anything to do with [college]." She was comforting me. She had her arm around me and everything. But at the same time she wasn't saying the right thing.

And my dad is not saying a word. Her description was that he was caught off guard because he was half asleep. But he was still hearing everything. After I told them and me and my mom are both crying. I don't know what my dad is doing.

* *

Lenny found coming out to his siblings was both easier (his sisters) and disappointing (his identical twin brother Lonny). Given these mixed reactions, I asked Lenny whether if he could take a magical pill to make him straight, would he? "At this point, I would choose to be gay. I am very content with it." Less chirpy and more solemn after the interview, Lenny thanked me, shook my hand, and left.

Asher also didn't expect his parents to react positively. "I thought my parents would have a problem with it. I don't know why. Because it's not something we ever discussed. There were no indicators to say they would be fine with it. My dad would make gay jokes and stuff." Asher had no coming-out plans; rather, it just slipped out during a family argument. The backstory was that during Asher's freshman year at a university his parents switched him to a local community college for financial reasons. Except, unknown to them, Asher had begun dating his first real boyfriend, and he didn't want to leave. Eventually he relented under parental pressure and transferred. Lonely at his new school, Asher said to himself, "Fuck this, I'm not staying."

★ ★

I went up to them and said, "This is the reason I'm staying." I laid it out for them and I slipped, "I'm gay," in the middle of it . . . My mom, nice Jewish woman, glances at it and you can tell she wants to say something and she's fighting against it on the inside, you know, and then they just glance over at this and just think, "Let him go back." It was just easier for them to have me a little bit farther away at that point.

R: *They didn't say anything about it?*

No. We're a very good family in that we don't talk about our emotions, we don't talk about our feelings, we don't talk about who we are dating.

R: *How have they reacted since then?*

My dad actually mentioned it for the first time . . . "If you are a gay man, you should not go into ecology. Most ecologists who work for the government work out West in small towns . . . Again, not a lot of gay men. If you value having a husband and kids, you should go into medicine. There is more money. There is more jobs and more job mobility." It was very practical. It took him three years before he could recognize it.

My mom has been much easier. She overcompensates kind of. She will be like, "Oh my God! I just saw this great thing about gay people!" And I'll be, "Okay, thank you." I had a, not a boyfriend, a friend with benefits but more than friends with benefits this spring, and he called me when I was home and like said some very nasty things and my mom overheard some it and she was very compassionate about it. But that was really the first time we talked directly about my sex life . . . She was like, "Well, have you been tested?" and I was like, "Yes and I don't think it's an issue." Again very practical.

* *

Rather than hysteria, crying, and the silent treatment, Asher's parents reacted in form for them: practical. Asher thus felt supported by his parents, and he was surprised because his father had been raised in an antihomosexual family. As for his mother, "They are Jewish so I don't think it's an issue. So whenever an issue comes up, they always vote with the Democrats."

In contrast to the practical, calm, unemotional approach of Asher's family was the drama of **Tyler**'s family. Tyler admitted that his Catholic Republican parents "scare the shit out of me," and he had no plans to disclose to them until circumstances dictated otherwise. The outcome he feared never materialized although their reactions did shock him (and I'll abbreviate the rather lengthy ordeal).

* *

The thought of it, telling them haunted me at night. I would stay up at night thinking about it thinking they are not going to pay for college. I don't know what I am going to do . . .

I was determined to see him [boyfriend] on our one-month anniversary . . . My mom contacted me to be like, "Where are you? Did you leave the number?" And I was like, "Friend's house! Sorry I forgot!" And then she was like, "You are lying to me . . ." My mother did not sound happy. She picked me up from the train station. She was like, "You need to stop lying to me. I need to know what's going on" and . . . we drove back to my house in total silence, and I went into my room when we got home and she was like, "You better come over and tell me what's going on." So I basically shut my door and spent thirty seconds building my confidence, went into her room, sat down on her bed with her and was like, "Mom I'm gay, and today I went to go see my boyfriend." And it was a shock. She didn't see it coming. She was even more shocked when I told her I had been out to my school for months. We cried, but she told me that she loved me no matter what and even though this isn't the choice she would have picked for me, she knows it wasn't something that I could control. So that made me break down in tears because I was so scared and that was a better response than anything. So we cried and stuff then my mother started being like, "You have to tell your father . . ."

[Two weeks later] I basically just sort of the blunt, "Dad I'm gay" type thing, and he was more like, "Are you sure?" And then he was more concerned because he was trying to tell me that this was going to be a harder life, like, "People are going to hate you for this. You are going to be at higher risk for STDs" and stuff. He too was like, "I'll always love you no matter what." So a really positive experience.

★ ★

So confident was he of his parents' love that Tyler was furious when his mother didn't vote for marriage equality. "'You are ridiculous. You are homophobic. You say you accept me, but you don't if you don't want me to get married.' I was very hard on her. I feel like it may have changed now [a vote for marriage equality]."

None of the young men reported exceptionally negative reactions from their parents. Even the silent maternal treatment **Jonathan** received was lifted after he brought his boyfriend home.

Went Great

When I asked *why* their parents responded the way they did, I received many blank looks, as though the young men had never thought about it or felt the reason must be apparent given the facts of the life stories they'd shared. However, several young men, all of whom received positive parental reactions, discovered the reason for their parents' reaction.

After one father found gay porn on the family computer, he immediately assured his son that he and his mother would always love and support him, though they feared he'd have a difficult life. "We love you for who you are," he said. Confused, he asked his mother, "Why didn't Dad freak out?" "Because," she explained, "he had gay tendencies in high school."

Another youth attributed his parents' positive reactions to the fact that they were both in theater. A family meeting was called, and his mother was greatly relieved when he announced he is gay. She'd feared that a severe medical problem was the reason for holding the rare family meeting.

On other occasions parents sensed their sons' feelings of stress and suspected the culprit might be gay related. One mother, seeing the sadness in her 13-year-old son, told him, "I know you're gay. You ought to accept it and get on with your life." **Dean**'s mother progressed from being antigay after she caught her son having sex with another boy to now considering Dean's boyfriend to be another son. When Dean officially came out to his mother when he was 15, she said to him that she "still loved me and be safe and use a condom."

Derek's progressive parents had gay friends and gays in their family tree. Yet Derek suffered in silence until his mother picked him up for Christmas break.

★ ★

I had been kind of flirting with this guy and he and one of my other friends like came down to say goodbye to me. And he's a lot more, not hugely flamboyant but I could see it in her eye when she saw. And then on the drive home, I was telling her about both of those friends, and my mom, I forget exactly what she said, but she kind of looked at me and she was like, "I suspect I'm not getting the whole story." And I was like, "What do you mean?" And she was like, "I think there's some bisexual or homosexual things going on here. Which one? Homosexual?" And I was like, "Yeah, maybe . . ." So it was kind of an awkward [seven-hour] car ride. I asked her like, "So what does this mean?" And she was like, "Nothing. I just have to think about it."

I was more worried about talking to her than anybody else. I actually have a memory of her when I was in like freshman year of high school, we were just joking around as a family, she and my dad and my brothers, and she was like, "None of you are gay, right?" And we were all like, "Nah." And my dad kind of looked at her and said, "If you are, that's fine. We're totally accepting." And my mom was like, "Yeah, but none of you are gay." And so there was just a little a bit of iffiness there . . .

I had promised myself if she had asked me, I wouldn't deny it. But I hadn't quite worked up the courage to do it. So it kind of took me by surprise. And then my dad was really offended that I hadn't told him. He was really upset just because it meant that I didn't trust him . . .

He actually wrote me a letter and I wrote him a letter back and stuff. The reason he was upset was just because he thought he and I were really close and he was offended that

I hadn't confided in him. What I tried to explain to him was the reason I hadn't told him was because I knew he wouldn't react badly and I knew he would accept it and I was so worried about mom that I was preoccupied with that. And I think he accepted that.

★ ★

Similarly, an academic break, not originally created for youths to come out to parents, elicited another family disclosure. Ted took one risky step farther than Derek by inviting his boyfriend to meet the family. It became a cause of celebration, a bottle of champagne.

★ ★

And the day before he arrived, I knew that I needed to tell my parents because it was going to be very obvious to them that my relationship was a little bit more than friends. At least in some ways, which physically it wasn't or emotionally which it was. It was one o'clock in the morning and I was like I have to tell my mom at least and I'll tell my dad tomorrow morning when he drives me to work. And I did. I told my mom and she opened a bottle of champagne, and I told my dad and he said, "All right, well I wish you hadn't told me today in the car like but go to work and I'll see you later." So it was extremely positive . . .

But my mom had known for a year because I went to Europe with a friend of mine who was a girl and we spent a month there and when I came back she asked, "Did you even feel anything towards her, no romantic feelings?" And I was like, "No!" And she's was like, "She's really beautiful" and I said, "When she wakes up in the morning her face is all puffy and it's like really disgusting," and my mom was like, "Okay got it!"

* *

Got it, most parents did, if not before, then eventually, with a range of almost unpredictable reactions for unpredictable reasons. Religious identification, social class, ethnicity, politics, and geography were unreliable predictors. The personal touch could be helpful—including parents who had their own same-sex attractions, gay family members, or gay friends. Perhaps most critical, though only hinted at in these interviews, was the nature of the parent-son relationship. If a parent truly loves a son, all else is irrelevant.

This was illustrated in a letter made public by a Ms. McClain who wrote to her son Zach after he came out on his Facebook page.

* *

I want you to know that I love you unconditionally. I love you with my actions, not just my words. I'm so proud of you. You are the bravest person I know. I'll fight for you always. Your sexual orientation does not define you. You are still the boy who forever won my heart. The only thing that concerns me is the number of empty soda cups and tea bottles in your room. Throw them away before ants come inside. I love you always, Mom.

* *

My guess is that many mothers (and fathers) could and would have written the same letter.

Hey Bro, Hey Sis

The young men came out to their sisters and brothers before or after their parents, either directly or indirectly, by design or by accident, and with varying levels of need-to-tell importance. Some siblings were deemed too young to know, or their parents said they'd tell them. It was generally of lesser urgency to disclose to siblings, and, perhaps reflecting this reality, nearly all in-the-know siblings reacted positively. Perhaps the siblings knew because they had seen gay porn on their brother's computer, caught him having sex in the home, read his Facebook page, or just "put two and two together" when they met his "friend."

Although they were not necessarily a critical stepping-stone for a boy's coming-out process, the siblings' responses nevertheless were usually life affirming for their gay brother. For example, **Asher**'s sister had heard rumors about her brother making out with his track co-captain. Asher texted, "I'm gay." She texted back, "This is great! We can go talk about boys."

Tyler's disclosure to his older brothers resulted in a night that he'll celebrate for the rest of his life—motivation for others who debate whether to disclose to siblings.

★ ★

We were out on vacation, and it was in Florida, and we all went out drinking together, and when I had had enough drink I felt that I had the confidence. We were in the hot tub . . . It was great brotherly bonding, and I basically blurted out, "Guys I'm gay." My exact words were, "Guys I'm gay. I'm gay as fuck." They took it better than anything I could have imagined. They were like, "We're always be here for you. We love you no matter what." Then they started being like, "Which one of our friends do you think are hot?" And I was like, "Guys stop!" It was funny. A night that I will never forget.

★ ★

Dion's brother took brotherly love one step farther, even without an explicit disclosure.

★ ★

[My brother] is like very strong, and if he heard anybody talking about me, he would beat them up. I would kind of do whatever I wanted, and he was like in the background keeping all these people in line. I didn't hear about these things. My brother knows that I am, and he, I never told him, but I think he just kind of knew it. And we are extremely close. I talk to him probably four times a day. He's three years younger . . . He's more conservative than I am. A lot more conservative. But he will defend me if my dad or anybody tries to talk about me or anything.

R: Why didn't you come out to your brother?

Because he is very old fashioned. Which is very funny as far as like views of morality really has nothing to do with the gay thing, just more of the sex thing.

★ ★

In some families, however, the young men predicted that sibling disclosure wouldn't go well. **Nicholas** thought that his fraternal twin brother wouldn't be happy. "I hate to get into stereotypes, but he is very much a rednecky conservative type of person." He's also wasn't keen on telling his 12-year-old sister because she would be "just gossiping it to everyone she knows because she's the kind of drama person like that . . . The next thing you know she's going to be like OMG! to all of her friends and boom, everyone knows."

The most complicated family situation was **Lenny**'s. He has two older sisters and an identical twin brother, Lonny. Lenny was choking up when he came out to his sisters, but they said, "No problem" and "Great!" Lenny had anticipated the same reaction from Lonny, who was also a film major but at a different college. Once they were home together, Lenny prepared. "I mean we're not lovey-dovey, but at the same time I knew he wouldn't think differently of me for it." Lenny wasn't wrong, yet Lonny had little to say, which dumbfounded Lenny. "You know, someone that is your twin for twenty-two years and then they tell you something that you don't expect. Because I asked him if he had any idea and he said 'No,' which really shocked me because I thought he at least walked in on me [masturbating to gay porn] a couple times or something." Lenny booked 60 percent odds that Lonny is gay as well but hasn't come to terms with it. Lonny has never dated women or spoke of them in a sexual or romantic way.

* *

Anyone who knows twins knows them as super close. It was in high school that we grew very apart. It wasn't like one big fight or anything. It was like a gradual playing a video game together or something like that or doing something together and fighting a lot. Just like any siblings. But there was also the factor of us both being super shy and we were both identified as "the twins" and stuff. At least I knew for that I always wanted to be my own person and, you know, to be known as "Lenny who does this" and to be known as "Lonny who does that." We both wanted to go to different colleges to further do that. Which we did, and now it's better. During high school we barely said anything to each other.

It was mildly positive. He said he didn't have a problem with it and then was immediately talking to me about his movie. But at the same time, I know I wanted him to like ask me more questions or something. Honestly, him not asking me questions may be more of an indicator for me that he may be in the closet himself, but I don't want to perpetuate that either. The stage of our relationship is very interesting. I haven't really spoken to him since coming out to him.

★ ★

Lenny opened his cell phone to show me a picture of Lonny. Except for being shorn of his thick blond curls, they look identical.

Coming Out to Parents

Missing from these stories are parents who rejected or traumatized their son, because none of them did. That's not to say it doesn't happen, only that clinicians, public health officials, and the media greatly distort their numbers. Perhaps, at most, less than 2 percent of parents reject their child—which is 2 percent too many. In such accounts, however, there is obvious prior family dysfunction, and the disclosure exists within that life history. Most parents who initially reacted negatively do eventually come around to embrace their son.

Real-life consequences exist if we promote these extremely negative horror stories, not only because they're rare but also because they might well prevent or delay disclosure to parents. This can be particularly tragic for you and your parents if your anxieties are unreasonable or unfounded. You're denied potential life-affirming interactions that can draw your family together. And, as we know, for most mental health outcomes family support is critical.

Examples of anticipated disclosure fears are plentiful and have been duplicated on social media when youths record live their coming-out-to-parents episodes. The most moving and revealing that I have seen is Alden Peters's documentary film *Coming Out*. Alden recorded on camera his coming out to his older brother, mother, younger sister, younger brother, and finally his father. There is drama, humor, and acceptance, and ultimately all of them love him even more—for good reason.

On YouTube, twin brothers Aaron and Austin Rhodes came out to each other at age 16 and established a huge viewing hit when they disclosed to their father three years later by phone. Afterward on *Ellen*, they admitted that it was "the scariest moment" of their young life. Would that be their last phone call with him? They cried nearly uncontrollably, but their father's reaction was "now we can talk about anything. I was very proud of my boys."

The Monastero twins came out to each other and to their parents on camera with classic parental reactions (their father calmly continued to eat his jerk chicken). From all appearances, the twins' fears were, once again, far greater than the reality.

Advice on when and how to come out to parents is abundant online. The Everyone Is Gay organization offers these suggestions to college students for disclosing over Thanksgiving break:

- First, enjoy your meal.
- Have a plan, especially if things go poorly.
- Expect all other conversations to stop cold.
- Choose a relaxed time, not when the turkey is being pulled from the oven.
- Allow for at least a thirty-minute conversation.
- Ask questions such as "Do you have any questions?" and "Can I tell you more about myself?"
- Don't make the day only about you. Move onto other activities.
- Remind the family that you are still you.

Many of the young men I interviewed had expected the worst and were happily surprised by the positive responses (or lack of a negative one) they received from their parents. The worst reactions were parents who threw a tantrum. The result was maybe some yelling and misunderstandings, but no homelessness, no college tuition revoked, and no rejection. Often the circumstances were orchestrated, but just as often they were accidental. Mothers were usually, but not always, told before fathers. Far more often than the mothers, the fathers were nonplussed by the news and then went about their business as usual. Occasionally questions such as whether the young man was certain, or had been molested, or had tried to be straight were asked, and they were met with eye rolls or challenges by their gay son. Some parents already knew or suspected, or they feigned shock. The subsequent reactions included the silent treatment (usually ranging from hours to a week), crying (some out of concern, others from relief), and celebration (from hugs to champagne). True, parents might not be fond of talking about this subject, but over time they transition to acceptance, if not publicly then privately. At this point nearly all the coming-out to parents stories I've heard turned out basically okay, if not immediately then eventually. The parent-child relationships were sufficiently patched, and the young man leads a good gay life. The bottom line is that most parents love their son, and now they know him a little better than they did before.

Nicholas's parents can be counted in this positive mix. A year after my interview, Nicholas saw me on campus and excitedly announced, "I did it! Not thrilled, as I knew. But I've no dreadful story to tell you." Over break, he'd found that "the timing was right." So another coming out story to parents was completed successfully.

Mostly Gay

I could possibly be happily married to somebody, and they could be a woman. I guess I wouldn't say that's impossible, but I wouldn't say that I would be sexually attracted to them.

(DION, AGE 17)

Thus far I've written as if all the young men I interviewed identify as *totally* gay when in reality half of them reported they're *mostly* gay. Are they merely *totally* gay but unwilling to relinquish the hope that the right woman will come along? Or perhaps are they objecting to a sexual identity that locks them into an exclusive, airtight sexual box? Are they sexually or romantically fluid gay men? Are they hesitating to eliminate potential future changes in sexuality, so they're leaving the door open a crack to being possibly less than exclusively gay? Alternatively, are they young men who maintain romantic attachments to a few women or find particular women sexually desirable and are thus legitimately mostly gay?

I see no reason to intrinsically doubt these reports of nonexclusive sexuality. Not all guys are exhaustively one thing or another, especially given that sexuality exists along a spectrum and allows for many nuances, degrees, and possibilities. *Mostly gay* easily endures as a point along a sexual continuum from *totally straight* to *totally gay*. Young men vouch for this in-between status, and it is these developmental histories that are the subject of this chapter.

The first group comprises the young men who are mostly gay in name only, hence giving credibility to the doubters. The second group, however, is the young men who are legitimately along the spectrum, though not all are mostly gay in the same way.

Actually, I'm Gay

Of the twenty-one who identified as mostly gay, nine are quite likely totally gay because their written surveys didn't list any sexual or romantic attraction, fantasy, genital contact, infatuation, or relationship with girls or women, at least not recently. However, during the interview they expressed reservations about being totally gay.

Several identify as mostly gay because of *politics*. Not believing in exclusive or simple identity boxes, the politicos rejected all such attempts to lock them into an absolute category. When I asked about his preferred identity, one youth replied, "If you make me give you a title, then I'm *queer*." Another said *pansexual* because "I like it. I like gay culture, but I also hate it. Part of me is good at being gay. I could give you the Judith Butler's response, and I do believe it is repetition of performance so it seems natural. I take a cultural studies perspective." Understand?

Others choose mostly gay for *cultural* reasons. In response to his family's mandate to marry, one Asian American youth hopes to rid himself of all sexual attractions to make everything "ideally fine." He is mostly gay because he interprets his lifelong erotic "homosexual desires" as merely a reflection of his need for emotional attachment with males, though he also wants to be naked with another guy. "I was called 'girly,' and I couldn't understand why guys go to girls when boys are not interested in me. In high school I get sexually attracted to other males and not girls. I wish there was a male I could get emotional and rely on and be around all the time. I don't want to be turned on by either sex, no crushes, no fantasies."

Another mostly gay variety is the young man who is *emotionally* attracted (not necessarily romantically) to some women or finds women beautiful (physically, not necessarily sexually). He may or may not have had sex with or dated girls, and he doesn't anticipate doing either in the future. "Not that I don't like them, but I wouldn't want to jump on one." Another young man leaves the door slightly more ajar: "I'm awestruck by their beauty and want to be around them. Just make out and touch them. Maybe 1 in 50,000 girls." What to do with all that appreciation? Just to be safe, he is mostly gay.

A fourth reason for not identifying as totally gay is an unwillingness to close the *heterosexual door*, which blends several of the other three men. **Lenny**, **Geoff**, and **Jake** have come out relatively recently and aren't yet ready to give up hope that the right woman might come along.

Lenny has never had a crush on a girl, only on boys, but he's never dated girls or boys. Only recently has Lenny had sex with a guy, which was shortly after he came out the previous year at age 21. Lenny believes that eventually he'll consider himself totally gay, but until he garners more experiences he identifies as mostly gay. At that point, he anticipates he'll be "very content with it."

Although **Geoff** had held hands with his girlfriend in the bleachers during basketball games and taken a girl to his senior prom, he regrets never having sex with a girl. "I would have liked to see what it was like. But it's not a huge regret. I don't lose sleep over it."

Jake's transformation from in to out of the closet was not a straight line because he had engaged in serious heterosexual behavior and romance. Jake finds women emotionally appealing, and he can "legitimately feel like there are women that actually, I can imagine nothing better than making out with you right now, because I just want to." If circumstances had been different, he might have been heterosexually married today. Now, he wants a husband.

★ ★

Having sex with the guy in college because it was through that that I knew that that was a significant part of who I was. I could put a name on "I want more emotion from this sex." And I don't want to be clamped down about this.

R: How do you see your future?

Same-sex relationship.

R: Do you see yourself having sex with a woman?

No. I mean I wouldn't count the possibility of it ever happening, like I don't see myself having vaginal sex ever again. In the right situation, I could fantasize about mutual masturbation with a girl. I can't imagine going from the attraction into the situation, how it would happen necessarily, but I would enjoy it . . .

If you go into fantasy, a guy is going to pop up . . . So I think that when you fantasize about things, you scratch the easiest thing to get you off, and I think for me, that is men. But like no, I don't come across perfect men, sexually erotic men in my day-to-day life.

★ ★

Jake's journey isn't crystal clear to either of us. Although all his sexual attraction, fantasy, infatuation, sex, and romance are directed toward men, Jake identifies as mostly gay, largely because "some women are just really attractive, and I find it really hard to define exactly what it is that makes that a package but it happens." Being mostly gay allows Jake to keep the door "a little bit open" even as he recognizes what drives him to women (the emotional) and to men (the erotic).

A fifth reason is a catchall group—*idiosyncratic*, I'll call it. One youth claimed he is "gay with bisexual tendencies," yet he's never had a crush on or sex with a girl, only on boys, from an early age.

218

His self-designated identity baffled me until he closed the interview with an extended story of a recent, devastating breakup with the love of his life, his "first and last boyfriend." Now, he said, "I don't care so much about sex." After he recovers, my guess is he'll again identify as totally gay.

Categorizing **Asher** isn't easy. Sorting through his emotional and erotic connections make Asher one of a kind. He has had many close emotional attachments to both sexes, but the girls he dated were never an erotic connection, and his one sexual encounter with a girl was more than sufficient to satisfy his heterosexual curiosity. By contrast, his first sex with a guy happened during his senior year of high school, but their relationship became a rather unhappy one. "I've had close [female] friends where there has been emotional connections but no sexual connections. And those connections have always been much stronger than those connections with my male friends or male partners." Clarity didn't come when I asked whether he would take a magical pill to make him straight.

* *

I would prefer if you would turn me bisexual. I don't want to go totally straight because that's boring. I hear a lot about my friend's sexual encounters. Straight people tend to have much more boring sex. It would also just made it a lot easier to meet people. I could marry a girl if I found her emotionally appealing. I usually connect with women, which is why it would be nice to find them sexually attractive. Or maybe it would also make it easier for me to find a man. Who knows?

* *

His teacher might be onto something when she described Asher "as a lesbian trapped in a man's body." I'm not sure whether that qualifies Asher as mostly gay, bisexual, or something else, but he said he's mostly gay—and perhaps he's right.

Really, Mostly Gay

The other eleven young men identify as mostly gay with some small degree (usually between 5 percent and 15 percent) of attractions, fantasies, genital contacts, infatuations, or romantic relationships with women. Each has all or some of the five indicators. What all eleven share are a previous girl crush, current romantic feelings directed only toward men, and a small degree of sexual attraction to some women.

The verifiable mostly gay young men are of two basic sorts. One wants to be totally gay and hopes his future will direct him there. Another young man told me that, although he is far more attracted to males than females, "I'm still attracted to females, but it is not something I want to act on. I could be straight if there was a gun to my head." Not quite so dramatically, another young man imagines his ideal as being in a committed sexual and romantic relationship with a guy: "I do find some girls very, very attractive, and I'd be willing to have sex with her. Sex wouldn't be bad or boring and on par with sex with a guy."

Three young men represent a second type of mostly gay—each comfortable with his mostly gay status with no desire to change. For example, **Derek** had three high school girlfriends, including one while he was having a gay fling. But it is not just any girl or woman who attracts him: lesbians and masculine women physically turn him on. His last girlfriend, a field hockey player, was physically fit and beautiful, and they shared compatible personalities and musical interests. For him, an attractive guy has to be athletic, masculine, and not "like the effeminate side of the homosexual community." His current boyfriend, the captain of the lacrosse team and a "very hetero-normative guy," fits the bill. If in the future Derek were to have a relationship with a woman, it would need to be an open relationship. Derek said he prefers to marry a guy—he is, after all, mostly gay.

Dean is very choosy because only a few girls turn him on. "I don't like the fake ones who look like everyone else, the blondes and blue-eyes. Maybe more the punk." With guys it is more erotic and lustier. If Dean sleeps with a guy, they might subsequently become friends or he'll befriend him first and then have sex. With girls, once they are friends, he loses all sexual interest. Dean acknowledged that 10 percent of his attractions and crushes are for women. If the right one came along, he thinks he could marry her if she allowed him to have sex with guys as well. Dean said he wouldn't change his sexuality with a magical pill. After all, "I am who I am whether it's for a purpose or not. I love who I am."

Taking mathematical stock of his life, **Dion** calculated he's been attracted to only a few girls but to lots of guys. By age 17 he was fairly certain about his sexuality. But why only *fairly* certain? Dion wondered whether there is some small part of him that might be heterosexual. "It's very rare that I am sexually attracted to a woman, but there could be someone . . . I don't have someone like that now, that in the future I could possibly be happily married to somebody and they could be a woman. I guess I wouldn't say that's impossible, but I wouldn't say that I would be sexually attracted to them." With guys, however, Dion is drawn to the tall, tan, Nordic blonds. When he sees a guy across the room, he said, "It's visceral."

To Be or Not to Be Totally Gay

Self-identified mostly gay men could be unsatisfied gays who might or might not be on their way to being totally gay. Perhaps a young man who identifies as mostly gay is avoiding the politically exclusive sexual boxes, or he simply doesn't want to limit his options. He might be holding out hope for a miracle—not that he'll turn straight because he's given up on that score. He loves his male eroticism, but if the right woman came along he might go for her. Few of those I spoke with were overly optimistic.

Other mostly gay young men, however, are legitimately on the spectrum, at a point between "bisexual leaning gay" and "totally gay" with a degree of sexual attraction to women, at least to certain types of women. He might deduce he's *mostly* because of his romantic rather than his sexual orientation, though it's difficult to decipher whether his romantic interest could be understood as feelings of emotional connectedness with women, or an appreciation of their beauty, or something better described as a hardcore infatuation and feelings of romantic love.

If you believe sexuality is composed of three categories (gay, bisexual, straight) rather than many points along a continuum, the mostly gay young men are a contradiction. It's not just sexual or romantic attraction to men versus women that is critical but the frequency and intensity of these attractions. It's not merely a matter of sexual performance, because he can get it up for either sex, or of romantic feelings, because he can kiss either sex with the best of them. Rather, his penis rises to the occasion more quickly and he kisses with more passion when it's a guy. When a guy cheats or breaks up with him, he's more distraught, even shattered. Although cultural and personal hopes can intervene and superficially cloud these issues, he remains *mostly gay* in terms of the strength of his erotic and romantic preferences. I predict that few will have anything other than casual sexual encounters or infatuations with women. It's their homoeroticism that reigns supreme.

Few of the young men I spoke with believe sexual and romantic orientations are one and the same, which raises larger questions of discriminating between sex and love. Erotic ecstasy is apparent in their genitals and fantasies, but what about love? What distinguishes an emotional relationship from a romantic relationship? What is true love? The discussion of love is our longest chapter, which is telling.

First Love

Had a crush on Chad . . . It was so ridiculous how much I was in love with him, and I loved skiing and his family. I kept it inside, and I was jealous when others were his friends, and I hated his girlfriend. (JEREMY, AGES 13 TO 18)

Anthony and Patrick

At age 16, **Anthony** discovered Patrick, the love of his life. They recently celebrated their third year together, though they are now attending different colleges. It was not love at first sight, but something else—a mystical aura, an eye contact—that connected them. Their story, at least from Anthony's perspective, is a little convoluted, but I'll try to make it clear. I'll add that when he talked about Patrick, Anthony was the most animated he ever became during our interview.

★ ★

First dating was Patrick who I'm dating now . . . Everyone knows on Facebook who is a gay person, and you can literally draw lines connecting people, either had a past together and connect everybody and all would be connected . . . Patrick said he kept hearing this name and, "Who is this kid?" I remember seeing him at our football homecoming in October before we dated, and he had friended me on Facebook the week before, but I didn't know who he was. Sorry but I'm going everywhere with this . . .

Wasn't sure [if he was gay], and I saw him at the homecoming game with all his friends who were drunk or high at the time and walking in with this huge crowd, making noise, and all looking at them. Had all attention, that group of people at the high school.

He and me made eye contact as [he was] walking by and just stared at each other, and the next day in the hallway and saw each other again, and I was staring at him, staring at him in the eye and he looked away after a while pretending he didn't see me and walked away, and few days later he messaged me on Facebook and claimed to be drunk. I thought he was very attractive, and so when he said he was drunk we talked a little bit. I didn't text him the next day because just figured he was drunk and made a mistake and wouldn't reconnect me at this time.

We ended up talking, kept talking and dated ten days later. He initiated the dating. Back seat of his car. You're going to judge me! If you were to ask me questions about my earlier past, it kind of follows the same trend, but because I didn't know a lot of guys and was overeager, overzealous, I remember we had gone on a date and met in the mall, went somewhere, talking on beach, hit it off really well and wanted each other, and we ended up having our first kiss and I blew him in the back of his car. First date but before we were officially together. He had orgasm, not me. I was in one of my past hookups, I guess I wasn't able to get hard, so I was nervous and didn't want it to come up and I don't really care, even now, don't care if I don't finish. I don't really mind because it's a relation-ship thing. I'm not, not selfish in the area. So we did and I didn't . . . It was good experience but felt guilty because felt like a slutty thing to do. I remember thinking, "How did that happen?" But it was positive somewhat because of my guilt I guess.

R: *First time you had real sex?*

It was also in back seat of his car, but at the time I had not met his family so didn't have places to go and he hadn't met mine . . . I was just kind of shocked by the experience. It was not exactly my first time, but I topped first and then I basically told him I couldn't finish. I was nervous, but "I think I want to bottom for you." We were dating at this point. I remember I wasn't that bad about it, didn't hurt, the sex itself wasn't painful but it was uncomfortable. It was also very very emotional, and that is why it was positive. The physical wasn't so great, but it was a very emotional, positive experience . . .

R: Have you experienced true love?

Yeah, with Patrick. I know that you or any adult will think otherwise, and I understand that. Being gay and not knowing a lot of people but I wasn't depressed but I was down because I wasn't with anyone, and I had convinced myself literally that I wouldn't be happy until I went to college and met someone and that wasn't going to happen now. So honestly think that Patrick made me so happy, and I needed that in my life then and now . . . We told each other fairly early on that we loved him, within a month and everyone was like, "It's a little early for that," but I can tell you now that my feelings in that month are the same as they are now. I remember really lying in bed watching a movie and he was hugging me from the side, and I remember thinking that this feels right. I didn't tell him I loved him then, but it was what I needed and feels right and really, really happy.

* *

That's a *love story* that's hard to beat! It's an infatuation that grew quickly to romantic love and an attachment. Many straight couples have a similar story in that they were both teenagers when they met, they attended the same school, they became physical quite early, and they were public about their relationship but hid it from their parents. It's a story filled with doubts, bliss, and hopes about the future.

Nearly every young man I interviewed wants a "Patrick" in his life—to love and be loved and to share lives together. I organize their tales of love and romance by the age at first love: beginning in middle school, then high school, and finally college/work. I'll close with those who haven't experienced a first love and the reasons they gave for its absence.

Each Other's Other

Passionate love is not the same as romantic love. You can have a crush but never be attached, have an infatuation that's a first step toward romantic love, have an infatuation and an attachment at the same time, or never develop a crush on the guy you love. And, of course, it's not an all-or-nothing proposition. Degrees of infatuation and romantic love are common. You can move from being possessed by an infatuation for a particular guy to a romantic love that grows even as the infatuation decreases. It's complicated and likely reflects the personal style of each guy in the pairing.

To define romantic love, here are telling behaviors and feelings. Fill in the blank with the person of choice.

- I am prepared to share my possessions and future with _____.
- I would feel lonely without _____.
- _____ knows everything about me.
- I hope my feelings for _____ will never end.
- _____ is the person who can make me feel the happiest, the most emotionally connected.

If you agree with each statement, you're on the attachment spectrum.

Infatuation is arousing, and romantic love is soothing, a more comfortable state to be in, although it too has its insecurities.

- Does he love me as much as I love him? *Impossible to answer.*
- Who's texting him? *Trust is critical to develop.*

- When is the right time to say, "I love you?" *You'll know, but don't expect the reciprocal statement, at least immediately.*
- Will he say it back, then or ever? *Don't force it, but let him say it when he's ready.*
- Is this for life? *Perhaps, though the love will change over time.*
- Will we marry? *At least it's now an option.*
- Does he want kids? *Slow down, but a topic for serious discussion.*
- If it ends will it happen again? *Likely, though it won't be identical. You've been changed.*
- Will it tell me something about myself? *Yes, to be discussed over time.*
- Is this true love? *Eventually the answer will be evident.*

How you find your forever love, how you learn what attracts you, how you discover the ways in which love is expressed, how you know the relationship is progressing, and how you understand that it's over and why it's over are not familiar territory for most young lovers. Maybe it's the same for straight youths, or maybe gays are unique because the two are both guys. One notable difference is that few straight guys break up with their girlfriends because they're pretending to be gay. Yet more than a few gay guys have called it quits with a guy because one of them is pretending to be straight. Journeys to love have their own agenda.

I'd also like to point out a noteworthy minor theme. We've seen it in the young men's stories of their first sex and their crushes, and we'll see it here as well. Some of the young men reported that they would rather be touched or loved by a male than to touch or love another male. As one young man stated it, "I more want to be a boyfriend than have a boyfriend." This highlights a particular need—to be wanted or taken care of by another male. Does this reflect the primacy of the romantic over the sexual? I'm not sure.

Young Love

Infatuations begin early, frequently before puberty, but they seldom evolve into full-blown love affairs. So, too, *true love* waits until high school or beyond—but not always.

Jeremy, who was raised in a rural conservative community, had his first crush, first coming out, first sex, first romance, and first true love with the same guy, Chad. Although their relationship flourished, ultimately it wasn't forever. The ending was particularly devastating.

★ ★

Chad moved to the school [in seventh grade], and I was assigned to be his buddy and we hung out. I was his first friend . . . Joke of others that we were gay because always hung out, [but] we never got anything for being gay in the small school . . .

It was so ridiculous how much I was in love with him, and I loved skiing and his family. I kept it inside, and I was jealous when others were his friends, and I hated his girlfriend. I told him in ninth when we were hanging out in my tree house and I was being obvious. He knew that my older brother and sister are gay. He finally asked me if I was gay, and I said I was. He was exactly the same. At the time he did not understand my true feelings for him. He was the first person I told. I never told him my feelings . . .

We were celebrating New Year's Eve, and he came onto me and started kissing. We were 15, maybe 16, and then I knew for sure. Oral sex for both. We didn't talk about it. We did it all the time, including anal sex. It was not just getting our rocks off because was kissing and cuddling. Both had an orgasm. He put his hand on my leg and kissed me while he rubbed my thigh. Then I took over, and I initiated the oral sex.

Felt awesome, amazing, euphoric, incredible! I was so in love with him it just felt right. We just never talked about it. I'd say weekly all through high school until he moved in with my parents because his parents moved his senior year and they wanted him to finish here. We talked about it his senior year, and he said he loved me and was terrified of others knowing.

He ended it, this after our attractions for six years. No contact since. He started dating the girl he had dated in eighth grade when he moved in. We stopped talking. Ended badly. He said he was straight.

R: Was it true love?

Yes, absolutely with Chad. Head over heels, ridiculous. That New Year's Eve because first time had gay experience and first huge crush, and the two were put together, and it was a bomb, passionate, life changing.

R: Biggest regret?

Wished I never had the affection for my best friend. Wished it was different and we'd still be friends . . . I know I can't change it, but wish never had the attraction to Chad because it ended so badly when he moved out in one day.

★ ★

A case of gay loathing also interfered with 14-year-olds **David** and Sam. They volunteered at a community service organization, and Sam correctly read David's feminine mannerisms. David had always wanted to be with someone more masculine, and Sam fit the bill. They discretely dated for two years. At the five-month mark, they began having oral sex, and they had sex twice a week. Ultimately, however, neither sex nor the relationship could heal Sam's self-denial.

★ ★

He was kind of a meat-heady type. He broke up with me because I think he was bisexual or was just so terrified of coming out after. I could tell that it really bothered him for a long time. He was worried that we wouldn't have a future together, and it was just digging himself into a deeper hole with this relationship, so in the end he decided that it was too much for him . . .

I actually ran into him afterwards, and we talked for a little bit, and it brought back everything that was so good about the relationship. And we were really really close to getting back together, but then I pulled away for a second, for the first time ever, thought about things rationally. And that was the last time I spoke to him.

★ ★

A pair can also split simply because it's the natural, inevitable course of the relationship. One young man recalled, "I loved and cared, but deep down I knew it wouldn't last." Perhaps these words suggest a toxic combination of inexperience, an uncooperative partner, and lots of what-ifs. Even though a relationship doesn't last, the memories and lessons learned linger. As one young man tearfully said, "I'm a better lover for it. I did better the next time."

Adolescent Lovers

Your romantic urgings can be as intense as they are for any straight teen. Relationships flourish in high school, though they're handicapped when same-sex dating isn't tolerated. Although the prohibition against taking another boy to the prom is on the decline in many communities, it still affects millions of guys. And it's getting easier to find the boy of your dreams, but not always.

As you likely know, romantic relationships of any vintage have their ups and downs, with gratifying, frustrating, and uncontrollable moments that test your mettle. Not all first romances begin with a friendship, become idyllic, and end with a family. Sometimes they begin as online strangers sexting each other and never evolve into real-life boyfriends. It takes two, and sometimes the other guy isn't cooperative. Of the young men I interviewed, the stories ran the gamut from disasters to first loves that they believe will offer lifelong positive memories. I begin with the smashups, then move on to the victories.

Similar to **Anthony**, 15-year-old **Dean** went online and talked with a guy who lived a few miles away, and one day Dean stopped by the guy's house. Blowjobs were exchanged, and Dean assumed they were now dating. Because of family problems, the boy moved in with Dean's family, and inevitably they were caught doing it by Dean's mom, who promptly said she wouldn't allow that "gay shit in my house." Afterward, the boyfriend returned home, drank, got high, and cheated (all in one day). Dean, who was madly in love and having great sex with this guy, couldn't salvage their relationship. Negotiating reality has its maddening qualities.

Cultural issues also intervene with the passion of first love. There's such potential, yet neither youth is ready to say that they want to commit. Having sex turns out to be considerably easier than having a relationship or letting go of the relationship.

* *

He is the guy one should not date! For three weeks we were dating, and I was asking for sex. He's very much in the closet so could not go to his place. He was a great guy, talked long hours on the phone, a college sophomore in a Latino fraternity. We didn't see each other much, but I'd try calling and he was always busy. Very heart wrenching. When we did talk there was lots of silence, and other times it felt like phone sex, that he was getting off. He texted me and said, "Let's be friends," as he can't be out and wanted to hold onto his secret. Said it was cultural, his family. I hate him. It is time for me to get over him and move on.

* *

But moving on didn't happen, and the end was not in sight. Two years later when he was a college freshman, he joined the same Latino fraternity as his ex, and a year later he e-mailed his ex to tell him "how much I loved him and wanted a second opportunity, but again neither of us stepped forward. I guess we were on/off again boyfriends." Hope is about all they have at this point.

Another pair first kissed and made out on a romantic New Year's Eve as they watched the ball drop in New York City. The big question for the young man was, "Should I kiss him?"

* *

All our friends went to bed, and he invited me to sleep with him. Both did oral sex. It gratified all my feelings, realized I'm gay, and made me happy. I came to accept my gayness. It lasted six months. More sex after that, every week, and this was senior year in high school. He told me he didn't know what love was and not sure if he loved me. He said he didn't know if loving his computer was the same as loving me. I was very upset as we had both said we loved each other and that was a big step for me. He didn't mean anything it seemed. One can know love in high school. I pushed him away and said some very mean things, so far out of my life he can never come back. I was so upset, especially because he had gone to a bathhouse. I've recently apologized to him, and he wrote back saying he never wanted to see or hear from me again.

* *

Ted was 14 and then 16 when he learned that romance needs considerable development and two guys who are willing to cultivate it. If an intimate relationship remains secretive it will not flourish.

★ ★

He was someone in my math class, and he treated me differently than any other guy treated me . . . I remember he was also sort of enigmatic in a way. I didn't really know very much about him because he was never in my previous friend circles. But I walk into math class one morning, which is my first period class in my freshman year of high school . . . He would put his hands in the shape of a heart over his chest and that made me feel really good. Super positive.

R: Did you tell him you had a crush on him?

No. But it was very obvious, or I would assume it was obvious . . . I was very unsure of myself and very uncomfortable with the idea that I was gay . . . and then, as soon as I got into high school it became very obvious to me that I did not share the same attraction to women that many of my friends did. And it didn't necessarily have to do with sexuality. It had to do with the sexual and romantic aspect of it. And that guy, the one with the heart over his chest, was sort of like the tipping point in a way where I started to realize how much the emotional side of things mattered.

★ ★

That crush became history, and the second didn't fare much better. The emotional intimacy was present, but, again, if a partner is unable to acknowledge his sexuality, a positive outcome is difficult to achieve.

★ ★

Evident to everyone . . . completely in love, and we basically spent all of our time together. This was between my junior and senior year of high school. As soon as that was over, we were on the phone every day and texting all the time . . .

[In college they roomed together.] People assumed that we were in a relationship. We had the largest closet on campus housing, physically, but there was definitely another level to it. I waited a long time for him to come out. I would try to make him be a little bit more sexual. He comes from an extremely conservative background . . . It was very committed but not sex, no intimacy, only emotional.

★ ★

Ted was "quite sure" the guy wanted the two of them to be in a relationship, but the guy decided he could not be gay, so Ted moved on.

Gay relationships evolve, change shape, and are redefined. A high school freshman sensed his best friend was flirting with him, which was intriguing. While walking in public, he jokingly dared the boy to kiss him, and much to his surprise the boy contemplated it. Their friendship grew, and their romantic energy was obvious to their friends. Totally infatuated, they respected and sacrificed for each other, and expressed genuine love for each other. Ultimately, life transitions intervened, and they split, though they'll "always be connected."

★ ★

We're at the high school LGBT Center and he asked me to sit on his lap. Then he came over and sat on mine. He had a long scarf and it covered his jeans, so I was messing around his waist and undid his zipper and got two fingers in and was massaging. No resistance. It was a step in the right direction and was one more thing of how much we liked each other. He was a best friend, with benefits. Yet neither of us stepped forward and said, "Be my boyfriend." Then this past summer

236

I went to his house to say goodbye before I came to college, and we were alone. He sat on my lap as I was on the computer, and it was a reconnection. This time we had oral sex. Each grew in different directions, and when it ended we still loved each other. I respect and value him, and it'd be sad if I never saw him again. My first true love, my first boyfriend.

★ ★

It was not an ending but an outcome neither imagined at the time—a relationship in absentia, fully intimate, and a family always.

Given common life changes, teenage romantic partners can drift apart as each attends college or begins a career. This reality complicates relationships, but it can also be a convenient excuse to end a relationship that should not continue. During his senior year **Asher**'s ex-girlfriend introduced him to Danny, a fellow church member who was also in theater.

★ ★

Both of his parents were lesbians. He had a lot more experience than me. He was very patient and kind of coached me along. We realized we couldn't do it in either of our houses, and he had a big truck [his mom's] so we went out and we had like a nice thing . . . He showed me how to do it. I didn't have anal sex until college. It was just oral sex. He initiated it. I never initiate the sexual contact . . .

It was pretty regular. We once did it right before practice in the parking lot. This is one of my favorite stories. We showed up to practice, our school had red sweatpants for both. He was theater and I was track, but we accidentally switched pants, and he accidentally shows up to theater in red track pants and I show up to practice in red theater pants. By accident! We just switched.

We were known as dating. I tried to take him to prom, but I wasn't allowed to buy a ticket for him. It lasted until June of that year when we talked about it.

R: *Future sexual contact between the two of you?*

No. I guess looking back, I wasn't overly physically attracted to him. Which as I grew older, it made it harder for me to interact with him sexually.

★ ★

The two zipped up, packed, and went to separate colleges, and are now casual friends. Love is insufficient if the two are not right for each other.

Though his relationship eventually floundered, **Tyler** said he'd do it all over again.

★ ★

I consider my first serious relationship happened towards the end of my junior year with Perry, and we actually had dated for eleven months. I went to Friday nightclub gay thing, and I met a gay friend there. Perry was also friends with him, and then we friended each other on Facebook and started talking on Facebook then we Skyped and then we agreed to go on a date.

R: *Did it become physical?*

I think it was like six weeks after we met and started dating . . . A week after that, we gave each other blowjobs, then two weeks after that we continued to do blowjobs and we basically only saw each other on the weekends . . . So it was two weekends after the first blowjob that we attempted to have anal sex. It didn't work. I wanted to top and he was a virgin, and it was like not working. But then after a week after that is when we did and it worked.

R: *Do you still have contact with him?*

He broke up with me for a week after the first three months and there was a week break and we got back together, and then at the ten-month mark he broke up with me again. And then begged for me back basically a couple days later, and I got back with him and we were back together for another week and he dumped me, and then we actually, that ended at the end of my senior year. We got back together when I was back here at college, and we were back together for a month and then I broke up with him. Mostly, he broke up with me, broke up with me, broke up with me, and then I broke up with him. My relationship with me and him, we don't communicate. I wanted to be friends still and he didn't. He is more of the, "If we are not together, we are out of each other's lives . . ."

We loved each other, but we were not right for each other probably. It was more like just in general things where we would annoy each other, and I'm sure that happens in relationships. Deep down, we really cared about each other. We never wanted to walk away upset at each other . . .

My freshman year, I had gotten out of my relationship, and I was more interested in coming to college, being free, getting the experience, having a single dorm room that I could bring guys back to. I mean like obviously I don't think I was obscene or ridiculous in what I did. I didn't go out every night and pick up a guy. But during my freshman year, I had slept with four people. And to me, that was a big deal considering I had only slept with one person before coming to college.

R: *What is your biggest regret?*

I broke up with Perry for that time. And I also regret what I did that led me to break up with Perry which is, now I'm going to feel like a terrible person on tape . . . I guess I thought in my head that this isn't going to work and I convinced myself of that and the weekend, Halloween weekend, there was a Gay Mafia party, and so I went out to the party and I drank and I got drunk, and I brought a guy back to my room, and I knew I was going to break up with Perry that weekend but I couldn't figure out how to do it, so I felt like, in my drunken mind looking back on it now I knew it was not the right idea. I was like I will give myself a reason to break up with him and reason for him to never ever try to win me back because I knew if he tried, he would get me back. So I hooked up with the guy. It was just a blowjob, but I told Perry the next day and I broke up with him. And I told him that we can't be together, and I haven't spoken to him since.

R: *Have you experienced true love?*

Yes, with him . . . Where I am now I am almost completely romantic. I am done doing the "Let's hook up with a bunch of guys." I miss what it felt like to be with Perry.

★ ★

Life gets in the way but as Tyler reminds us, first love seldom totally disappears from memory. Gay pairings can break hearts, linger without resolution, or last forever.

Young Adult Love

After high school the world of potential romances explodes for those who move out of the family home. It's raining men! For example, at college there are more choices and more opportunities for exploratory dating (nothing to lose), sex without commitment (hookup sex), a boyfriend, and romantic love. Plus, a young man is likely more emotionally accessible and is entertaining new perspectives about what he wants from life. And, of course, there's always the Internet to help him find whatever he's looking for.

As a result, the uncertainties also expand. Is breakup sex a good idea? It may be fun, but will it reignite an unpleasant past? Is returning to an ex-lover for another go-around stupid? Will you ever find anyone as good as the one you lost? Will you ever find another boyfriend, period?

Even after breakups, the possibilities of renewal can linger, including for **Dion** and his first love at age 19. "I think love means different things to different people and I am very aware of that, and I guess some people mistake love for infatuation or lust or excitement or just the thrill of having something new." Though he and his second boyfriend cared deeply for each other and always will, it was by Dion's reckoning "a terrible relationship." However, three years later he believed he might marry him some day. Lessons are difficult to learn—"terrible relationship" and "might marry" can overlap.

Opportunities for casual hookup sex highlight the separate entities of sex and romance. Difficult relationships are those in the middle, as **Liam** discovered. He had sex with several guys during his freshman year of college before he met a really hot guy at a party and they spent not just the night but the week together. They had sex the first night, became infatuated the second night, and proposed marriage the third night. This was a bit too quick for Liam. The second time he became so infatuated had a very different trajectory. His senior year Liam met a gorgeous graduate student, and they developed an intense friendship. One night the gorgeous guy slept over in the same bed, and they didn't touch, not until Liam "pretended to 'accidentally' put my hand on his shoulder. My heart was pounding, so much chemistry. He took my hand and kissed me. It's been two years, and we are very much in love . . . I would propose to him if I could." Now, by law, he can.

Geoff also discovered the love of his life, though the evolution was slow and their future remains undetermined. Similar to Liam, it also began as a friendship (but with "benefits").

* *

He lived in my dorm last year. We started out during the first few months of school just being really good friends. We have a lot of similar interests, and things kind of took off. We realized we had the potential to be more than friends. We liked each other . . .

R: *Is there a point at which you began dating?*

Formally it was over Christmas break, and we were together hanging out and I asked him to date me formally. We felt like we needed a formal thing even though we were exclusive by that point already.

R: *Is this the first guy you had genital contact with?*

No. Yes. We knew we liked each other, but we weren't sure if we wanted to date each other. We thought we were just better suited for friends, so I kind of messed around a little bit in between so I'm trying to remember who was first. I think he was first . . .

R: *What did formally dating mean to you?*

It didn't really change anything in terms of, "Now we're dating, let's have sex." I mean that happened before. Or, "Now we're dating we have to go on dates and ask each other how our days were." That stuff all happened before. So for us it was just more of an official thing. This is our [first] anniversary if you will. It was just a date for us. For me, it validated or verified our relationship in a way. It was the real thing now. No longer just messing around.

R: *Was that a commitment to monogamy?*

Yeah, I think so. Well I had mentioned that when we were kind of friends with benefits . . . and not that we set definite rules when I asked him out. It's not like, "You shall be monogamous," but I think that's just kind of understood in our relationship. It's never really come up. I don't think it will. Knock on wood. It's not like he has ever come up to me and said, "I really like this guy. How about I do both of you?" We are each other's. And we can certainly have other guy friends. But no romance . . . Now, if there is ever sort of an issue or any kind of concern, it doesn't have to be negative, we are comfortable enough to talk about it.

R: Do you guys live together?

I'm still in the dorm but he lives two doors down.

R: Have you guys talked about the future?

A little bit. Obviously, it's hard to make conclusions when you are 20 years old. But at this point in our relationship, I feel that we are very compatible and so does he. Obviously, we have had some disagreements and arguments but nothing major, and granted we've only been dating a yearish. But we've talked about what the future can hold. It's kind of nerve-wracking a bit because we're not sure of grad school or work or whatever.

★ ★

Issues that break up straight relationships also shatter gay ones—cheating being one. Online, **Jonathan** found his first hookup, first sex, and first relationship. He was "a masseuse and a flight attendant, and we started talking online, and we ended up meeting a few times in person, and he was the first person who made me feel okay with being sexually intimate with another man. I was 22." A few months later, Jonathan boarded flight attendant number two ("I swear this isn't a pattern!") and delivered him home to meet his family, where he was readily accepted. They lasted several years, and their relationship ended just months before the interview. Jonathan wasn't prepared to commit to monogamy, creating "quite a mess" that couples counseling couldn't resolve. Though they loved each other, love wasn't enough, and neither was the promise to "marry him and settle down and have 2.5 kids and a house."

Unwillingness to forsake novel, casual sex is a dilemma facing many young men, especially those just beginning their sexual careers who also want a long-term, sexually exclusive relationship. **Derek** faced this with his two boyfriends as well as the issue of cheating (his and theirs). He brought his first boyfriend home for a "Thanksgiving Surprise," but another surprise waited him months later. Derek believes in true love (and long stories): so would it be boyfriend number one or boyfriend number two?

★ ★

When we were doing housing our sophomore year, everybody told us don't live together because you'll end up hating each other. So we did the next closest thing, which was we each had [dorm] singles and they were right next to each other. So basically lived together. We slept in the same bed. We had one room for sleeping, and one room for the rest of our stuff . . .

With my first boyfriend, he and me really really hit it off. He had more sexual experience with guys than I did, so he kind of coached me through everything for the first couple months, definitely the honeymoon phase, and beyond. Probably as long as six or eight months, he and I were very convinced that we were going to be together for a really long time. That crumbled . . .

The fall of sophomore year was fine for the most part, but towards the end I actually went home and met this kid that was a couple years younger than me and he messaged me on Facebook and we started talking, and I didn't even realize he was hitting on me. And I just decided, I felt like I was kind of mentoring him, so he and I got together for coffee and just chatted and stuff. But I ended up just thinking, "Wow, this is a really cool kid. I like him a lot. Oh, there are other people out there than my current boyfriend." And then I came back to school and shortly thereafter, the incident where my boyfriend cheated on me happened and that was just like it.

R: *Did he tell you?*

I had to do some digging. I suspected it. Actually what happened, we had a party it was him and I and two of our gay friends who were a couple at the time. We all drank too much. I drank a bunch, threw up, and passed out. Just like went into my room and fell asleep. I woke up the next morning, and my boyfriend was in bed with me. One of the other guys was in the other room, and there was an empty condom wrapper. And at first I thought, "Oh it was just them." But I talked with the guy that was still there, and he said "No," his boyfriend had gone home really early. He decided he was too tired. And then I was like, "Oh wait, did you and my boyfriend?" And he was like, "No! I passed out here really early, too." Things were not lining up. So I did some snooping on Facebook, and there was weird stuff in conversations, and eventually it came out that my boyfriend and the one that had left, I still don't know exactly what happened, but they did have sex.

R: Your current boyfriend?

We have been together for a year and three months. I'm a long-term guy. So my current boyfriend is actually the kid that I met and had coffee with. When my first boyfriend and I broke up, I kind of went back to him and said when I was confiding in him and talking with him, and he and I hung out more and more and more. This was the summer after sophomore year now. This was a few months later. And he and I started dating that summer . . .

R: Most significant sexual or romantic event?

When my first boyfriend cheated on me. That, as far as my sexual development went, that took me from the mentality of a monogamous thinking in the distance type person to thinking about promiscuity and thinking about the fact that I wanted more experience, and it really redefined how I thought about myself sexually.

R: Biggest regret?

Cheating on my current boyfriend with my ex-boyfriend. That was a big no-no. That was the first event that disrupted the sanctity of my second relationship with a guy. Since then, it has become a lot more rocky.

★ ★

Sometimes lessons are difficult to learn, even for young men who are quite bright.

Hasn't Happened Yet

If you are without a true love experience, you might believe you'll never have one. You may also be happy not to be in love, or you may say that you'd like to wait. Why? Several of the young men gave their reasons:

- Deficient self-development. First he has to like himself before becoming intimate with another. Eventually he hopes for true love. "Oh god, yes!"
- No reciprocation. He thinks he's in love because it "hurts inside," then discovers his love object has a girlfriend or boyfriend.
- Cultural, religious, or class mandates. He's been sexual with a guy, but nothing can ever come of it because he has to marry the girl that's right or chosen for him.
- Too busy. He has gay sex, but a relationship takes too much time and energy, and he'd rather spend time with friends and on his education.
- The appeal of hookup sex. He can't do friends with benefits if he has a boyfriend.
- Fear of rejection. He feels breaking up will hurt too much. "He'll crush my heart, an open wound. I get more emotionally involved than I think."
- Gay relationships ultimately fail. "They don't go anywhere anyways. It would harm me and not be beneficial."

Lenny spans several of these reasons. As a thoughtful 22-year-old, Lenny was perplexed by the notion of true love. After coming out the previous year, meeting a guy, and having sex (his first time), he now questions whether he fell in love with him. Certainly, he had "feelings."

★ ★

I became completely infatuated. But that is extremely rare for me. I only had one other person like that. And that was in high school, but rarely do I ever get that attracted to someone. Because I remember at the time I was so attracted to him but I also didn't know quite what to do with it. I didn't know what I wanted from him. I didn't know how to approach it. I didn't know if I should have said, "Hey, I want to get to know you more so I can eventually date you or if I can continue having flings with you or something." Right now I'm in a stage where it's not like I'm not identifying myself as wanting or not wanting a relationship . . . I also feel behind, and I want to be able to meet other gay men my age and not be bogged down by the fact that I am still a newbie.

R: Have you experienced what you think is true love?

The one in high school I just thought was the perfect person then that evolved into something more negative. Now I don't think as highly of him anymore. That just kind of went away, so it's hard for me to say if, you know, if what I felt for, actually I am not sure. I feel like it was close. I felt like all the elements were there except for how do I find this person in a prolonged capacity like living with this person. Stuff like that. I feel like there were a lot of components that I haven't experienced with him yet and maybe know that. I don't have contact with the high school guy. That did not evolve.

I am not sure if he has heard through the grapevine that I have come out. And looking back on my interactions with him, I don't know if he had a suspicion. Basically he was one of my good friends, and I was very aggressive then in being friends with him. But it was hard because we were friends but I wanted more than that, and I would never do anything to get more than that. I guess it probably confused him why this friend of his was constantly wanting to do things, and at one point he just got the wrong idea and just thought that I wanted to be him and he sent a message to me online that was like, I was kind of caught off guard, he just kind of blew up and that left me feeling very upset and I just didn't really respond to that. And we kind of made up but since then it's always just kind of been like . . .

R: *Is he straight?*

Yes, but he hadn't dated anyone in a while, so I always had that like hope, and he is like mildly ambiguous in terms of his personality.

R: *How do you see your future in terms of sex and romance?*

I have been thinking about it, and it's not clear in my mind yet in terms of marriage and what I want yet, but I am also trying to figure out if it is something that I will eventually want and regret not having done. Or at least figuring out a way to do it my own way whether it's through some other bond that isn't marriage. Right now, and probably for the next couple years, it's not important for me to have found a lifelong soul mate. However, it is important to me that I do want to. It's tricky because I want to date other guys in the capacity that people would date in high school. It's more of just trying out relationships. And I feel a little bit more pressure now. I feel like guys around my age have already done that and they are looking for people who are more perfect for them . . . Ideally over the next few years I would like to have more experiences. More sexual experiences and also more experiences like going out with a guy and just making that more normal for me. I know my first date is going to be extremely awkward for me.

* *

One message is *don't fall in love with a straight guy*, or else expect to be hurt. Another is know thyself and what you want in life in terms of sex and romance. The third message is that sexual lust and romantic feelings are difficult to manage when you are young and hopeful.

True Love—A Tricky Concept

Nicholas's answer to whether he's ever been in love was classic Nicholas. "Goddamn that's a tricky question! Love, yes. True love, possibly. I don't know. I am still trying to figure out what love is." Let's take a look at the complexity in Nicholas's developmental trajectory.

Nicholas admitted to being "in multiple places on that multiple times. Definitely when I first started, I was like, 'Okay relationship maybe, maybe not soul mate, but definitely monogamous relationship.'"

One possibility was the first guy he had sex with, which was during his freshman year at college. They dated for a month. Did Nicholas love him? "At the time, maybe kind of I might have thought that, but I think it was more of like an emotional attachment. Okay we are dating and I like him. Like what a stereotypical teenager thinks love it. Not really love but I don't think it was love, but there was definitely some sort of feelings somewhere. It's not quite dating, but it's not like hooking up. It's just, you know, semi-dating." That sounded confusing, even for Nicholas.

After an "ugly, messy breakup" with his second boyfriend (who cheated on him), Nicholas entered his "pity hookup slut mode. Not that I am proud of it but it definitely. I would not be who I am without having gone through that." We will soon return to "true love."

★ ★

R: Where did you find those guys?

Grindr mostly. I might have also had a few parties in the sense that you know like if you are always looking for a relationship, you don't get a view of what it is until you step back and start doing something else. The same as like when you are driving really really fast, it's only when you stop or slow down you're like, "Wow I was going fast!" So like having that for a few months, and you know I eventually got out of that and started dating more . . .

★ ★

In part this was due to Nicholas having lost a potential boyfriend, a guy who'd planned on asking Nicholas out until he discovered the Grindr activity. "Oh oops. I fucked that one up" was Nicholas's response, because he'd been very attracted to the guy.

In his sophomore year Nicholas dated a guy long distance. He felt an attachment and "a feeling of some sort of love and commitment there, and then it broke off." Committing himself to never again do a long-distance relationship, he is now in another that holds great promise. "So I am still learning and trying to understand what love is. I think I've experienced it in at least some way, shape, or form."

There's nothing inherently gay about Nicholas's story—it's about the messiness of sorting through sex, romance, love, and their connections. Before I let each young man escape the romance section, I ask them, "What is in your future when it comes to sex and romance?"

He's My Soul Man

I'm a hopeless romantic. It is safety, home, love, someone who accepts me. (YOUTH, AGE 19)

You've had sex with a guy, with or without romance, or you've fallen for a guy, with or without sexual contact. Sex and romance are with the same guy or different guys. But what is most important to you? It's a simple question with complicated answers because, as always, it depends.

Anthony had a quick, certain answer: he is far closer to the romantic than the sexual end of the continuum, though he hastily added that he loves sex. His primary life goal is to find love and he will never forego it. Love will never be secondary. Anthony has found his soul mate, and the type of *traditional future* he envisions was endorsed by most of the young men I spoke with. By a long shot, most prefer an idealized future in which they fall in love and have a lifelong, romantic, monogamous relationship with the man of their dreams. This counters the stereotype that gay youths just want sex, sex, and more sex. Some do want lots of sex, and sex is certainly pursued, with various levels of intensity and purpose, but what most impressed me was the longing many of the young men expressed for an intimate, emotionally significant attachment to another guy. In this, I sense they are rather typical of young men of their generation.

Focus on Sex

The young men who are exceptions to this traditional trajectory were hesitant to call it quits on having lots of sex with lots of different guys. One young man loves being gay because "it's easier for us to be promiscuous, less is expected of us like having to have kids or having to be in a romantic relationship, and it's easier to focus on selfish things like career, take care of ourselves." He admitted he might be an outlier because he is a free-spirited maverick.

More typical is the young man who wants it all, with the priority right now of having lots of (careful) sex. "If someone clicks then great. I'm not saving myself for anyone, but if I find him then I'd go for it." For him, sex is a series of auditions, though he recognized that given "my looks and big dick I break lots of hearts." (I never said all gay youths are humble!) He speculated that he'll be more focused on a relationship in his late 20s, but until then he's happy to let the tryouts and shattered hearts continue.

Asher answered the sex/romance question with gusto: "as much sex as possible, with multiple friends with benefits." Then he slightly backtracked because of the realization that his college career is coming to a close. Given that "love is a temporary chemical change in the brain that will go away" and that a relationship should be based on "really great intellectual and emotional connections," he believes that now, in college, is the ideal time to find such a guy. Asher, however, has given himself few chances to meet his potential forever guy.

★ ★

I'm also highly, I don't know what to call it. I am very picky when it comes to that. I have not met any really outdoorsy granola gays yet. I do creative writing. I was in a class, and

252

it was my minor for a while. All of my writing was about homosexuality because I was coming to terms with it still . . .

I wish I hadn't hooked up with as many people. Sometimes I feel like I have a reputation in the community. I wish I actually dated people. I wish I hadn't broken up with some of the people I did date. Because I just didn't give them a chance. I found a flaw and decided I didn't like it. Sometimes I would make decisions based on guys that I realized were really stupid. I wish I hadn't done that.

* *

Likewise, **Jonathan** isn't prepared to settle down with just one guy—which was how he always imagined a romantic relationship would be. His biggest life regret is his sexual rampage from ages 17 to 21 with, by his count, seventy-three partners. He was "horny and didn't want to masturbate." The net effect, according to him, was arrested development. He had sex with people "that I just absolutely regret being with just because of the way that the experience made me feel. I had no interest in them at all, and that kind of tempered my sexual growth because I feel like being with them I became a much more hardened person." Jonathan said he "had to recover and figure out why I did this for so long." To become healthier, he vowed to be more thoughtful and rather than just focusing on physical characteristics (tall, athletic, muscular), he's now looking for intelligent conversations, friendship, and a connection. What's his plan? "I'm trying to figure out what I enjoy sexually and trying to find sexual partners that are like me so that I can explore things further. Since I feel like I've had a very strange growing up into my gayness, I feel like I still have a lot more exploring to do before I settle down with one partner."

Although most of the men envisioned a romantic relationship in their futures, some thought that these relationships might not mimic the stereotypical vision of a straight marriage. A few explicitly rejected the institution of marriage as an intrusion by the state into personal affairs. This, however, was clearly a minority view. Most accepted rather than rejected the *marriage option*. Before moving to those who were absolutely certain that they were headed toward marriage, we'll look at some of the unique alternatives that several of the young men imagined for themselves.

Unconventional Options

The most common alternative to orthodox marriage for gay youths is having a sexually open but romantically closed relationship. Couples with open agreements usually have rules or conditions that limit when, where, how often, and with whom outside sex is permitted. For instance, the rules might be only casual hookups, no anal, no overnights, only strangers, never in the home, only threesomes, only when one is traveling, only once per week/month, and with promises to tell or not tell. Such contracts benefit couples by providing boundaries for the relationship, supporting a nonheterosexual lifestyle, and fulfilling the couple's sexual needs.

Jonathan, who had the sexual rampage under his belt, isn't willing to settle down with one partner until he's at least 30. Will it be monogamous? "An open relationship is where I am in my mind right now . . . primarily, to put it really crudely, I don't want to have chocolate every day. I feel like there will be one person where I want to be solely romantically involved with, but sexually I feel like there are so many things that I don't think one person will be able to fulfill for me." So his answer is to be open sexually, closed romantically.

Dion's solution varies slightly. He wants to start with a monogamous sexual relationship and then evolve it to an open one. However, he is less than certain about the workability of this arrangement.

★ ★

Well sex-wise, there are probably very few people who have more sex than I do. Sex will always be there. Sex is not hard to come by. Relationship-wise, I think I'm a complicated person. I know I am. It's not something I'm bragging about because I don't think it's a good thing . . .

I want a monogamous relationship, but I don't feel like it needs to be. I feel like if you have a relationship, I feel like it needs to start that way . . . There needs to be a firm base, and if time goes on and if someone were to have sexual interactions or encounters with other people, I would be okay with that as long as our relationship remained healthy . . .

I am very worried that I'm going to be married several times . . . I'm not quite sure if I'll wait for the right person. I think there could be love but they could not be the right person, and I wouldn't wait and go ahead with it. Would the relationship be monogamous? Probably at first, and I keep saying that I don't have a problem with it. But it would really depend on the person I'm with, and even right now there's this guy that I've been with for a while and we never officially dated and I care about him deeply, but I'm also very hesitant because I'm not sure. He's not really all that into sex. And I don't need a whole lot of sex if I'm being fulfilled and everything else is there then sex isn't all that important . . . I think I would have to feel very secure and appreciated.

★ ★

Others can't imagine themselves in a monogamous relationship, either because they believe such relationships aren't attainable or because they aren't something that the young men wants. Some continue to believe that gay relationships are just plain wrong or unnatural. The *not natural* argument convinces several that successful gay relationships are unrealistic because the male genome, for both gay and straight men, has evolved for males to sleep around, spread their seed, and never form lifelong, monogamous relationships. Not all scientists would agree, especially those who argue that forming romantic attachments is hard-wired into both male and female brains regardless of sexual orientation to facilitate long-term pair-bonding and enhance high levels of social intelligence. Romantic love, devotion, and commitment are not only about having and raising children but also about transforming us from apes to modern humans. Gay people are not exempt from this evolution. To favor "my heart rather than my dick" is not going against human evolution.

Young gay men, 18 to 25 years of age, reported in one study being more similar to straight women than to men in being more upset with *emotional* than sexual infidelity, and this was true regardless of how long they had been in their relationships or whether they were the cheaters or the cheated-on. These young gay men were in touch with their evolved selves.

The young men I interviewed proffered other unique solutions to the sex/romance question. One felt that romantic crushes interfered with pure sex, which was what he wanted. Another felt that all same-sex relationships had expiration dates, so he had resigned himself to being an eternally single guy. "Straight men have women to force them into marriage. Realistically, can I be expected to follow my heart rather than my dick?" Another confessed that when he is in a relationship he wants lots of sex with different guys, but when he is single and having lots of sex he wants a monogamous relationship. Although none of them endorsed a polyamorous lifestyle (plural romantic *and* sexual relations with multiple men), it could be considered as a possible solution.

Despite these reservations and individual preferences, for the vast majority it was straightforward: find *the man*, someone like **Anthony**'s Patrick, by the time they are 30.

True Love

One young man proudly announced, "I'm a hopeless romantic. It is safety, home, love, someone who accepts me." He is clearly in love with love. Nearly every young man hopes it will happen to him by the magical age of 30, though some fear that true love will pass them by. Why were they afraid? One claimed he is a victim of a gay culture that values and glorifies casual sex and demeans marriage. Is he right?

Ted wrestled with the open versus monogamous dilemma, even as a friend was keeping count of his own sexual exploits, which now numbers in the eighties. "That's fine for him and I appreciate that but I, that's not me." When trying to name the guys he'd had sex with, Ted lost count and offered to bring me his list. (I declined.) "I can count them on all of my digits or three, between ten and fifteen probably."

Ted indicated that his strong preference is to have a real relationship, but then he qualified his original statement. "No, I'm not going to say that! I much prefer having a long-time emotional relationship with somebody. I don't necessarily know whether I would want an open or monogamous relationship. It's very much dependent on the guy. I can only say in previous relationships, I only wanted it to be monogamous because I like the idea." However, Ted loves partying, dancing, getting totally wasted, going crazy several times a month, and being the "dance savage" more than he loves finding a romance.

Having casual sex ("short-term promiscuity") while waiting for *the man* to come into his life is a minor inconvenience for **David**, who placed himself on the romantic side of the scale. "Those few times where I haven't had contact in a really long time and I want to chalk up sex," he said, but then he waivered. Until he finds the guy he will marry at age 25, he will content himself with monogamous relationships and occasional flings.

Given the cheating of his first boyfriend, **Derek** cautioned, "Be careful." Although ultimately Derek wants a relationship, he is now grappling with how to get there and whether it is even possible. He isn't optimistic.

★ ★

Externally, I am very close to the romantic side. Internally, I am much more towards the middle. One of the reasons that my first boyfriend's cheating on me was such a big deal was because I had only ever been with two guys, him included. He had a lot more experience, and I just got jealous of the experience. I wanted to have more contact. That turned into a whole huge fiasco because I cheated on him and it was not good.

So I came out of that relationship thinking, "I want to mess around." I want to have a lot more sex with a lot of different people and get more experience. But socially, that was kind of a lot harder to do than I thought it would be. It's also just a lot harder to do it at home.

★ ★

After adding more sexual experiences, Derek predicted he will once again favor the monogamous path, with the right guy this time.

Tyler described himself as also a romantic. Now that he's 20 he's done with the "let's hook up with a bunch of guys" syndrome.

* *

If my next relationship could last forever, I would make it that way. I want to find somebody who I fall head over heels for who loves me just as much and who I can grow up and marry and have a family with. And that's what I really want. And the problem is, at the age I'm at right now, no one else wants that.

R: *Would this relationship be a monogamous relationship?*

Completely monogamous. If the guy wants to sleep with somebody else, then break up with me first. I make that very clear. I am not the kind of person who will like turn a cheek to you doing something with someone else.

* *

Not surprisingly, **Nicholas** hated my question.

* *

Shit that's a hard question. Are you purposely leaving the question really open? I am attracted to, it's a pretty wide margin right now because I am opening the doors a little bit to say that I want a relationship not just a, you know. I am looking for a long-term relationship guy, and I want somebody who is sort of equal to me in stature whether that be intelligence or finance or physical size build whatever. I have a very hard time finding people who listen and talk about their emotions, who are able to actively talk about how they feel and particularly how they feel about their emotions. That is my particular frustration.

* *

259

Nicholas's romantic type contrasted with his one-night stand type, "the leaner, jockey, takes control and knows what they want." Others also linked desirable sex partners with physical, "superficial" characteristics such as physique, genitals, and body hair. With the qualities they seek in their future husbands, however, emotional intimacy and friendship take precedence, the personal dynamics rather than the physical attributes. **Asher's** checklist included a guy who wants a townhouse in the city, a nice farm in the country, two to four adopted kids, and a few dogs. Another youth's itemized list included a partner who wants to live "in the wild with me, kind of a Brokeback Mountain kind of thing." **Nicholas** prefers pets to children: "I never really liked little kids. I'm okay with pets." All important to consider!

It's a Serious Issue

I'll close with **Dean**, who philosophically struggled with our conversation largely because finding sex is easier for him than maintaining a relationship.

★ ★

I don't believe in love per se. Love is an unbreakable force with no control over and I don't believe in that . . . Hard for me to feel feelings. I can cry at sad movies. Hard time to decide if I ever truly loved anyone because of all the expectations . . . It has been a recent realization, and it is okay but now I'm thinking of all my past relationships with people. Like this person, we promised to spend the rest of our lives together, totally happy, never bored, protect each other all the time, want to see each other happy, healthy [but it ended].

If I wasn't in a relationship my sexual activity would be at peak. I like variety. I go out to have a good time, and sex is part of that. There are no rumors about me because I'm open, and people can tell my reputation. When I drink I get slutty and flirt with everyone. If I go to a gay bar I look for the hottest guy there and I take him home. Helps my self-esteem. I've gone to where no one wanted me to go and everyone wants to go.

I have fantasies and crushes on what I can't have . . . I'm not good with romance . . . It is hard to have a good or healthy relationship. I'm fine on my own, and I love sex. Relationship is really great for some. I can be in a relationship and be happy, and when not in a relationship I want to be with somebody, to come home to someone. Yet I want to do what I want.

* *

Although the young men fancied a variety of futures, most have at least a notion that theirs will include a romantic relationship—whether open, closed, or some variation with rules. The man of their dreams should appear by age 30, which would allow him to settle down, marry, and be in a monogamous relationship. I doubt that in these expectations they vary much from straight guys.

For the doubters, who have reservations that they deserve love or can maintain a relationship with another man and remain sexually loyal, underneath it all, love and romance with the same man is what they want. For them, now is the time for erotic fun, experimentation, and sexual variety, and tomorrow will be the time for romance, intimacy, and security. How the two will actually play out developmentally mystified many. With embarrassed laughs, more than one proposed that the ideal future romantic relationship would be sexually open for him but closed for his partner. For how that arrangement actually works out, I would refer them to the divorce rate among straight men.

After I'd read the interview transcripts multiple times, two observations struck me. First, most young gay men currently desire the near singularity of a *soul mate*. Whether a young man feels he deserves one, believes he can ever find one, or believes such men even exist, in his ideal world he'd have one. Second, rather ironically, each young man seems convinced that he's the only gay man alive who wants a soul mate! If only these "exceptions" could find each other . . .

Being Young and Gay in America

Butters: "Now you know my terrible secret!" Stan: "You're gay?
I don't mind you're gay. That's okay with me."

(SOUTH PARK, 2002)

I don't see Frankie's sexual orientation at all—it doesn't define
him. He's a great person. (ZACH RANCE, BIG BROTHER 16)

My final question, "If there were a magical pill that would make you straight, would you take it?" evoked deeply opinionated views over a range of topics. Perhaps sensing that the interview was coming to a close, most of the young men seized the opportunity to express final thoughts about gay life and their fellow millennial gays. I listened and recorded. What most distressed them were *flamboyant gays*, *queer gays*, and *sex-crazed gays*. In addition, if the young man was "straight acting," he was angry with the assumption that *gay jocks* have an easy life being gay and fitting in with mainstream society. First, I'll begin with their near universal conviction. With few exceptions, these young men believed that those of their generation have accepted their sexuality.

Acceptance

We're familiar with reports of nonstop, vicious, and at times life-taking violence that gay youths face, especially at school. Recent white papers from gay and government organizations concur: gay youths report feeling unsafe at school, largely because they receive verbal harassment, threats, and physical abuse from peers, teachers, and school administrators alike. A careful read of these official policy statements reveals that although these events do happen, the vast majority of the harassment that gays receive is minor and is usually unrelated to sexuality per se—that is, it's the type that youths of any sexuality collect simply because they bother to exist. He is too heavy, too skinny, or too short; he has the wrong skin color or religion or social class; he doesn't dress right or has an unpleasant odor or personality; he doesn't act like a typical guy, is too annoying, or is just plain weird. If there's bullying, it's from a small number of peers, usually one or two guys acting in concert who are ready to attack others regardless of sexuality.

Having heard these reports on social media, the young men assumed that their schools were the rare exceptions. On occasion one of the young men would witness friendly bantering among straight youths ("That's so gay!") or would observe outright ridicule of a "feminine" male classmate. Nearly all claimed that their high schools were safe places to be gay, though this was less true in some communities (rural, conservative, religious) and locations within the school (buses, gyms, lunchrooms). Coming out seldom resulted in harassment and rejection. More commonly they received responses such as "great," "awesome," and "duh." Anyone uncomfortable with same-sex sexuality knew it wasn't cool to be overtly homophobic and kept his mouth shut and walked away. Middle school was worse, of course, but that was true regardless of the characteristic bullies targeted.

These young men belong to the "nice generation," reflected in their confidence, connectedness, community orientation, and openness to change. These characteristics have been echoed in nearly every public poll comparing millennials with their parents' generation, who frequently expressed outrage with gay issues. This held across many facets of modern life.

- More gay and trans individuals are now represented on broadcast, cable, and streaming shows—up to 4 percent on prime-time broadcasts.
- Although most Americans now say it's "okay" for a professional sports team to have gay athletes, those under 30 are less bothered if an athlete is shown kissing his boyfriend.
- Millennials believe gay sex is more morally acceptable than casual sex between two heterosexuals who have no intent of forming a relationship.
- Spectrum Clubs have been established at U.S. military academies. Gay service members now talk openly with their straight friends about their boyfriends.
- A prominent comic book superhero character, Iceman, recently "cometh out," following a long line of comic book characters. The publishers reported that displaying sexual and gender diversity has improved the sales of comics.
- Gay characters on Broadway are routine, and they are distinctive for what they seldom contain—no cowering in the closet, no threat of AIDS, and no self-loathing related to sexuality.
- *Out Magazine* named President Obama its gay Ally of the Year for 2015, citing his support for marriage equality, repeal of don't ask don't tell, prohibition of federal worker discrimination, expansion of hate crimes legislation, and promotion of gays in the military. The president felt honored: "I was proud to say love is love."

As a closeted teenager, baby boomer playwright Mark Gerrard considered the most interesting thing about himself was being gay, and he lamented losing that outsider, "special" status among today's generation. He's right: for the nice generation, being gay no longer means living on the outside.

- Jacob, a straight high school junior in Las Vegas, on realizing his gay best friend didn't have a date to the prom, reached a creative resolution—they'd go together, as dates.
- In Carmel, New York, high school seniors Dylan and Bradley were voted "Cutest Couple."

Now you say, "That's great, but I want to join a college fraternity—that bastion for (presumably) wealthy, politically conservative, white, and straight young men." You're in luck because the *bond of brotherhood* has been extended to openly gay youths as well, whether the fraternity is oriented toward Jews ("Homophobia Isn't Kosher" read one sign) or blacks (where progress is slower but evident), or is located in the South. Whereas fraternities once admitted gay youths unknowingly, now "no one cares." In a Kansas fraternity, one straight brother said of his fellow gay brother, "It wasn't his defining factor. He was just a person like everybody else in the fraternity." Reports of fraternity guys bringing their male dates to spring formals are no longer news. Kansan Zach George should have talked to Villanova swimmer Ryan Murtha about calling a coming-out meeting. George had expected the worst, but he received the same kind of acceptance Ryan had reported; one fraternity brother joked, "OK, can we watch football now?" Everyone laughed, including Zach, who promptly went to his room and cried tears of joy.

Still, you might wonder why you would want to join a fraternity. You would have many of the same reasons as the straight guys, such as forming lifetime bonds, as well as reasons unique to you, as explained by the writer of "10 Ways Being Gay in a Fraternity Is Awesome." Fraternities offer lots of eye candy, protective wingmen, trusted confidantes, in-house fashion gurus, popularity among the girls, and male bonding. Plus, you get to become an educator on all things gay: What's gaydar? What's a bear? Doesn't it hurt?

If you were to announce your gayness over the PA system (as Ellen DeGeneres's sitcom character did) or indulge in public displays of affection in the school hallways (as *Glee*'s Kurt and Blaine did), would anyone really care? When another guy dared to intimidate **Tyler**, his friends took revenge on the perpetrator. Rumors about sexuality can garner teasing, but few gay youths are targets of vicious bullying. Here's a typical report of gay bantering.

★ ★

People joked about me being gay and I did as well. It never felt harassing or attacking, but joking, fun. Never have been harassed. In this environment being different was embraced. It was not tolerated at my school, to be teased or harassed because of being gay, and no one would think of doing it. There was teasing in middle school but not serious. High school, not an issue.

★ ★

The one young man I interviewed who was most frequently bullied in school attributed it not to his sexuality but "because I was the class clown, obnoxious, and depressed." When he came out in his rural, working-class school, his peers reacted positively except for two ex-friends who called him a "faggot." Did he feel unsafe? No, he and his boyfriend openly dated and were voted by his senior class as *cutest couple* with 90 percent of the vote. "We never hid it, and we kissed and held hands in school." The bigger problem was adults. "We were not in the yearbook. The school said they were okay with it but didn't want it to happen because of parents and the repercussions."

To their credit, adults are coming around. David Denson, age 20, who is a major league baseball prospect, "bawdy" hip-hop dancer, and singer (with a Sam Smith-type voice), came out to his mother his senior year of high school. "I love my son dearly," his mother said, "and I love him unconditionally." This year, he also gained the unconditional support of his Baptist father ("If this is how you feel, I'm going to always love you. That's my son. I'm backing him 100 percent"), as well as his baseball teammates.

In his e-mail to me, Adrian contended he hadn't been bullied in his urban high school for two reasons.

★ ★

I have, surprisingly even to myself, not faced any major bulling or victimization. I believe this is for two reasons. Firstly, I am Latino and believe that the Latino community is more accepting of homosexuals than any other race because of their strong ties to family. Secondly, because I do not act "typically gay." I am not very feminine. Although I do not do sports or video games, other than that I act as a "straight" man. I do not have, nor pretend to have a voice higher than my own. I am not obsessed with fashion nor any female idol as some gay teen/men are. For this reason, people do not generally think I am gay, so I have never been targeted for that reason. And for this same reason I am not considered as "the gay kid" among my friends. I hope this has been helpful. I tried to speak as honestly as possible.

* *

The Flamboyant Gay

The stereotype that elicited the most voracious negativity from the gay young men I interviewed was the "super femmy gay." Their objections were both political and personal. Politically, they believed that "sissy" behavior sheds a negative light on all gays and thus sets back gay normalization and acceptance. Few want to be personally associated with them, as the following quotes vividly demonstrate.

- "I don't get along with them. I don't enjoy their cattiness and the bickering and the drama."
- "Bother me. Get on my nerves, bitchy, picky."
- "Makes me want to be more masculine, more butching it up."
- "Flamboyant, but not me, but makes us look bad. Why they have to be that way?"
- "OK, don't flaunt it. It's stupid. If just gay then be it."

The message they were sending? Tone it down—the vocal inflections, tight jeans, smirks, hand gestures, show tunes, and cattiness. We are boys, not girls, leading a boy's life. Be considerate of the image created. *Femme models* are not what the youths wrestling with coming out need to see.

Several of the feminine youths insisted those most vocally negative toward them were just closeted, straight-acting gay youths with a masculinity to defend. However, the interviews cast a much wider net that filled with those who were most aghast, at times even angry with glitzy, extravagant displays: the gay youths who are just slightly less flamboyant but definitely on the feminine side themselves. Perhaps such youths have most suffered the consequences of not being sufficiently masculine.

The assumptions here are twofold: one, these expressions are under self-control, and, two, they should be suppressed. No one spoke about the first issue, but several defended the inherent right of every teenager to freely express his gender identity. They believed that boys who act girly are our brothers and should not be harassed, although they also recommended the transgressions should be confined to private venues. But doesn't that assume they're under conscious control?

It is true that gay youths are, *on average*, more feminine than straight youths. Gay youths are rated and rate themselves as high on gender nonconformity—the degree to which a boy has the behaviors, expressions, characteristics, and interests of girls. This is true whether he is an infant, toddler, child, adolescent, or adult and is based on the direct observation of his behavior, family home videos, and survey questionnaires. It's the way he walks or talks, expresses his emotions, or prefers particular occupational or recreational interests.

Exceptions, of course exist, including **Derek**, **Asher**, and **Dean** who are as masculine as any straight man. Other young men appeared only slightly gender atypical—perhaps not so much feminine as not masculine or as feminized in a particular area of their lives. Perhaps he's masculine, yet an architecture major. He's masculine facially but not in his hand movements. He's athletic but interpersonally sensitive.

The objects of this gender derision are never particularly happy with the prejudice meted out on them by their brethren. To fully accept themselves they must incorporate their authentic gender expressions with their sexualities. One young man gained a sense of power and self-acceptance through his femininity. He'd grown up in an impoverished industrial community, and he wore cowboy boots, a cowboy hat, and a cowboy moustache to our interview.

★ ★

As a child I'd play with prissy, pretty things. When I couldn't I made a really mad face because I was angry. I could tell I was supposed to feel weird, that it was wrong playing with beads, dresses and not boy toys. I'd play with the girls. Elementary school was the worse time. Oh yes! I was a very feminine boy. In junior high I knew I was gay. I did not respond and it worked out well, and people stopped teasing me in a joking way. Because I was good at art, which was a shield, and I was popular because of that, they left me alone. In senior high were rumors I was gay, but lots stopped immediately when I came out. They said, "He's nice, we can talk to him." So not picked on. It was a "wow" factor I had. It's a power I have over people.

★ ★

Similar to others, he was teased because of his femininity, not his gayness, and it happened more as a child than as an adolescent. Although he loves his femininity, he knows the score: "In a world of effeminate gays, the masculine gays are most desired."

Sure, the gay jock might desire me as a sex partner, but will he love me tomorrow? If he wants me as a bottom, will he want me as a romantic partner? Clearly, these long-standing conflicts within the gay community have not been resolved by the current generation of young men.

Gender nonconforming young men adapt. One claimed he has great fashion taste and freely comments on the physical appearance of his fraternity brothers when they "dress like turds with their sweatpants and jock jerseys, their hair is a mess, or if clothes don't match." Another doesn't appreciate motorcycles, sports, or anything mechanical—or show tunes. However, "I love to gossip about Kelly Clarkson and Brittany Spears. Guess I'm kinda gay."

The Gay Queer

Overlapping the gender-expression flap was the animosity directed at the gay queer—the radical politico who's visible on every campus and in the media. Several young men uttered profound dismay that the *troubled gay queer* is the image of gayness represented in classroom discussions and public discourse. Yet they also admitted that it was these same queers who planned, directed, and managed the official gay events on campus, stocked the student leadership at the gay resource center (which can include various subgroups of sexual and gender minorities represented by the initials LGBTIQQAAFH2UCPPTTO), and populated the organizations and group meetings. They were contrasted with, as one bluntly asserted, the "90 percent who have our shit together. Being gay is not all just about rainbows." As a result, many would never be caught dead at gay political rallies or meetings, with one exception—the initial reception, which was attended by hundreds angling for a chance to meet the new gays on campus. The organizational half-life of this first audience is usually one week or less.

Even if he politically agrees with a particular stance advocated by queer youths, he resents their techniques (shouting, die-ins, kiss-ins) and appearance (feathers, nudity, rainbow everything). His non-queer priorities are gay-friendly dinner parties, social dances, fraternity and athletic events, marriage equality, children, not making a big to-do or display of sexuality, and accommodating mainstream culture. The young men I interviewed just wanted to go about their business being a student, socializing with friends, and looking for romance: "I don't want to incur their displeasure, but I don't associate with LGBs because they are dealing with things I did in middle school. I want to be supportive, but I just don't go to any of their things." In their own ways, perhaps each contingent advances the well-being of gay youths. I have little optimism that young gay men, miles apart in their lifestyles, will find much common political ground—similar to their straight brothers who also don't agree on everything.

The Gay Slut

Another issue that drew wrath was the perception of gays as *sex maniacs* who crave hookups with anonymous others and are obsessed with sex apps. Will the stereotype rub off on everyone?

- "I'm judgmental of the group as a whole. Majority are sex crazed. It's only the physical that's so important to them. The slutty stereotypes are true."
- "Scares me at times, the stereotypes I don't want to be associated with like having AIDS."
- "I don't like some of gay culture and it frightens me, like the promiscuous aspect. Not because they're gay but the way they act, and I don't want to be associated with that."
- "I didn't want to be ostracized with sex depravity, and I thought that it would subject me to the possibilities of being ostracized."

Those who desired romance over sex frequently had these views. They would rather find their soul mate than their next sex partner. They weren't alone—in fact, they were in the majority. And those who were chalking up the numbers of their conquests often intend to change once Mr. Right comes along. It's worth noting that several of the high rollers in number of sex partners were struggling with issues of impulsiveness and obsessive compulsive disorder.

The Gay Athlete

Not fully appreciated by many of the young men were the struggles faced by the straight-acting gay boys. If they stayed closeted, their straight peers would continue to admire their athleticism and masculinity. If they were to come out, they feared that they'd lose their privileged status. This might be the primary basis for the antigay stance of some of the masculine gay boys—they don't want to be associated with the weakness and unmanliness that they believe their straight friends so abhor.

This was Scott Heggart's view before he came out. A six-foot, four-inch high school sports star in football, basketball, softball, and hockey, Scott had experienced the machismo of sports from the time he could walk, and the worst thing a boy could hear was "fag" or "homo." With his growing awareness of his same-sex sexuality, "I'd started to understand who I was, what it meant. And if I was being true to myself, I probably would have come out in grade 6, but I didn't want to be that person."

Scott was gripped by a downward spiral of self-loathing, made worse in his world of masculinity and jocks. From his family's perspective, their "happy boy" turned sour and withdrawn. Finally, 15-year-old Scott reached out to his family, and, as he expected, they supported him. His older brother assured him, "I still love you. I still consider you my best friend." His father advised, "If you loved your child before you found out they were gay, that shouldn't change."

Telling his teammates, however, was another matter. To cope, Scott posted videos anonymously of "an openly gay jock" on his YouTube channel. He discovered that he had underestimated his straight teammates. A fellow hockey player wrote, "What you did man, it takes a lot of courage and I'm proud of you. And I've been talking to a lot of people and they all say the same thing." Scott's inbox was filled with supportive comments—"I wouldn't have had the balls to do that"—and apologies for hate speech. Scott eventually attended the high school prom with his boyfriend Brock.

To enhance a policy of "zero tolerance for the hurtful, chronic assaults against gay athletes, imagined and real," a campaign exists to help masculine, athletic gay teenagers accept themselves for who they are. Two of these are the "You Can Play Project," founded by professional athletes, and "Athlete Ally," founded to help straight allies change athletic culture by calling attention to the homophobic language and demeaning humor in sports.

Where are the comparable websites for the unabashedly sissy boys who are coping with their femininity? I've searched and asked others, and I haven't found any yet. They should exist.

The Magical Pill

If you believe the traditional view of a young gay life as living hell with rampant levels of internalized homophobia due to bullying, discrimination, and gay stereotypes, you'd expect the typical response to whether to take the magic straight pill to be a resounding, "Hell yes! Give me the magic pill already! Do you have it with you?" Or they should rush to the nearest pharmacy to buy it. Instead, the typical conversation was more akin to:

No, because it wouldn't be me.

R: *Wouldn't your life be better?*

Yeah, but I like being gay.

In early adolescence the teens might have been tempted by such a pill, but fewer would have been during high school, and nearly none are currently interested as young adults. All in all, the imagined pill dissolves without consumption.

Why not take the pill, especially after a young man has realized he's gay, which is seldom the best news he'll receive on that fateful day when he stops playing head games with himself? The complications being gay would be deleted if he were straight, dating a woman, and playing hockey.

- "I wanted to be like other people, to be similar to them and not diverge off from what they were doing. I didn't want to be different, and no one was out in my high school."

- "I sometimes wished I could just hang with guys and not worry about boundaries because of my homosexuality. I would love to just be assimilated with everyone else and not stand out."

- "Being gay ruined the image of perfection of myself. It'd be so wonderful if I'd get married, and it'd be the perfect package. Being gay just didn't fit my plan."

But then, wouldn't any boy, regardless of his sexuality, who is "out of the ordinary" because of his skin color, social class, appearance, disability, or personality say the same thing? The young man who said he'd have taken the pill "for the sake of my teenage self" is similar to many straight youths growing up in America who are concerned about fitting in. There are bigger issues here than same-sex sexuality.

However—and it's a *big however*—even if being a gay adolescent isn't the most prudent thing to be, most believe it makes them unique, with an internal life they'd like to keep:

- "Love who I am now and can't see that changing."
- "I wouldn't have all the things that I like about myself."
- "I wouldn't change because I love having sex with guys, but that's not a good answer."

No, that's a great answer.

Of course, the moments exist when you would love to pass and not be reminded of potential battles. The overwhelming sentiment is that it isn't about changing themselves, but changing society:

- "I like being attracted to guys, but it is an extra challenge. I'm obviously living in a society, and I want to be normal and have fewer hardships. I strive to be normal, but wouldn't take a magical pill."
- "It was hard to grow up homosexual, hard to be different, but it was exciting. I wished the social standards were different, not me."

The current seismic cultural shift has pleased many—professional athletes coming out, marriage equality, moral acceptance of homosexuality, and the normalization of being gay. Even the one young man I interviewed who attempted suicide now sees things differently. "I did not wish being gay in high school. It's not a choice, but back then I would have taken the pill if I could have but now, no." Two gay teachers supported him at the time, and he proudly declared, "I don't want to change. I am the way I am, and I embrace it." He was the leader of his college's LGBT student center, which was where I interviewed him.

Let Me Be Me

"I am the way I am, and I embrace it" is the mantra of the young gay man in this millennial generation. His life isn't fraught with rejection, harassment, isolation, wild sex, sexual diseases, or lovelessness. He's not naïve. It's an imperfect world, and far too many are willing to make his life difficult because he dares to differ from the norm. He's smart, popular, athletic, funny, creative, and adored by friends and family. This is true when he's a child, an adolescent, and now, especially, as a young adult. He's healthy, patriotic, rebellious, romantic, and would love for America to wake up to the reality of his life. Not surprisingly, he would never want to be anything else. He knows not all gay youths share this view, and he'd like to change that.

It's about things being better, not in the future but right now. If the future gets better (which he assumes it will), awesome. It's society not him that should take the magic pill and get with the program of sexual and gender diversity. When one young man and his parents visited New York City he was initially embarrassed because "we kept seeing these very flamboyant gays." Then he recalled what he learned in his high school Gay Straight Alliance. "I really, really love gay people and their differences. I celebrate and appreciate sexual diversity."

That said, the young men I interviewed are not primarily about gay pride, celebration, or even visibility. Most expressed some version of wishing the entire *gay thing* would just disappear so that he could be himself. Being gay shouldn't be *such a big deal*.

- "I'm fine with it. I don't necessarily need to be gay, just happy with whatever. My sexuality is a part of me and not my defining self. Has shaped who I am and wanting to be around those who accept me. It's hard but just a part of me. It's so politically contentious, and I'd like it to be less so."
- "I shouldn't be known by my sexuality."
- "Wouldn't change it. Wish it hadn't made me different or so hard to be me. Heterosexuals are okay with it and genuinely interested in my life."
- "It is unappealing to be simply defined. Not because it is bad or will hurt my career, it's just not the first thing that I want people to know about me."
- "I don't say, 'Hi, I'm gay and my name is . . .' That's not me. It's not that I was going to speak about it publicly. Being gay was not my defining characteristic."
- "Being gay is a lot, but I wished it was less important in my life. It divides people into groups. I wish there was more of a gradient. Then it would less define me. I don't scream it, but I don't hide it."

Many are doing just fine and have nothing to prove. My only argument with these young men is that not all gay youths are where they are, especially those who suffer from poverty, broken homes, and physical/mental health problems. At times, those young men might want to scream.

The young men live at a time that has increasingly normalized gayness. As I finish this book I read about a 10-year-old who openly identified as gay three years ago. When a classmate badgered him, Amelia, his mother, wrote about him on her blog:

★ ★

This time the gay kid, my gay kid, got pissed. He fought back. And the bully ran away. Then the gay kid, my gay kid, went home and talked to his parents about it. And you know what? I'm glad he got angry. That's a damn sight better than ashamed. He should be angry, because no one has the right to tell my kid that something he is is wrong. There should be no place for shame, because he has nothing to be ashamed of.

★ ★

As I'm editing the book, I received an e-mail from a 16-year-old who wanted advice not about being gay, coming out, or bullying but about his fifteen-month relationship with his boyfriend. Yes, they cuddle while in school, but is this infatuation or romantic love? This could just as well have been written by a straight boy about his new girlfriend.

Regardless of their sexuality, an increasing number of gay youths and those who love them agree that it's not okay to deny sexuality, to reject sexuality, or to compartmentalize sexuality. And with this I'll turn it over to a straight guy, Zach Rance, who was reflecting on his relationship with Frankie Grande (together, "Zankie") on the television show *Big Brother 16*.

★ ★

One thing I think that should definitely be on record is that it doesn't matter if someone's gay or straight. It doesn't matter. People don't need to judge anyone from their sexual orientation, and we need to move on from that. Everyone in the world. It doesn't matter if you're gay or straight, it doesn't matter what you wear, it doesn't matter what you look like, we're all people in the world, and we all have feelings. I think that's the main thing to me. I don't see Frankie's sexual orientation at all—it doesn't define him. He's a great person. He's a great human being. He's extremely smart, he's extremely funny, and to me that's all that matters. He's a very kind person. I just want that to go on record—sexual orientation doesn't matter, and the whole world needs to move on. That's just what we need to do.

★ ★

Postscript: Anthony's Return

I harbor both a fear and excitement to learn more about what it means to be gay in this world and most importantly to learn more about myself—to sustain confidence and pride in myself.

(ANTHONY, AGE 20)

Anthony is going abroad for a semester in an antigay country. Being gay in a new place will be far more challenging for him than it was in his high school and college. The day before he left, I asked whether he had any final reflections or advice for you, my readers. Of course! He wrote an essay regarding coming out, going to a gay bar, and the end of his romantic relationship with Patrick. Here, I quote liberally from his e-mails.

Coming Out

Over the summer **Anthony**'s family paid a visit to their ancestral home in Assisi, Italy. Now a young adult, Anthony engaged his relatives in new and deeper conversations.

* *

I was unaware if any of my younger cousins knew if I was gay or not. Not that I was afraid, but unaware if it needed to be addressed. My aunt admitted to me that she had a discussion with her twelve-year-old son who had later claimed that after seeing me again I did not "seem gay." She took the opportunity to emphasize the point that it is not a characteristic that ultimately defines.

I began thinking aloud at how I had never told any of my extended family. After coming out to my mom, my one request was that she didn't tell anybody, particularly my dad. I had not put it together until then, but through speaking I pieced together that she had apparently reached out to every-body to tell them—from my aunts, uncles, and even my Tea Party grandmother. I began to feel heated and a bit be-trayed, and I could sense the tension I had left in the minivan.

★ ★

That night Anthony and his sister shared drinks, sandwiches, and stories about how their mother had disclosed their "secret lives" without consent. His sister had a cautious perspective—they didn't know or appreciate what their mother had gone through when Anthony came out to her. Yet why would she have gone against his express wishes?

★ ★

I found some peace in sharing this moment and solidarity with my sister, and it was a moment that could not have come without exposing our selves and our secrets to one an-other. There is no textbook way to come out, and I admit to my unusually fortunate circumstances of acceptance by my family and peers. And yet, I have always held onto a strong fear of others knowing this fact and others about me before I can reveal it myself.

Coming out should definitely be child focused, but it cer-tainly affects parents and families regardless of the level of acceptance. What I do know is that she said she told my dad that night and that they cried together, she told me it was for a fear that my life would have to be harder because I am gay. I can assume it was a secret that she couldn't stand weighing on her and sought out my dad for guidance.

Would I advise another parent to do the same thing? Most likely not given the circumstances of how accepting others in the extended family would have been. Mine is pretty conservative, but all was well.

I think there is a pace to coming out, telling a few close friends and family first. I remember shaking when telling my first few friends, but with each acceptance it got easier and I felt empowered. I think that this is a positive experience that could have been shared between my extended family and I, or avoided if I did not feel comfortable with that information being disclosed to somebody in particular. We get along very well, and she has told me she would never judge, but my life could have continued on without my grandma ever knowing.

* *

As Anthony reflected on his disclosure, he recalled his inner strength when his mother asked whether he was sure it wasn't just a phase. Here Anthony offered clear advice to parents.

* *

When I put my foot down that it wasn't something to be questioned she was upset that I was being "righteous" or bold about my response. In my head, it was something that I had questioned, cried, prayed, and deliberated so much about before telling her that I wasn't ready or willing to have somebody else question it for me. What I'm trying to say here is that coming out was a pivotal moment in my life, and I assume it was for my mother as well—we both had our respective emotions and reactions.

That being said, my motto in life is usually "no rash decisions." If you think this is a point of contention, try bringing it up to your child as they probably don't see the same justification or experience the same emotions about keeping it a secret. The emotion they're probably experiencing the most is fear, and exposing this secret to others would be exploiting this fear.

My advice would be to let it remain at their pace, as I tailored the way I came out to people in different ways and I assume your child would appreciate the dignity of explaining it themselves. I'm not trying to downplay parents' emotions in this, but realize this is one of those moments where you need to prioritize the child. I think you can seek guidance from family or friends at a smaller scale with those that would not have reacted negatively. In the ideal scenario, an offer to be present in a room with the child while they come out to another family member could open a discussion and a source of comfort. I don't think anybody should be rushed into coming out, and I have many friends still in the process throughout college who haven't told their parents. Each individual has his or her pace, and it should be respected.

★　★

Good reasons exist to come out and expose yourself, and Anthony nailed them—to receive the acceptance and understanding that we all need and to change others. "Many of my friends who I told in middle school told me that their opinions on gay people had changed after I came out to them, as they realized that I was still 'me.'"

Coming out is private, but also universal. "Generations and opinions are being bridged and challenged when faced with personal examples to combat preconceptions. It is a task and certainly a burden, but I still hold onto moments when friends of family have admitted their opinions have changed or extended to me their acceptance and understanding."

Going to a Gay Bar

Anthony also wrote about visiting his first gay bar.

★ ★

I am really not the expert, and I only went once (still not 21). From what I remember at the club, there were wall-to-wall shirtless or scantily clad guys lined like sardines (should I have gone for a more appealing metaphor? Whoops), it was a lot of fun and our group of friends danced with each other. I remember being intimidated at first but mostly excited, being with a group of friends definitely gave me a sort of communal confidence that I was able to have fun and sing along to Beyoncé with the rest of the boys.

My humble advice would be first, to go with a group of friends to have a shared experience, a support system, and always somebody to dance with. It's an intimidating experience, but in these situations I say "go for yourself," without the expectation of meeting somebody there.

★ ★

Anthony's advice is to go see for yourself because you have an opportunity for anonymity and freedom to freely express yourself in a safe space—and have lots of fun with friends.

The Love of His Life

Nearly every young man wants a *Patrick*, something **Anthony** is now without. How do you know if this is your once and forever shining prince, your soul mate? I am slightly abbreviating his extended story.

★ ★

In the beginning of Patrick and my relationship I was 16, and had just begun growing out of my self-proclaimed "ugly duckling phase," while my self-confidence and maturity lagged a bit behind. What began as disbelief that a guy I had found myself so attracted to could have any interest in me became a relationship where I constantly compared myself to his past or our older, more muscular mutual friends.

I admired him for his confidence, his ease in navigating changing social situations, and his ability to take the role as a leader in our group of friends in planning or navigating— characteristics I idealized and wanted to emulate. Through our relationship we shared and guided each other through profound growth and understanding of our sexuality and ourselves. It took some road bumps and fine-tuning, but most importantly channels of open communication and unconditional understanding.

We became a team, and he introduced me to our quirky, expressive, and queer group of friends . . . who had found some solidarity with others who did not fit into the world of school uniforms and conservative heterosexual culture. These are people who helped me shed insecurities and gain confidence in my body and myself with their example of free expression and true pride in being gay . . . These are people I still keep in contact with and can share all of the high and lows of navigating life as a gay teenager and now young adult.

With the ease of expressing myself to this group, I sought out a college that I knew would be a very accepting environment based on sexuality so that I could continue living my life this way. After having already completed a year of long distance with Patrick being a year older, we were confident that we could continue making it work . . . We relived a sad departure week in and week out.

Towards the end of the year, I began to realize that I had been removing myself from my college environment and had passed up on more meaningful connections on weekends with my friends at school. I felt attached to my phone and communication during each night out, and experienced difficulties being satisfied with myself or being alone. After spending a final summer together, we both returned to school and I realized that my life at home and life at school had irreconcilable differences. I wanted to seize the short time I had at college to experience it more fully.

I broke it off and it was rough, I left it with a message that I believed we could stay friends, as no fight or disagreement had set off its resolution.

* *

The breakup trajectory was set in motion by a critical decision, familiar to young couples regardless of their sexuality: whether to be sexually monogamous. Much larger issues, however, were clearly at work.

* *

Patrick approached me with the thought of having a threesome with the friend who was also visiting. I laughed it off, as it had been something previously discussed at the beginning of our relationship as something I would not be comfortable doing—mostly based on self-confidence and a worry of feeling left out . . . The night ended with a bit of a fight and us sleeping on opposite sides of a blowup mattress, which wouldn't have been too conducive to a threesome anyway.

We took some time after this and met up a few days later to discuss what had gone on . . . He apologized to me for pushing and not thinking along the same lines, but wished I had been more open about why I felt that way so the fight wouldn't have happened in the first place. I brought up a lot of fears about going through college and breaking up at the end of the day, missing experiences along the way. We loved each other, but we stated that objectively the fight brought into question how we felt about continuing being in a very committed relationship, or if we should consider not being exclusive or break up . . . There was a bit of off and on between us though we ultimately stayed together over the summer and feeling like there were irreconcilable differences.

Navigating single life at college became another challenge. My college was saturated with a hookup culture that not often sustained itself past a first or second night—a world I was completely foreign to. I saw the ups and downs around me, and stuck to my guns with the belief that there were meaningful connections to be made even if I kept it at my own pace. I found some disappointment that despite seeking out such an inclusive and open environment, I failed to find anybody I truly clicked with.

I held my own and remained there for him as he had done for me in the beginning of our relationship. And within a few months, he apologized to me and showed his appreciation for my patience and toleration of his feelings. I'm happy to say we remain friends today.

Although things didn't work out between Patrick and I, I can confidently say that I loved him until the day I didn't. Weird phrase, I admit, but the idea is that even through struggles it was an incredibly fulfilling relationship while we were together. After observing my long-distance relationship and those of my friends, some who have stuck and others that have failed, is that you need to be able to live your life for you. Patrick was often my crutch when it came to going out or dealing with the emotions of starting a new school. It was incredibly helpful, but I came to some of my more profound growth when I faced things on my own.

* *

Achieving profound growth once independent but also with Patrick was a tricky balance to negotiate. It can be difficult to know when to stay in a relationship and when it's best to go your own way.

* *

Communication is key, but be able and confident to spend a day or weekend night by yourself. Being attached to my cell phone was a big deterrent from experiencing things around me, and I wish I had taken more opportunities to live in the moment. If you're on the fence about it my honest advice would be to break it off while you are still on good terms. I speak from experience so I have a bias, but a big part of the reason I did it when I did was that I didn't want it to end with a fight or give a reason for us to not continue communicating. A transition to friendship is easier than a transition from being an "enemy." I'm not trying to scare anybody out of this. It's best to be realistic. Patrick and I were long distance for 2 years, and I don't regret it at all.

* *

Anthony regretted not breaking up in person, and the timing was bad as he was starting classes and transitioning back into "separate lives while dealing with the heartbreak." And there was the guilt. "I knew it was harder for him than me, and I had to deal with that guilt on top of it."

As Anthony moves toward the future, he'll never forget Patrick, who'll always be a part of him.

* *

I am a big believer that the goal of a relationship should be to learn from one another. Patrick taught me so much during our relationship, and I wouldn't have had the confidence, friendships, or affinity for politics or reading the newspaper that I do now. That being said, after spending almost 3 years together with 2 of them over an hour away I felt like we have taught each other what we could. There are meaningful connections to be made, and I think [getting back together] would feel like too much of a step back or tied to too much history.

* *

Will Anthony find another Patrick? The short answer is sure, but he'll be different. Over the summer he connected with a guy from an entirely different religion, region, and social class with a vastly different gay history. Anthony was "impressed by his openness and confidence against a world that defined him by his sexuality." This young man had much to teach Anthony.

* *

I had sheltered myself from the real world and those who may disagree with me. I had found my first meaningful connection since Patrick with a guy quite unlike myself, and thus we had more to teach one another. At one point he asked me if I ever wished that I were straight, and I answered without too much thought that I had stopped thinking of being gay as a disadvantage years ago. With more reflection, I realized the naivety in my response. I am very proud to be openly gay, but realized I was not contributing to progress by surrounding myself with those who felt the same way as

I did. He realized each time he wished he wasn't gay he was really wishing for the acceptance of others instead of accepting himself. We talked about how it had provided us with insight on what it means to be a minority in the U.S. and the solidarity we had been able to find with other marginalized groups or for greater causes of LGBTQ equality.

After a few days of hanging out we definitely expressed to one another that we were hitting it off and really enjoyed each other's company, and we both didn't know how to feel realizing our time would be cut short and split thousands of miles away. In my head I really feel like he's the first guy I clicked with so seamlessly since Patrick, and it was recent so I have been thinking about him . . . He is also, in my opinion, the most attractive person who has ever had any interest in me, which is all exciting, flattering, and intimidating at the same time . . .

I was headed to a semester abroad, where being gay is not deemed appropriate based on culture and religious beliefs. I do not expect to be a channel for acceptance by example, but I harbor both a fear and excitement to learn more about what it means to be gay in this world and most importantly to learn more about myself—to sustain confidence and pride in myself in the face of adversity . . . I wanted to go on this abroad trip to live my life for myself and not determine self-worth based on a relationship with another guy, and thus I'm not trying to hold him back from living his own life or getting too caught up in my thoughts to miss out on my own.

* *

As he navigates his way through the world, Anthony is gracious "for those before me who had suffered and fought for progress, and for a hope that those ahead of me will grow up in a more accepting world." Yet far more needs to be done to "align with struggles of marginalized groups in the US . . . I have hope that I will foster meaningful connections and most importantly find those I can share openly with and learn from along the way."

Final Thoughts

After **Anthony**, I have little to add except the following:

You cannot change the direction of your sexual and romantic attractions.

1. Trying to become straight is wasted time and likely to be a source of great pain and suffering.
2. Regardless of your sexuality and gender expression, accept nothing less than your full rights.
3. No matter how weird you feel you are, we're all weird.
4. Live a life worthy of celebration because, indeed, the *gay kids are all right*.

This book fulfills the promise I made to Anthony and the other young men I interviewed to *tell our stories* as we live them, with honesty, humor, and joy.

APPENDIX

NOTES

ACKNOWLEDGMENTS

INDEX

Appendix: Methods

The young men interviewed in this book were participants in one of two research projects. In all respects, the protocol followed the ethics guidelines mandated by my university.

Friends and Lovers

From April 2008 through April 2009, 160 young men across a range of sexualities between the ages of 17 and 27 years (mean: 20.0) volunteered for my "Friends and Lovers" study. The research was advertised as an interview study with young men about their "friends and lovers since you were a child, teenager, and now." With their help we would increase our understanding regarding the sexual development of young men of all sexual orientations from earliest memories to the present time.

Seventy percent identified as Caucasian, with the rest identifying as Asian American (13 percent), African American (7 percent), Latino (6 percent), or Native American (3 percent). Of these young men, 72 percent were university students, and the remainder was enrolled in a local community or commuter college or was working. Their academic majors were widely distributed across the social sciences, biological/life sciences, engineering, and humanities. The most desired career trajectories were, in order, working in finance, marketing, or business; becoming a teacher or professor; working in the medical field; becoming a lawyer or an engineer. Nearly three-quarters reported they were either middle or upper middle class. Two in ten reported that their families were working class or lower middle class. Two-thirds were raised in small or medium-sized towns or suburbs, or in a small city. Nearly one-third grew up in an urban area, and few were from rural/farming communities.

Flyers were posted in freshman and sophomore residence halls and in college cafés; notices were posted in online newsletters and on a fraternity mailing list; and ad cards were distributed by undergraduate research assistants and by participants who gave the ad cards to their friends. Each young man notified the primary investigator (me) that he was interested in participating. Details were sent to the responders regarding the project's purpose along with informed consent forms, the preinterview questionnaire, and the interview times. Each participant was informed that he could return the completed questionnaire or bring a hard copy with him to the interview. The questionnaire consisted of basic demographic data collection: age, education, major, citizenship, ethnicity, social class, community size, and career objectives, and high school and/or college activities, clubs, and organizations.

The interview was held in a private location in an academic building and lasted from 40 to 135 minutes, with an average of 73 minutes. At the beginning of the interview, each participant completed a questionnaire about what percentage of his sexual attractions, sexual interactions (genital contact), infatuations/crushes, sexual fantasies, and romantic relationships was directed to males and females when he was a child, an early adolescent, an adolescent, and currently, and how he anticipated he would be and would like to be in the future. The interviews were not tape-recorded, so the quotations throughout this book (usually with the generic "a young man") are not verbatim but are extremely close to this. I took extensive notes with a shorthand technique that I developed to record nearly every word. I transcribed these notes immediately following the interviews.

Eight of the individuals who volunteered for the study did not respond to further e-mail contact to set up an interview time. Thus, 93 percent of the young men who contacted me completed the research. Of those who were sent the questionnaire, 100 percent returned it, and 100 percent who set up an interview completed it (three did not show at the appointed time but contacted me and rescheduled).

The participants were paid a twenty-dollar incentive for their time. All but one agreed to be contacted in succeeding years for the opportunity of participating in longitudinal follow-up questionnaires, interviews, or experiments.

Of the 160 young men, 27 identified as gay or mostly gay. These included three, **Dean**, **Jeremy**, and **Liam**, whose stories are featured in this book. The others provided comments that are frequently included in the text.

Personality and Sexuality

Dr. Gerulf Rieger, a postdoctoral fellow in my Sex & Gender Lab, and his undergraduate research assistants recruited 229 participants in 2012. Of these, 109 were men between the ages of 18 and 32 (mean: 21.9). The research was broadly advertised as a laboratory-based study investigating issues of sex, gender, and personality. The primary purpose was the assessment of sexual orientation through a new technique, pupil dilation.

At the time, 66 percent of the men were undergraduate college students, and an additional 17 percent had completed their undergraduate education and were working. Others were in graduate school (9 percent), had completed some college and had dropped out (6 percent), or had just finished high school (2 percent). Seventy-five percent identified as Caucasian and the rest as Asian American (12 percent), Latino (5 percent), mixed ethnicity/race (5 percent), or African American (4 percent).

Advertisements for the study were placed on a Facebook page, in several residence halls and fraternities, and on several websites catering to those on athletic teams. To increase recruitment of sexual minorities, a notice was posted on a Craigslist web forum oriented toward sexual minorities. Young men contacted the laboratory by e-mail, and written informed consent was obtained after they arrived at the university laboratory. They participated in the physiological portion of the study and then completed a survey administered online using a Web surveyor tool, which included a seven-point sexual orientation scale identity, ranging from exclusively straight to exclusively gay. One question at the conclusion of the survey asked about their willingness to participate in an hour-long interview to "track your sexual and romantic development from first memories to the present day." All but four agreed to be contacted.

Of the 109 men, forty-eight identified as gay or mostly gay; of these, fourteen scheduled a follow-up interview for an additional incentive of twenty dollars. These included **Anthony**, **Asher**, **David**, **Derek**, **Dion**, **Geoff**, **Jake**, **Jonathan**, **Lenny**, **Nicholas**, **Raj**, **Ted**, and **Tyler**. All names are pseudonyms. One interviewee not included in this book had considerable incomplete information. Informed consent was obtained for tape-recording the interviews. A paid research assistant transcribed the recordings, and these are the source of the quotes in the book. The quotes have been altered only to mask personal identifying details and to delete extraneous information (such as a rant against a political party or an analysis of the participant's mother).

Reflections on Methods

Whether these gay youths look like America in their basic personal and social lives I do not know. It is not my intent to present each as representing anything other than himself. Although the forty young men are diverse in many respects (social class, personality, religion, ethnicity, region), they are not "representative" of young gay men in the United States. Underrepresented are Latino, African American, and Native American young men, and those growing up in large urban areas, with limited education, and with few socioeconomic resources, and who are unwilling to share their personal life with a stranger. Originally I believed young men who were uncomfortable with their sexuality or were not out to others would not participate in this study, but I was wrong on both accounts, as is apparent in the life stories.

NOTES

Tell Our Stories

The views I express in the "rarely suicidal" section are not frequently shared by other gay scholars and political activists. For an excellent discussion of these issues, see T. Waidzunas, "Young, Gay, and Suicidal: Dynamic Nominalism and the Process of Defining a Social Problem with Statistics, *Science, Technology, and Human Values* 37 (2012): 199–225.

For script theory, see J. H. Gagnon and W. Simon, *Sexual Conduct: The Social Sources of Human Sexuality* (Chicago: Aldine, 1973).

My first sexual-minority research is found in R. C. Savin-Williams, *Gay and Lesbian Youth: Expressions of Identity* (New York: Hemisphere, 1990), and data on the lack of differences between gay and straight individuals can be found in *The New Gay Teenager* (Cambridge, MA: Harvard University Press, 2005). Since then I have located other research: B. K. Gorman, J. T. Denney, H. Dowdy, and R. A. Medeiros, "A New Piece of the Puzzle: Sexual Orientation, Gender, and Physical Health Status," *Demography* 52, no. 4 (2015): 1357–1382; R. P. Juster, N. G. Smith, E. Ouellet, S. Sindi, and S. J. Lupiendoi, "Sexual Orientation and Disclosure in Relation to Psychiatric Symptoms, Diurnal Cortisol, and Allostatic Load," *Psychosomatic Medicine* 75 (2013): 103–116; J. Konik and M. Crawford, "Exploring Normative Creativity: Testing the Relationship between Cognitive Flexibility and Sexual Identity," *Sex Roles* 51 (2004): 249–253; P. S. Loosier and P. J. Dittus, "Group Differences in Risk across Three Domains Using an Expanded Measure of Sexual Orientation," *Journal of Primary Prevention* 31 (2010): 261–272; D. Perry, K. Walder, T. Hendler, and S. G. Shamay-Tsoory, "The Gender You Are and the Gender You Like: Sexual Preference and Empathic Neural Responses," *Brain Research* 1534 (2013): 66–75; L. P. Wadsworth and S. A. Hayes-Skelton, "Differences among Lesbian, Gay, Bisexual, and Heterosexual Individuals and Those Who Reported an Other Identity on an Open-Ended

Response on Levels of Social Anxiety," *Psychology of Sexual Orientation and Gender Diversity* 2 (2015): 181–187; M. A. Yule, L. A. Brotto, and B. B. Gorzalka, "Mental Health and Interpersonal Functioning in Self-Identified Asexual Men and Women," *Psychology and Sexuality* 4 (2013): 136–151.

For more on the importance of self-esteem in general, see U. Orth and R. W. Robins, "The Development of Self-Esteem," *Current Directions in Psychological Science* 23 (2014): 381–387.

Ryan Murtha's coming-out talk to his team in quoted in C. Zeigler, "Villanova Swim Team Takes Gay Teammate to Chipotle for His Coming Out Party," *SB Nation: Outsports,* February 4, 2015, www.outsports.com /2015/2/4/7957015/ryan-murtha-gay-swimmer-villanova-chipotle.

Why Am I Gay?

Jenny Graves provides an overview of her ideas about genetics in J. Graves, "How Our Genes Could Make Us Gay or Straight," *Washington Post,* June 4, 2014, www.washingtonpost.com/posteverything/wp/2014/06 /04/the-science-of-sexuality-how-our-genes-make-us-gay-or-straight/. **For two excellent overviews on the biology of sexual orientation,** see G. D. Wilson and Q. Rahman, *Born Gay: The Psychobiology of Sex Orientation* (Chester Springs, PA: Peter Owen, 2005); and S. LeVay, *Gay, Straight, and the Reason Why: The Science of Sexual Orientation,* 2nd ed. (New York: Oxford University Press, 2016).

For a review of the older boy effect, see R. Blanchard, "Review and theory of handedness, birth order, and homosexuality in men," *Laterality: Asymmetries of Body, Brain and Cognition* 13 (2008): 51–70. Blanchard's talk on this topic is available online as R. Blanchard, "How and Why Do Older Brothers Influence Sexual Orientation in Men?" (lecture, Michigan State University, November 2012), www.researchgate.net/publication/254862003 _Blanchard_Michigan_State_University_2012.

For articles that discuss the changes in ex-gay leaders, see I. Lovett, "After 37 Years of Trying to Change People's Sexual Orientation, Group Is to Disband," *New York Times,* June 20, 2013, www.nytimes.com/2013/06 /21/us/group-that-promoted-curing-gays-ceases-operations.html;

and C. M. Wong, "John Smid, Former 'Ex-Gay' Leader, Marries a Man in Oklahoma," *Huffpost Queer Voices,* February 2, 2016, www.huffingtonpost .com/2014/11/19/john-smid-ex-gay-wedding-_n_6186524.html.

First Sexual Memory

For a brief review of the development pathways from first sexual memories to romance, see R. C. Savin-Williams, and K. M. Cohen "Developmental Milestones of Sexual-Minority Youth," *International Review of Psychiatry* 27 (2015): 357–366.

Sex Play

For data on children, see A. Kågesten and R. W. Blum, "Characteristics of Youth Who Report Early Sexual Experiences in Sweden," *Archives of Sexual Behavior* 44, no. 3 (2015): 679–694; I. Larsson and C. G. Svedin, "Sexual Experiences in Childhood: Young Adults' Recollections," *Archives of Sexual Behavior* 31 (2002): 263–273; and W. N. Friedrich, J. Fisher, D. Broughton, M. Houston, and C. R. Shafran, "Normative Sexual Behavior in Children: A Contemporary Sample," *Pediatrics* 101 (1998): E9.

First Crush

For Elaine Hatfield's publications on love, see her bibliography page at www.elainehatfield.com/articles.htm. Included among these publications is an extended passionate scale for children, adolescents, and adults.

For the infatuation scale, see S. J. E. Langeslag, P. Muris, and I. H. A. Franken, "Measuring Romantic Love: Psychometric Properties of the Infatuation and Attachment Scales," *Journal of Sex Research* 50 (2013): 739–747.

The Joy of Puberty

An overview of sexuality in general and puberty in particular can be found in S. LeVay, J. I. Baldwin, and J. D. Baldwin, *Discovering Human Sexuality,* 3rd ed. (Sunderland, MA: Sinauer, 2015).

For more information on relative differences in physical dimensions, see A. F. Bogaert, "Physical Development and Sexual Orientation in Men And Women: An Analysis of NATSAL-2000. *Archives of Sexual Behavior* 39 (2010): 110–116; and A. F. Bogaert and S. Hershberger, "The Relation between Sexual Orientation and Penile Size," *Archives of Sexual Behavior, 28,* (1999): 213–221. **For findings that raise questions about measuring penis dimensions,** see D. Herbenick, M. Reece, V. Schick, and S. A. Sanders, "Erect Penile Length and Circumference Dimensions of 1,661 Sexually Active Men in the United States," *Journal of Sexual Medicine* 11 (2014): 93–101.

A recent review of sex education can be found in L. Josephs, "How Children Learn about Sex: A Cross-Species and Cross-Cultural Analysis," *Archives of Sexual Behavior* 44, no. 4 (2015): 1059–1069. **For data on U.S. sex education in particular,** see R. Klein, "Listen Up, Legislators: People Want Better Sex Education Than What Many States Require," *Huffpost Politics,* April 10, 2015, www.huffingtonpost.com/2015/01/09/sex-ed-yougov -poll_n_6438080.html; R. Klein, "These Maps Show Where Kids in America Get Terrifying Sex Ed," *Huffpost Teen,* April 8, 2014, www.huffingtonpost .com/2014/04/08/sex-education-requirement-maps_n_5111835.html; and A. Temblador, "Why Is LGBT-Inclusive Sex Education Still So Taboo?" *Huffpost Queer Voices,* February 2, 2016, www.huffingtonpost.com/2015/03 /07/lgbt-inclusive-sex-education-_n_6819854.html.

For a discussion of general adolescent health, see L. Steinberg, "How to Improve the Health of American Adolescents," *Perspectives on Psychological Science* 10 (2015): 711–715.

The Good, the Bad, the Porn

Jason Winters's blog discussions of pornography can be found at www.drjasonwinters.com/blogs/psychology-of-sexuality?category =Pornography. Maria Konnikova's views are found at http://aeon.co /magazine/psychology/does-too-much-porn-numb-sexual-pleasure/.

For more on the effects of porn, see M. McCormack and L. Wignall, "Enjoyment, Exploration and Education: The Understanding the Consumption of Pornography among Young Men with Non-Exclusive Sexual Orientations," *Sociology,* February 23, 2016, doi: 10.1177/0038038516629909; and G. M. Hald and N. M. Malamuth, "Self-Perceived Effects of Pornography Consumption," *Archives of Sexual Behavior* 37 (2008): 614–625; and R. Arrington-Sanders, G. W. Harper, A. Morgan, A. Ogunbajo, M. Trent, and J. D. Fortenberry "The Role of Sexually Explicit Material in the Sexual Development of Same-Sex-Attracted Black Adolescent Males," *Archives of Sexual Behavior* 44, no. 3 (2015): 597–608. The National Union of Students survey is reported in A. Young-Powell, "Students Turn to Porn for Sex Education," *The Guardian*, January 29, 2015, www.theguardian .com/education/2015/jan/29/students-turn-to-porn-for-sex-education.

For more on the relationship between puberty and porn watching, see I. Beyens, L. Vandenbosch, and S. Eggermont, "Early Adolescent Boys' Exposure to Internet Pornography: Relationships to Pubertal Timing, Sensation Seeking, and Academic Performance," *Journal of Early Adolescence* 35, no. 8 (2015): 1045–1068. For the American Society of Addiction Medicine's definition of addiction, see www.asam.org/for-the -public/definition-of-addiction.

OMG! A Wet Dream

For more on wet dreams, see D. Brennan, "Wet Dream FAQ," *WebMD*, December 22, 2015, http://teens.webmd.com/boys/wet-dream-faq; Division of Adolescent and Young Adult Medicine, Boston Children's Hospital, "Wet Dreams," *Young Men's Health*, October 15, 2014, http:// youngmenshealthsite.org/guides/wet-dreams/; and J. B. Lancaster, "What Are Wet Dreams?" *TeensHealth*, November 2015, http://kidshealth.org/teen /sexual_health/guys/expert_wet_dreams.html.

Masturbation

For data on masturbation, see S. LeVay, J. I. Baldwin, and J. D. Baldwin, *Discovering Human Sexuality*, 3rd ed. (Sunderland, MA: Sinauer, 2015); C. Robbins, J. D. Fortenberry, M. Reece, D. Herbenick, S. Sanders, and B. Dodge, "Masturbation Frequency and Patterns among U.S. Adolescents," supplement, Society for Adolescent Medicine Annual Meeting Program Issue Adolescent Clinical Care: Integrating Art & Science, Toronto, Ontario, Canada, 7–10 April 2010, *Journal of Adolescent Health* 46, no. 2 (2010): S36–S37; and D. Herbenick, M. Reece, V. Schick, S. A.

Sanders, B. Dodge, and J. D. Fortenberry, "Sexual Behavior in the United States: Results from a National Probability Sample of Men and Women Ages 14–94," *Journal of Sexual Medicine* 7 (2010): 255–265.

First Girl Sex

The readings for the previous section have additional applicable information for this section as well.

First Boy Sex

See the following readings for more on reasons to have sex: L. Z. DuBois, K. R. Macapagal, Z. Rivera, T. L. Prescott, M. L. Ybarra, and B. Mustanski, "To Have Sex or Not to Have Sex? An Online Focus Group Study of Sexual Decision Making among Sexually Experienced and Inexperienced Gay and Bisexual Adolescent Men," *Archives of Sexual Behavior* 44 (2015): 2027–2040. Also check out the references for chapter 13 of my book: R. C. Savin-Williams, *Gay and Lesbian Youth: Expressions of Identity* (New York: Hemisphere, 1990).

Studies that have documented gaydar include K. O. Tskhay and N. O. Rule, "Accuracy in Categorizing Perceptually Ambiguous Groups: A Review and Meta-Analysis," *Personality and Social Psychology Review* 17 (2013): 72–86; G. Rieger, J. A. W. Linsenmeier, L. Gygax, S. C. Garcia, and J. M. Bailey, "Dissecting 'Gaydar': Accuracy and the Role of Masculinity-Femininity," *Archives of Sexual Behavior* 39 (2010): 124–140.

For more on the generational differences in sex and identity, see R. C. Savin-Williams and K. M. Cohen, "Developmental Trajectories and Milestones of Lesbian, Gay, and Bisexual Young People," in "Homosexuality and Mental Health," ed. G. Mundle, L. Mahler, and D. Bhugra, special issue, *International Review of Psychiatry* 27, no. 5 (2015): 357–366.

I'm Gay—Probably, Certainly

The most often cited studies on sexual identity are V. Cass, "Homosexual Identity Formation: A Theoretical Model," *Journal of Homosexuality* 4 (1979): 219–235; and R. R. Troiden, "Becoming Homosexual: A Model of Gay Identity Acquisition," *Psychiatry* 42 (1979): 362–373. For more recent critiques, see R. C. Savin-Williams, "The New Sexual-Minority Teenager: Freedom from Traditional Notions of Sexual Identity," in *The Meaning of Sexual Identity in the Twenty-First Century*, ed. J. S. Kaufman and D. A. Powell, 5–20 (Newcastle upon Tyne, United Kingdom: Cambridge Scholars, 2014).

Something to Tell You

To read more coming-out stories, see I'm from Driftwood: The LGBTQ Story Archive (http://imfromdriftwood.com) and SB-Nation: Outsports (http://www.outsports.com).

The staff production of the Alden Peters documentary *Coming Out* (2015), which was funded through the Kickstarter website, talk about their process here http://youtube/v9gT_L9W3kE. For updates on the film, see the Facebook page (www.facebook.com/ComingOutDoc).

For a corporate blog post with information about social trends reflected on Facebook and a summary of that company's statistical research, see B. State and N. Wernerfelt, "America's Coming Out on Facebook," *Research at Facebook*, October 15, 2015, https://research.facebook .com/blog/403359139870267/america-s-coming-out-on-facebook/.

Tom Luchsinger tells his story in "King of the Double Life: Olympic Hopeful Tom Luchsinger Could Hide Being Gay from the Cameras but Not the Mirror," *SB-Nation: Outsports*, December 14, 2014, http://www .outsports.com/2014/12/14/7391989/tom-luchsinger-gay-swimmer.

Hey Mom, Dad, Bro, Sis

The source for Tom Luchsinger's story was provided in the previous chapter. **For the data on families,** see E. A. McConnell, M. A. Birkett, and B. Mustanski, "Typologies of Social Support and Associations with Mental Health Outcomes among LGBT Youth," *LGBT Health* 2 (2015): 55–61; V. Samarova, G. Shilo, and G. M. Diamond, "Changes in Youths' Perceived Parental Acceptance of Their Sexual Minority Status over Time," *Journal of Research on Adolescence* 24 (2014): 681–688; and R. C. Savin-Williams, *Mom, Dad, I'm Gay: How Families Negotiate Coming Out* (Washington, DC: American Psychological Association, 2001).

Zach's mother's letter can be read at S. Malm, "'You Are Still the Boy Who Forever Won My Heart': Mom Writes Heartfelt Response to Son Who Comes Out as Gay on Facebook," *Daily Mail*, September 5, 2013, www.dailymail.co.uk/news/article-2412145/Moms-heartfelt-response-son-came-gay-Facebook.html. The Rhodes twins' coming out video can be watched here: Rhodes Bros, "Twins Come Out to Dad," *YouTube*, January 14, 2015, https://www.youtube.com/watch?v=L3K0CJ8usPU. The Monastero twins' coming-out video can be watched here: TheMonasteroTwins, "Twins Coming Out to Parents Live," *YouTube*, August 11, 2014, https://www.youtube.com/watch?v=FxEypK7z50c.

For specific Thanksgiving advice, see M. Wollan, "How to Come Out at Thanksgiving," *New York Times*, November 20, 2015, www.nytimes.com/2015/11/22/magazine/how-to-come-out-at-thanksgiving.html.

Mostly Gay

Several research reports address the topic: Z. Vrangalova and R. C. Savin-Williams, "Mostly Heterosexual and Mostly Gay/Lesbian: Evidence for New Sexual Orientation Identities," *Archives of Sexual Behavior* 41 (2012): 85–101; and the forthcoming article in the journal *Archives of Sexual Behavior*, R. C. Savin-Williams, B. M. Cash, M. McCormack, and G. Rieger, "Gay, Mostly Gay, or Bisexual Leaning Gay? An Exploratory Study Distinguishing Gay Sexual Orientations among Young Men."

First Love

The attachment scale was developed in this study: S. J. E. Langeslag, P. Muris, and I. H. A. Franken, "Measuring Romantic Love: Psychometric Properties of the Infatuation and Attachment Scales," *Journal of Sex Research* 50 (2013): 739–747.

For more discussion of the unique issues facing gay youth in romantic issues, see L. M. Diamond, R. C. Savin-Williams, and E. M. Dubé, "Sex, Dating, Passionate Friendships, and Romance: Intimate Peer Relations among Lesbian, Gay, and Bisexual Adolescents," in *The Development of Romantic Relationships in Adolescence*, ed. W. Furman, B. B.

Brown, and C. Feiring, 175–210 (New York: Cambridge University Press, 2000); L. M. Diamond, "Love Matters: Romantic Relationships among Sexual-Minority Adolescents," in *Adolescent Romantic Relations and Sexual Behavior: Theory, Research, and Practical Implications*, ed. P. Florsheim, 85–107 (Mahwah, NJ: Lawrence Erlbaum, 2003); and R. C. Savin-Williams, "Are Adolescent Same-Sex Romantic Relationships on Our Radar Screen?" in *Adolescent Romantic Relations*, 325–336.

He's My Soul Man

For a discussion of attachment and romance issues, see C. C. Hoff and S. C. Beougher, "Sexual Agreements among Gay Male Couples," *Archives of Sexual Behavior* 39 (2010): 774–787; G. J. O. Fletcher, J. A. Simpson, L. Campbell, and N. C. Overall, "Pair-Bonding, Romantic Love, and Evolution: The Curious Case of *Homo sapiens*," *Perspectives on Psychological Science* 10 (2015): 20–36. For research on infidelity, see D. A. Frederick and M. R. Fales, "Upset over Sexual versus Emotional Infidelity among Gay, Lesbian, Bisexual, and Heterosexual Adults," *Archives of Sexual Behavior* 45, no. 1 (2016): 175–191.

Being Young and Gay in America

Reports on bullying and unsafe schools can be found at these websites: the Gay, Lesbian, and Straight Education Network (www.glsen.org); the American Psychological Association (www.apa.org); and Parents, Family, and Friends of Lesbians and Gays (www.pflag.org). For more about acceptance reflected, see R. P. Jones and D. Cox for the Public Religion Research Institute at www.publicreligion.org.

To read more **about the Pew Research Report,** see S. Tanenhaus, "Generation Nice: The Millennials Are Generation Nice," *New York Times*, August 15, 2014, www.nytimes.com/2014/08/17/fashion/the-millennials-are-generation-nice.html. For more on the GLAAD report, see J. Egner, "More Gay and Transgender Characters Are on TV, Report Shows, *New York Times*, October 27, 2015," www.nytimes.com/2015/10/28/arts/television/more-gay-and-transgender-characters-are-on-tv-report-shows.html.

For examples of positive straight responses, see A. Morrison, "Straight Teen Asks Gay Best Friend to Prom," *CNN.com*, May 1, 2015, www.cnn.com/2015/04/24/living/feat-straight-teen-asks-gay-best-friend-to-prom/; E. Cawthon, "N.Y. High School Names Same-Sex Couple as 'Cutest' in Yearbook," *CNN.com*, June 5, 2013, www.cnn.com/2013/06/04/us/new-york-same-sex-couple-yearbook/; R. L. Swarns, "Out of the Closet and into a Uniform," *New York Times*, November 16, 2012, www.nytimes.com/2012/11/18/fashion/military-academies-adjusting-to-repeal-of-dont-ask-dont-tell.html; B. Stelter, "Gay on TV: It's All in the Family," *New York Times*, May 8, 2012, www.nytimes.com/2012/05/09/business/media/gay-on-tv-its-all-in-the-family.html; G. G. Gustines, "Coming Out as Gay Superheroes," *New York Times*, December 23, 2015, "www.nytimes.com/2015/12/24/fashion/coming-out-as-gay-superheroes.html; and D. Victor, "Out Magazine Names Obama Its Ally of the Year," *New York Times*, November 12, 2015, www.nytimes.com/2015/11/13/us/politics/out-magazine-names-obama-its-ally-of-the-year.html.

To read more about **gays in fraternities**, see The Odyssey, "Voices: What It's Like to Be Greek and Gay," *USA Today College*, November 28, 2014, http://college.usatoday.com/2014/11/28/voices-what-its-like-to-be-greek-and-gay/; Anonymous, "My Life as a Gay Fratstar," *New Voices*, March 31, 2015, http://newvoices.org/2015/03/31/my-life-as-a-gay-fratstar/; G. S. Parks, "Gay Men in Black Fraternities," *Huffpost Black Voices*, November 27, 2012, updated January 27, 2013, www.huffingtonpost.com/gregory-s-parks/gay-men-in-black-fraternities_b_2189499.html; M. Tarazi, "10 Ways Being Gay in a Fraternity Is Awesome," *Vital Voice*, August 14, 2014, http://thevitalvoice.com/10-ways-gay-fraternity-awesome/; and E. Donovan, "Voices: What It's Like to Be Openly Gay in a Fraternity," *USA Today College*, August 28, 2015, http://college.usatoday.com/2015/08/28/kansas-fraternity-openly-gay/.

For articles about **acceptance of gay athletes**, see M. Strachan, "Here's All the Proof You Need That America Is Ready for Gay Professional Athletes," *Huffpost Sports*, January 22, 2015, updated January 23, 2015, www.huffingtonpost.com/2015/01/22/gay-athletes-poll-professional_n_6525870.html; E. Swanson, "Americans Say Yes to Gay Athletes . . . Until

They Kiss," *Huffpost Queer Voices*, May 15, 2014, updated February 02, 2016, www.huffingtonpost.com/2014/05/15/gay-athletes-poll_n_5325963 .html; and B. Witz, "David Denson, Gay Baseball Prospect, Achieves a Key Victory: Being Himself," *New York Times*, August 21, 2015, www .nytimes.com/2015/08/22/sports/baseball/david-denson-baseball -prospect-achieves-a-key-victory-being-himself.html. More articles can be found on the SB-Nation: Outsports website at http://www.outsports.com. For two examples of the scientific literature on gender nonconformity, see G. Rieger, J. A. W. Linsenmeier, L. Gygax, and J. M. Bailey, "Sexual Orientation and Childhood Gender Nonconformity: Evidence from Home Videos," *Developmental Psychology* 44 (2008): 46–58; and J. M. Bailey and K. J. Zucker, "Childhood Sex-Typed Behavior and Sexual Orientation: A Conceptual Analysis and Quantitative Review," *Developmental Psychology* 31 (1995): 43–55.

Tyler Curry's personal account with many articles about his life can be found at www.twitter.com/iamtylercurry.

For Scott Heggart's personal story about being a young gay hockey player, see You Can Play Project, "You Can Play—Scott Heggart," March 26, 2012, http://youcanplayproject.org/videos/entry/you-can -play-scott-heggart. More on gay youths in athletics can be found on the websites of the organizations You Can Play Project (http://youcanplayproject .org) and AthleteAlly (http://www.athleteally.org).

For Amelia's story, see Amelia, "Bully My Son at Your Own Risk," *Huffpost Queer Voices*, February 4, 2015, updated February 02, 2016, www .huffingtonpost.com/Amelia/bully-my-son-at-your-own-risk_b_6577458 .html?utm_hp_ref=tw.

For an interview with Zach Rance, see B. Schultz, "Big Brother Star Zach Rance Sets Record 'Straight' on Frankie Grande Showmance," *Out*, October 07, 2014, www.out.com/entertainment/television/2014/10/07/big -brother-star-zach-rance-sets-record-straight-frankie-grande.

ACKNOWLEDGMENTS

Having worked with several publishers during my professional life, I am thrilled to continue with Harvard University Press because of the dedication of its staff, the supportive nature of HUP toward authors, and the Press's willingness to take risk. My editor, Andrew Kinney, following the HUP tradition, has been a pure delight to work with.

I am most grateful to Fritz Klein (founder) and John Sylla (chairman and chief executive officer) of the American Institute of Bisexuality (www.americaninstituteofbisexuality.org) for financial support during the past four years. My home department, Human Development; my college, Human Ecology; and my university, Cornell, have been unwavering in their encouragement and support.

Finally, I am able to write because I have one of the most loving and supportive husbands in the universe, Kenneth Miles Cohen, and the Cohen family he shares with me: Norman, Marilyn, Avy, Jill, Jessica, and Sarah.

INDEX